2003 Tax Legislation

Jobs and Growth Tax Relief Reconciliation Act of 2003

Law, Explanation and Analysis

As Signed by the President on May 28, 2003

CCH INCORPORATED
Chicago
A WoltersKluwer Company

This publication is designed to provide accurate and authoritative information in regard to the subject matter covered. It is sold with the understanding that the publisher is not engaged in rendering legal, accounting, or other professional service. If legal advice or other expert assistance is required, the services of a competent professional person should be sought.

ISBN 0-8080-0991-5

©2003, **CCH** INCORPORATED

4025 W. Peterson Ave.
Chicago, IL 60646-6085
1 800 248 3248
http://tax.cchgroup.com

No claim is made to original government works; however, within this Product or Publication, the following are subject to CCH's copyright: (1) the gathering, compilation, and arrangement of such government materials; (2) the magnetic translation and digital conversion of data, if applicable; (3) the historical, statutory and other notes and references; and (4) the commentary and other materials.

All Rights Reserved
Printed in the United States of America

Jobs and Growth Tax Relief Reconciliation Act of 2003

Ebb and Flow of Tax Law Changes: What's In, What's Out?

On May 28, 2003, President Bush signed into law the Jobs and Growth Tax Relief Reconciliation Act of 2003. The bill (H.R. 2) cleared Congress on May 23, 2003, following last-minute negotiations between the House and Senate. Passed largely along party lines and requiring a tie-breaking vote in the Senate by the Vice President, the Act marks the cornerstone of the Bush Administration's economic stimulus plan. The Act has an overall cost of $350 billion, with approximately $320 billion labeled as tax cuts, $20 billion allocated for aid to the states, and the remainder allocated to child tax credit refunds. None of the cost of the Act is offset by spending cuts or revenue-raising provisions. The size was dictated by the need to secure enough Senate votes for passage. In general, the reduction in cost was achieved by leaving in all of the tax cut provisions in some form but shortening the time that they are effective. The net result is one of the largest tax cuts in U.S. history, with its benefits heavily "frontloaded" in the early years.

Containing 10 key tax-related provisions, the scope of the Act is broad and sweeping, going to the fundamentals of tax law. Half of the provisions accelerate, albeit temporarily, tax cuts not set to take effect until 2006. Many of the remaining provisions enhance existing provisions of the Internal Revenue Code. Its true effect, however, must be gauged in the context of the introduction of yet another layer of complexity to the tax law. Together with the sunset of changes enacted as part of the Economic Growth and Tax Relief Reconciliation Act of 2001 (P.L. 107-16) and those contained herein, taxpayers face many temporary and phased-in/phased-out effective dates. The result is a revolving door of tax rate and other changes between now and 2010, making mid- and long-range tax planning difficult and more tax-driven than ever before.

Primarily focused on individuals, the Act includes reductions in the four top marginal rates and expands the two lower tax brackets. Marriage penalty relief is provided by increasing the standard deduction for married couples and by expanding the 15-percent bracket for joint filers. The child tax credit is increased, with advance payment of the increased benefit starting in July 2003. To ensure that these benefits are not eliminated by the alternative minimum tax (AMT), the AMT exemption was also increased. All of these provisions are effective only for 2003 and 2004, except for the rate reductions, which will be in effect through 2010.

Also included in the Act is a reduction in rates for capital gains and dividends to 15 percent for the four highest tax brackets and 5 percent for the two lower brackets. The 15-percent rate continues through 2008, while the 5-percent rate continues through 2007 and drops to zero for 2008. Two business provisions increase bonus depreciation from 30 to 50 percent through 2004 and increase Code Sec. 179 small business expensing from $25,000 to $100,000 for 2003 through 2005. In combination, these changes add up to a significant reduction in taxes, with many potential ramifications for taxpayers making financial and business decisions over the next several years.

About This Work and CCH

CCH's *2003 Tax Legislation: Law, Explanation and Analysis* provides readers with a single, integrated reference tool covering all aspects of the Jobs and Growth Tax Relief Reconciliation Act of 2003. Along with the relevant Internal Revenue Code provisions, as amended by the Act, supporting committee reports and other related official materials, CCH editors, together with several leading tax practitioners and commentators, have put together the most timely and complete practical analysis of the new law. Tax professionals looking for the Conference Report, including the related bill text, can find it in a separate CCH publication. Other books and tax services relating to the new legislation can be found at *http://tax.cchgroup.com/specialreport/federal*.

As always, CCH remains dedicated to responding to the needs of tax professionals in helping them quickly understand and work with these new laws. And, perhaps most importantly, CCH will be there to remind practitioners of the many prospective changes as the phase-ins and phase-outs take effect.

Mark A. Luscombe
Principal Analyst
Federal and State Tax Group

May 2003

OUTSIDE CONTRIBUTORS

Harley T. Duncan
Federation of Tax Administrators
Washington, D.C.

Michael J. Grace
Jackson & Campbell, PC
Washington, D.C.

Robert Keebler
Virchow, Krause & Company, LLP
Green Bay, Wisconsin

Sidney Kess
New York, New York

Tim Kochis
Kochis Fitz
San Francisco, California

Keith Nakamoto
PricewaterhouseCoopers LLP
Chicago, Illinois

Martin Nissenbaum
Ernst & Young LLP
New York, New York

Vincent J. O'Brien
Vincent J. O'Brien, CPA, PC
Lynnbrook, New York

Michael Schlesinger
Schlesinger & Sussman
New York, New York

CCH FEDERAL TAX GROUP
EDITORIAL STAFF

James de Gaspé Bonar
M.A., Ph.D.
Publisher

Mark Hevrdejs
J.D., LL.M., C.P.A.
Executive Editor

Joseph S. Gornick
B.A.
Executive Editor

Explanation and Analysis

Robert C. Ansani, J.D., LL.M.
Louis W. Baker, J.D., M.B.A.
Katherine Baransky, J.D.
David Becker, J.D.
Rebecca E. Begelman, J.D.
Maureen C. Bornstein, J.D.
Managing Editor
Glenn L. Borst, J.D.
Anne E. Bowker, J.D.
Douglas Bretschneider
Managing Editor
John O. Buchanan, J.D., LL.M.
Mildred Carter, J.D.
Tom Cody, J.D., LL.M., M.B.A.
Eileen Deane, J.D.
Kurt Diefenbach, J.D.
Managing Editor
Karin R. Dunlap, J.D., LL.M.
Karen Elsner, C.P.A.
Jacqueline Fajardo, J.D.
Shannon Jett Fischer, J.D.
Donna M. Flanagan, J.D.
Adrienne G. Gershon, J.D.
Laurel E. Gershon, J.D., LL.M.
Tony D. Graber, J.D., LL.M.
Bruno L. Graziano, J.D., M.S.A.
Carmela L. Harnett
Kay L. Harris, J.D.
Karen Heslop, J.D.
Jane A. Hoffman, C.P.A.
Portfolio Managing Editor
Dem A. Hopkins, J.D.
David M. Jaffe, J.D.

George G. Jones, J.D., LL.M.
Managing Editor
Tracy Jurgus, J.D., LL.M.
Thomas Kabaker, J.D.
Alfredo Karam, J.D., LL.M.
Nicholas J. Kaster, J.D.
Sean Kelley, CPA
Mark E. Kissinger, M.B.A., J.D., M.S.T.
Lynn S. Kopon, J.D.
Mary W. Krackenberger, J.D.
Thomas K. Lauletta, J.D.
Jennifer M. Lowe, J.D.
Laura M. Lowe, J.D.
Managing Editor
Mark A. Luscombe, J.D., LL.M, C.P.A.
Principal Analyst
Daniel J. McCarthy III, J.D.
Sheila E. McFarland, J.D.
Jela Miladinovich, J.D.
Sheri Wattles Miller, J.D.
Ellen Mitchell
Tracy Gaspardo Mortenson, J.D., C.P.A.
John J. Mueller, J.D., LL.M.
Managing Editor
Anita Nagelis, J.D.
Jean T. Nakamoto, J.D.
Jerome Nestor, J.D., C.P.A., M.B.A.
Managing Editor
Lawrence Norris, M.S.
Managing Editor

Karen A. Notaro, J.D., LL.M.
Portfolio Managing Editor
Linda O'Brien, J.D.
Marie O'Donnell, J.D., C.P.A.
Karin Old, J.D.
Stephen R. Paul, J.D.
Lawrence A. Perlman, C.P.A., J.D., LL.M.
Deborah M. Petro, J.D., LL.M.
Ricky E. Rems, J.D.
Neil A. Ringquist, J.D., C.P.A.
Warren L. Rosenbloom, A.S.A.
John W. Roth, J.D., LL.M.
Carolyn M. Schiess, J.D.
Karla A. Schreiber, J.D.
Phillip Schwindt, CPA
CCH Tax Compliance
Michael G. Sem, J.D.
James Solheim, J.D., LL.M.
Raymond G. Suelzer, J.D., LL.M.
Kenneth L. Swanson, J.D., LL.M.
Deanna V. Tenofsky, J.D., LL.M.
Laura A. Tierney, J.D.
David E. Trice, CFP
Dawn R. Wagner, J.D.
Richard N. Waldinger, J.D.
James C. Walschlager, M.A.
Kelley Wolf, J.D.
George L. Yaksick, Jr., J.D.
Nicholas J. Zafran III, J.D.
Ken Zaleski, J.D.

Washington News Staff

Jeff Carlson, M.A.
Paula L. Cruickshank
David A. Hansen, J.D.

Kathryn Hough
Catherine Hubbard, M.G.
Rosalyn Johns

Joyce Mutcherson-Ridley
William Pegler

Electronic and Print Production

Trent Allan
Lilian Bajor
Ce'on Barnes
Brian A. Berens
Miranda Blunt
Stella Brown
Angela D. Cashmore
Elizabeth Dudek
Tara K. Fenske
Jane Fridman
Mary Ellen Guth
Ann Hartmann
Kathleen M. Higgins
Jennifer Holland
Kristine J. Jacobs

Linda Kalteux
Kenneth R. Kuehl
Andrea M. Lacko
Faina Lerin
Rebecca Little
Chantal M. Mahler
Andrejs Makwitz
Helen Miller
Loretta Miller
Barbara Mittel
Molly Munson
Patricia Panek
Holly J. Porter
Diana Roozeboom
David Schuster

Monali Shah
Diane Shultz
Sanford Silverman
Eileen Slivka
Monika Stefan
Jason Switt
Katharine H. Trickle
Emily Urban
Marco Aurélio M. Vidor
James M. Waddick
James F. Walschlager
Jamie Wild
Lynn Wilson
Laura M. Zenner
Christopher Zwirek

How to Use

¶ 1

CCH's *2003 Tax Legislation: Law, Explanation and Analysis* provides you with CCH explanations and analysis of the Jobs and Growth Tax Relief Reconciliation Act of 2003 (H.R. 2). In conjunction with CCH editors, practitioners have provided practical guidance and planning strategies and identified pitfalls to be avoided as a result of the law changes contained in the 2003 Act. Included in this text are the provisions of the Internal Revenue Code, as amended, added or repealed by the new law, and the relevant controlling Committee Reports.

Here is a guide to the numerous features provided in this text:

HIGHLIGHTS

A summary of the Highlights of the 2003 Act provides references to the CCH Explanations to give you a quick overview of the major provisions of the 2003 Act. The Highlights are topically arranged by subject and provide a means of entry into the Explanations. See ¶ 5.

CCH EXPLANATIONS

CCH-prepared explanations of the Jobs and Growth Tax Relief Reconciliation Act of 2003 are arranged according to subject matter for ease of use. Each explanation includes a discussion of background or prior law that helps to put the law changes into perspective.

Incorporated throughout the explanations is expert commentary provided by practitioners. This commentary highlights planning opportunities and strategies engendered by the new laws. Pitfalls to avoid are identified. Charts and examples illustrating the ramifications of specific law changes are incorporated throughout the explanations.

Also included are references to CCH STANDARD FEDERAL TAX REPORTER, CCH FEDERAL TAX SERVICE, and CCH FEDERAL TAX GUIDE for related explanations. Subscribers to the electronic version can link from these references to the related material.

The inter-relationship of the law changes made by the 2003 Act and the effect on individual taxpayers and businesses is discussed in Chapter 1 of this work. The 2003 Act's impact on various taxpayer types are highlighted and sample scenarios showing the tax savings as a result of the 2003 Act are illustrated.

Each explanation chapter is preceded by a chapter table of contents. A detailed table of contents for the entire explanation portion of the *Law, Explanation and Analysis* text is also included for easy identification of subject matter.

Each individually numbered explanation paragraph ends with the applicable effective date of the provision discussed. The effective date is preceded by a star (★) symbol for easy reference.

The explanation paragraphs are followed by boldface amendment captions that (1) identify the Act Section and the Code Section added, amended or repealed and (2) provide cross references to the law and to the reproduced Committee Reports. *The CCH Explanations begin at ¶ 105.*

INDEX. Because the topical or subject matter approach to new legislation is usually the easiest to navigate, you may also access the material in the CCH Explanations through the extensive Index. The Index begins at *page 201*. The Index is also available on the electronic version of this publication.

AMENDED CODE PROVISIONS

CCH has reflected the changes to the Internal Revenue Code made by the Jobs and Growth Tax Relief Reconciliation Act of 2003 in the "Law Added, Amended or Repealed" provisions. Deleted Code material or the text of the Code provision prior to amendment appears in the Amendment Notes following each reconstructed Code provision. *Any changed or added portion is set out in italics.*

The applicable effective date for each Amendment Note is set out in boldface type. Preceding each set of amendment notes, CCH provides references to (1) the corresponding controlling Committee Reports and (2) the CCH Explanation related to that added, amended or repealed Code provision. Subscribers to the electronic product can link to the related explanation or Committee Report material using these references. *The text of the Code begins at ¶ 5001.*

NON-CODE PROVISIONS

The sections of the Jobs and Growth Tax Relief Reconciliation Act of 2003 that do *not* amend the Internal Revenue Code appear in full text in Act Section order following the "Law Added, Amended or Repealed" section of the text. Included is the text of Act Sections that amend the Economic Growth and Tax Relief Reconciliation Act of 2001 (P.L. 107-16). *The text of these provisions appears in Act Section order beginning at ¶ 7005.*

COMMITTEE REPORTS

The controlling Committee Reports officially explain the intent of Congress regarding the provisions in the 2003 Act. At the end of the Committee Report text, CCH provides a caption line that includes references to the corresponding explanation and Code provisions. Subscribers to the electronic version can link from these references to the corresponding material. *These Committee Reports appear in Act Section order beginning at ¶ 10,001.*

EFFECTIVE DATES

A table listing the major effective dates provides you with a reference bridge between Code Sections and Act Sections and indicates the retroactive or prospective nature of the laws explained. *This effective date table begins at ¶ 20,001.*

SPECIAL FINDING DEVICES

A table cross-referencing Code Sections to the CCH Explanations is included *(see ¶ 25,001)*. Other tables include Code Sections added, amended or repealed *(see ¶ 25,005)*, provisions of other acts that were amended *(see ¶ 25,010)*, Act Sections not amending Internal Revenue Code Sections *(see ¶ 25,015)* and Act Sections amending Code Sections *(see ¶ 25,020)*, so that you can immediately determine whether a provision in which you are interested is affected. In addition, an explanation of the sunset provisions contained in the 2003 Act *(see ¶ 29,001)* and a listing of provisions dropped in Conference *(see ¶ 30,001)* are provided.

A detailed table of contents for the entire *Law, Explanation and Analysis* text is also included for easy identification of subject matter.

¶ 1

Table of Contents

How to Use .... ¶ 1
Highlights .... ¶ 5

Explanation

Chapter 1 Taxpayer Impact with Sample Scenarios .... ¶ 105
Chapter 2 Individuals .... ¶ 205
Chapter 3 Business and Investment .... ¶ 305

Law and Committee Reports

Law
    Code Sections Added, Amended or Repealed .... ¶ 5001
    Act Sections Not Amending Code Sections .... ¶ 7005
Committee Reports .... ¶ 10,001

Special Tables

Effective Dates Table .... ¶ 20,001
Code Section to Explanation Table .... ¶ 25,001
Code Sections Added, Amended or Repealed .... ¶ 25,005
Table of Amendments to Other Acts .... ¶ 25,010
Table of Act Sections Not Amending Internal Revenue Code Sections .... ¶ 25,015
Act Sections Amending Code Sections .... ¶ 25,020
Sunset Provisions .... ¶ 29,001
Provisions Dropped in Conference .... ¶ 30,001

                                                                                     Page
Index 201

Detailed Table of Contents

CHAPTER 1. TAXPAYER IMPACT WITH SAMPLE SCENARIOS

Jobs and Growth Tax Relief Reconciliation Act of 2003
Overview .... ¶ 105

Jobs and Growth Act Impact on Individual Taxpayers
Overall effect on individual taxpayers .... ¶ 110
Effect on high-income taxpayers .... ¶ 112
Effect on middle-income taxpayers .... ¶ 114
Effect on low-income taxpayers .... ¶ 116
Effect on married taxpayers .... ¶ 120
Effect on single taxpayers .... ¶ 122
Effect on families .... ¶ 124
Effect on senior citizens .... ¶ 126

Jobs and Growth Act Impact on Investors
Overall effect on investors .... ¶ 130
Effect on retirement investors .... ¶ 132
Effect on education investors .... ¶ 134
Effect on estate planning .... ¶ 136
Effect on wealthy investors .... ¶ 138

Jobs and Growth Act Impact on Businesses
Overall effect on businesses .... ¶ 140
Effect on corporations generally .... ¶ 145
Effect on closely held corporations .... ¶ 147
Effect on pass-through entities generally .... ¶ 150
Effect on partnerships and LLCs .... ¶ 152
Effect on S corporations .... ¶ 154
Effect on REITs .... ¶ 156
Effect on small businesses .... ¶ 160
Effect on capital intensive businesses .... ¶ 165
Effect on labor intensive businesses .... ¶ 167
Effect on technology businesses .... ¶ 170
Effect on multi-national businesses .... ¶ 175
Effect on financial entities .... ¶ 180
Effect on personal holding companies .... ¶ 182
Effect on collapsible corporations .... ¶ 184
Effect on regulated investment companies .... ¶ 186
Effect on not-for-profit entities .... ¶ 190
Effect on employee stock ownership plans .... ¶ 192
Effect on governmental entities .... ¶ 195

Jobs and Growth Act Sample Scenarios
Sample scenarios for individuals .... ¶ 198

CHAPTER 2. INDIVIDUALS

Rate Reductions
Acceleration in individual income tax rate cuts .... ¶ 205
10-percent tax bracket expanded .... ¶ 210

Marriage Penalty Relief
15-percent tax bracket of joint filers expanded .... ¶ 215
Standard deduction of joint filers increased .... ¶ 220

Credits
Acceleration and advance payment of child tax credit increase .... ¶ 225

Alternative Minimum Tax
Minimum tax relief for individuals .... ¶ 230

Capital Gains and Dividends
Reduction in capital gains rates (see ¶ 305 and following)
Dividends taxed at capital gain rates (see ¶ 325 and following)

State Aid
Temporary state fiscal relief .... ¶ 240

CHAPTER 3. BUSINESS AND INVESTMENT

Capital Gains
Reduction in capital gains rates for individuals .... ¶ 305
Elimination of five-year holding period .... ¶ 310
Small business stock .... ¶ 315
Transitional rule .... ¶ 320

Dividends
Dividend income of individuals taxed at capital gain rates .... ¶ 325
Dividends passed through RICs and REITs .... ¶ 335

Depreciation
Increase and extension of bonus depreciation .... ¶ 350

Deductions
Increased expensing for small businesses .... ¶ 355

Corporations
Repeal of collapsible corporation rules .... ¶ 360
Reduced accumulated earnings tax rate .... ¶ 365
Reduced personal holding company tax rate .... ¶ 370
Corporate estimated tax payments for 2003 .... ¶ 375

Highlights

¶ 5

Sunset Provision. In order to comply with the Congressional Budget Act of 1974, the Jobs and Growth Tax Relief Reconciliation Act of 2003 contains two provisions that sunset some of the changes made by the new law. .... ¶ 29,001

INDIVIDUALS

EGTRRA Provisions Accelerated. Tax rate reductions included in the Economic Growth and Tax Relief Reconciliation Act of 2001 (EGTRRA) that were scheduled to take effect in 2006 are accelerated to 2003. This lowers the 27-percent rate to 25 percent, the 30-percent rate to 28 percent, the 35-percent rate to 33 percent, and the 38.6-percent rate to 35 percent. The reductions are in effect through 2010. .... ¶ 205

Ten-percent bracket expanded. The income cut-off for the 10-percent tax bracket see-saws, increasing from $6,000 to $7,000 for single filers and from $12,000 to $14,000 for married persons filing jointly in 2003 and 2004; dropping back to $6,000 for single filers and $12,000 for joint filers in 2005, 2006 and 2007; and returning to $7,000 for single filers and $14,000 for joint filers in 2008, 2009 and 2010. .... ¶ 210

Fifteen-percent bracket expanded for joint returns. The marriage penalty is reduced by increasing the 15-percent tax bracket for joint returns to twice that for single taxpayers in 2003 and 2004. For 2005, 2006 and 2007, the 15-percent bracket for joint returns is 180 percent, 187 percent and 193 percent, respectively, of the 15-percent bracket for single taxpayers. In 2008, 2009 and 2010, the 15-percent bracket for joint returns once again increases to twice that for single taxpayers. .... ¶ 215

Standard deduction increased for joint filers. The marriage penalty is reduced by increasing the amount of the basic standard deduction for married taxpayers filing joint returns to twice the amount of the basic standard deduction for single taxpayers in 2003 and 2004. After 2004, the standard deduction for married taxpayers falls to 174 percent of the standard deduction for single taxpayers and then gradually returns to double the single taxpayer's amount for 2009 and 2010. .... ¶ 220

Child tax credit increased. The child tax credit is increased from $600 to $1,000 per child for 2003 and 2004. Taxpayers whose 2002 returns indicate they are entitled to the credit for 2003 will receive advance payment of the increase in the credit for 2003. The child tax credit falls to $700 in 2005, 2006, 2007 and 2008; rises to $800 in 2009; and returns to $1,000 for 2010. .... ¶ 225

AMT Exemption Amount Increased. The alternative minimum tax (AMT) exemption amount is increased by $4,500 (from $35,750 to $40,250) for single taxpayers and $9,000 (from $49,000 to $58,000) for married taxpayers filing joint returns for 2003 and 2004. .... ¶ 230

States Receive Temporary Fiscal Relief. States will receive $20 billion in aid for fiscal years 2003 and 2004, with $10 billion devoted to Medicaid assistance and $10 billion available for other essential government services. .... ¶ 240

BUSINESS AND INVESTMENT

Capital Gain Tax Rates Reduced. For individual taxpayers, the maximum tax rate for most long-term capital gains falls from 20 percent to 15 percent through 2008. The 10-percent capital gains tax rate for lower-income individuals falls to 5 percent through 2007 and to zero for 2008. The reduced rates are also used when calculating alternative minimum tax (AMT) liability. Transitional rules apply to sales and exchanges made after May 6, 2003. .... ¶ 305, ¶ 320

Special Rates for Five-Year Property Eliminated. The optional 18-percent and 8-percent tax rates on capital gains arising from the disposition of property held for more than five years are eliminated. .... ¶ 310

AMT Preference for Excluded Gain Adjusted. When a noncorporate investor excludes gain from the sale of qualified small business stock, the portion of the exclusion that is treated as a tax preference item for purposes of the alternative minimum tax (AMT) is reduced to 7 percent. .... ¶ 315

Tax on Dividend Income Reduced. Dividend income received by an individual shareholder from a domestic or qualified foreign corporation is taxed at a maximum rate of 15 percent through 2008. For lower-income individuals, a new 5-percent rate applies to dividend income through 2007, and dividend income is tax-free for 2008. .... ¶ 325

RIC and REIT Rules Coordinated with New Dividend Tax. The rules for dividends passed through regulated investment companies (RICs) and real estate investment trusts (REITs) are coordinated with the new rules for taxing dividends. .... ¶ 335

Bonus Depreciation Increased and Extended. The additional first-year depreciation allowance is increased from 30 percent to 50 percent for property acquired after May 5, 2003, and placed in service before January 1, 2005 (or 2006 for property with longer production periods). Depreciation caps on vehicles are also increased. .... ¶ 350

Expensing Limits Increased for Small Businesses. The amount that a small business can deduct for depreciable property placed in service during 2003, 2004 and 2005, is increased from $25,000 to $100,000, and the capital purchase amount for qualifying property is increased from $200,000 to $400,000. Off-the-shelf computer software is added to the list of Code Sec. 179 property. .... ¶ 355

Collapsible Corporation Rules Repealed. Collapsible corporation rules are repealed through 2008. .... ¶ 360

Accumulated Earnings Tax Rate Reduced. The accumulated earnings tax rate is reduced to 15 percent through 2008. .... ¶ 365

Personal Holding Company Tax Rate Reduced. The tax on undistributed personal holding company income is reduced to 15 percent through 2008. ... ¶ 370

Corporate Estimated Tax Payments Deferred. Corporate estimated tax payments ordinarily due on September 15, 2003, are deferred until October 1, 2003. .... ¶ 375

¶ 5

Chapter 1

Taxpayer Impact with Sample Scenarios

JOBS AND GROWTH TAX RELIEF RECONCILIATION ACT OF 2003
Overview .... ¶ 105

JOBS AND GROWTH ACT IMPACT ON INDIVIDUAL TAXPAYERS
Overall effect on individual taxpayers .... ¶ 110
Effect on high-income taxpayers .... ¶ 112
Effect on middle-income taxpayers .. ¶ 114
Effect on low-income taxpayers .... ¶ 116
Effect on married taxpayers .... ¶ 120
Effect on single taxpayers .... ¶ 122
Effect on families .... ¶ 124
Effect on senior citizens .... ¶ 126

JOBS AND GROWTH ACT IMPACT ON INVESTORS
Overall effect on investors .... ¶ 130
Effect on retirement investors ...... ¶ 132
Effect on education investors ...... ¶ 134
Effect on estate planning .... ¶ 136
Effect on wealthy investors .... ¶ 138

JOBS AND GROWTH ACT IMPACT ON BUSINESSES
Overall effect on businesses .... ¶ 140
Effect on corporations generally .... ¶ 145

Effect on closely held corporations .. ¶ 147
Effect on pass-through entities generally .... ¶ 150
Effect on partnerships and LLCs .... ¶ 152
Effect on S corporations .... ¶ 154
Effect on REITs .... ¶ 156
Effect on small businesses .... ¶ 160
Effect on capital-intensive businesses .... ¶ 165
Effect on labor-intensive businesses . ¶ 167
Effect on technology businesses .... ¶ 170
Effect on multi-national businesses .. ¶ 175
Effect on financial entities .... ¶ 180
Effect on personal holding companies .... ¶ 182
Effect on collapsible corporations ... ¶ 184
Effect on regulated investment companies .... ¶ 186
Effect on not-for-profit entities .... ¶ 190
Effect on employee stock ownership plans .... ¶ 192
Effect on governmental entities .... ¶ 195

JOBS AND GROWTH ACT SAMPLE SCENARIOS
Sample scenarios for individuals .... ¶ 198

JOBS AND GROWTH TAX RELIEF RECONCILIATION ACT OF 2003

Overview

¶ 105

The Jobs and Growth Tax Relief Reconciliation Act of 2003 contains 10 key tax-related provisions, each of which is important in a variety of significant ways and to a variety of taxpayers. The $320 billion in tax cuts and $350 billion overall 10-year cost rank this legislation among the largest tax cuts ever passed by Congress. Unlike other large tax cuts, however, this one is a lot more "front-loaded"

¶ 105

because most of the cost (i.e., the tax-cut benefit) is attributable to tax breaks given for the next two to five years. Of the $350 billion in total cost, over half, $60.8 billion in 2003 and $148.7 billion in 2004, benefits the first two years. Each of the 10 provisions is projected to have a 10-year cost of at least $10 billion, except for the small business expensing provision, the early benefit of which is offset somewhat in later years.

Also, unlike other large tax bills of the past, the 2003 Act does not create many brand new Internal Revenue Code provisions. This is not a tax reduction act with new targeted deductions and credits. Yet, the scope of this tax act is broad and sweeping, going to fundamental elements of the tax law. There has been significant tax legislation in the past that made no changes to marginal rate brackets. This legislation has three provisions affecting marginal rate brackets. There has been significant tax legislation in the past that did not change tax rates. This legislation has three provisions reducing tax rates. Half of the provisions accelerate, albeit often temporarily, tax cuts that were already in the tax law with postponed effective dates. Still others—although not all—use existing law to enhance benefit provisions already in the Code.

The true significance of this tax legislation lies not in looking at each individual provision, but rather in looking at how the changes relate to and with each other, and what significance those inter-relationships should have on taxpayer behavior. This chapter examines these inter-relationships within this new tax legislation in order to gauge their impact on individual taxpayers and businesses, and the revised tax planning that they should now undertake.

JOBS AND GROWTH ACT IMPACT ON INDIVIDUAL TAXPAYERS

Overall Effect on Individual Taxpayers

¶ 110

This tax legislation is fundamentally focused on individual taxpayers. It includes a reduction in the four top marginal rates (¶ 205). It also includes a reduction in the tax rates on capital gains (¶ 305) and dividends (¶ 325). It also expands the two lower tax brackets, increasing the size of the 10-percent bracket (¶ 210) and eliminating the marriage penalty in the 15-percent bracket (¶ 215). Additional marriage penalty relief is provided for in the standard deduction (¶ 220). The child tax credit is increased (¶ 225). Finally, to ensure that these benefits are not eliminated by the alternative minimum tax (AMT), the AMT exemption amount is also increased (¶ 230). About the only people who will not derive some benefit from these provisions are single people in the 10-percent tax bracket without children or investments.

Effect on High-Income Taxpayers

¶ 112

Considerable commentary has suggested that high-income taxpayers would receive a disproportionate benefit from the lowering of income tax rates. However, at least according to statistics released by the Treasury Department, taxpayers with incomes in excess of $100,000 will end up paying a larger share of the total income tax burden after passage of the 2003 Act than before (Treasury Department, Office of Public Affairs Release (May 22, 2003), Distribution Table for the

Jobs and Growth Tax Relief Reconciliation Act of 2003). In any event, high-income taxpayers will be pleased to see the top income tax rate drop from 38.6 percent to 35 percent effective for the 2003 tax year. This move serves to accelerate the schedule established under the Economic Growth and Tax Relief Reconciliation Act of 2001 (EGTRRA) (P.L. 107-16) by three years (¶ 205). High-income taxpayers will also benefit from the drop in the long-term capital gains rates (¶ 305) and parallel treatment for stock dividends (¶ 325).

The top-rate reductions will have a positive impact on the after-tax incomes of high-level employees and on entrepreneurs who derive their incomes from sole proprietorships, S corporations, partnerships and other pass-through entities. These are individuals specifically targeted by the Administration to help drive economic growth in the near and long term.

Just how much of a change will the rate reductions mean for a typical high-income couple?

Example. Jack and Suzanne Birkwood, a married couple with two children under age 17, have $300,000 of income. Their income includes $10,000 in dividend income and $50,000 in itemized deductions.

	Proposal	Present Law	Savings	% of AGI
Adjusted Gross Income	$300,000	$300,000		
Itemized Deductions	45,185	45,185		
Personal Exemptions	3,172	3,172		
Taxable Income	$251,643	$251,643		
Tax	62,688	69,607	6,919	
Child Credit	(0)	(0)	0	
Tax After Credits	$ 62,688	$ 69,607	$6,919	2.31%

What other changes should high-income taxpayers be aware of? For one, the lowering of income tax rates generally should be considered when the next opportunity (June 16) arrives for paying estimated taxes. In addition, the capital gains changes, along with the new treatment of dividends, should prove to be a boon to high-income individuals who tend to be more heavily invested in stocks. This is evidenced by the fact that approximately 63 percent of dividend income was received by those individuals reporting incomes of over $100,000, according to the latest IRS Statistics on Income Bulletin.

Effect on Middle-Income Taxpayers

¶ 114

Middle-income taxpayers were not forgotten in the 2003 Act. Much has been written about the shock wave predicted within the next few years when the AMT is expected to become a concern for many middle-income taxpayers. Although the 2003 Act does not, as some had hoped, take direct aim at the heart of the individual AMT, at least it does its best to temporarily slow down AMT growth. This is accomplished by increasing the exemption amount to $40,250 for single filers and to $58,000 for married couples filing a joint return in 2003 and 2004 (¶ 230). In addition, the lower rates on capital gains (¶ 305) and dividends (¶ 325) are also applicable for AMT purposes.

In another beneficial change for middle-income taxpayers, withholding rates will be dropped to reflect the new lower income tax rates effective for 2003 (¶ 205).

¶ 114

Beginning this summer, middle-income workers will see more money in their weekly pay checks. Money, it is hoped, will be directed toward the purchase of autos and other consumer goods to help the economy through the third and fourth quarters of 2003. Taxpayers should be cognizant of at least one possible issue with respect to changes in withholding rates: If withholding for the second half of the year is adjusted to reflect a full year's reduction in marginal rates, taxpayers should be prepared for a potential increase in withholding starting in January 2004.

Effect on Low-Income Taxpayers

¶ 116

Effective in 2003, the 10-percent income tax bracket is expanded to $7,000 for individuals and $14,000 for married persons filing jointly (¶ 210). This was not supposed to occur until 2008 under the schedule provided by EGTRRA. In addition, the income levels applicable to the 10-percent rate bracket will be adjusted for inflation beginning in 2004. However, to temper this good news, the 2003 Act calls for the 10-percent bracket to return to the schedule previously established in EGTRRA—$6,000 and $12,000, respectively, in 2005 through 2007.

Although not typically a concern of low-income taxpayers, the special five-percent rate on long-term capital gains (¶ 305) and dividends (¶ 325), available to persons in the lowest brackets, could prove to be a welcome benefit in certain situations. For example, a young person above age 13 who is still in school or who has a very low-paying job, but who has been gifted stock from a parent or grandparent, could use the additional savings to help build a down payment on a starter home, to pay graduate-school tuition or to begin his or her own investment portfolio.

Effect on Married Taxpayers

¶ 120

Married taxpayers were singled out for particular benefit in the 2003 Act. In fact, according to statistics provided by the Treasury Department, 45 million married couples will receive average tax cuts of $1,786 and marriage penalty relief is expected to reduce taxes for 34 million couples by an average of $589 (Treasury Department, Office of Public Affairs Release (May 22, 2003), Effects of Major Individual Income Tax Relief Provisions in the Jobs and Growth Tax Relief Reconciliation Act of 2003). Of specific interest to married taxpayers are the accelerated expansion of the 15-percent bracket (¶ 215) and the acceleration of the increased standard deduction for joint filers (¶ 220).

The size of the 15-percent bracket for married couples filing jointly will be twice that available to individuals filing as single for 2003 and 2004. However, beginning in 2005, the size of the bracket will be determined according to the schedule allowed under EGTRRA. Similarly, the basic standard deduction amount for joint filers will be twice that available to single filers (currently $4,750) for 2003 and 2004, dropping back to the percentages set forth in EGTRRA beginning in 2005. Although these changes will not eliminate the marriage penalty for all married taxpayers, they will go a long way toward achieving that goal. Future Congresses will undoubtedly feel the political pressure to not let this relief lapse and, in fact, may be hard pressed to allow a return to the schedule set by EGTRRA.

Explanation

Effect on Single Taxpayers

¶ 122

Single taxpayers were not necessarily the object of any particular relief provisions in the 2003 Act, but will, of course, benefit from the same rate reductions (¶ 205 and ¶ 210) and investment incentives (¶ 305 and ¶ 325) as other taxpayers.

Example. Deborah Engell, a single taxpayer, has $100,000 of income. Her income includes $3,000 in dividend income and $15,000 in itemized deductions.

	Proposal	*Present Law*	*Savings*	*% of AGI*
Adjusted Gross Income	$100,000	$100,000		
Itemized Deductions	15,000	15,000		
Personal Exemptions	3,050	3,050		
Taxable Income	$ 81,950	$ 81,950		
Tax	$ 17,302	$ 18,813	$1,511	1.51%

Effect on Families

¶ 124

Much as in the case of married taxpayers, taxpayers with children under age 17 are the beneficiaries of several important provisions of the 2003 Act. First among these is the acceleration of the increase in the child tax credit from $600 to $1,000 for 2003 and 2004 (¶ 225). Perhaps even more important for those who are hoping that tax benefits will stimulate the economy quickly, beginning in July, 2003, a portion of the credit ($400 for each qualifying child) will be paid in advance to those taxpayers who claimed the credit for 2002.

The impact of these provisions on families should not be taken lightly. In fact, the Treasury Department estimates that 34 million families with children will benefit from an average tax cut of $1,549 (Treasury Department, Office of Public Affairs Release (May 22, 2003), Effects of Major Individual Income Tax Relief Provisions in the Jobs and Growth Tax Relief Reconciliation Act of 2003).

Effect on Senior Citizens

¶ 126

Senior citizens did *not* receive at least one piece of relief that many had been hoping for, that being the repeal of the 1993 increase in the taxation of Social Security benefits. However, according to the Treasury Department, 12 million seniors will receive an average tax cut of $1,401 under the 2003 Act (Treasury Department, Office of Public Affairs Release (May 22, 2003), Effects of Major Individual Income Tax Relief Provisions in the Jobs and Growth Tax Relief Reconciliation Act of 2003). The new lower rates on capital gains and dividends (¶ 305 and ¶ 325) will be a big plus for senior citizens, with the Treasury estimating that seven million seniors will see an average decline of $1,088 in taxes as a result of these changes.

JOBS AND GROWTH ACT IMPACT ON INVESTORS

Overall Effect on Investors

¶ 130

When President Bush first made his tax proposals for action by Congress this year, the centerpiece was the elimination of what the President referred to as the double taxation of dividends. The Jobs and Growth Tax Relief Reconciliation Act of 2003 does not exactly accomplish the President's goal in that regard, but this is not necessarily bad news for investors. For one thing, the 2003 Act will not require computation of the excludable dividend amount that was part of the President's original plan, and, thus, eliminates the accompanying record keeping by companies and their shareholders. In addition, the 2003 Act will have an impact on a broader spectrum of investors since it will not only lower taxes on dividends (¶ 325), but also on most long-term capital gains (¶ 305).

What possible changes should we be looking for in investor behavior in response to the 2003 Act? For those investors who are wise enough (or lucky enough) to have appreciated securities in their portfolios, the new lower rates on long-term capital gains presents an opportunity to sell some or all of these holdings and to use the proceeds to rebalance their investment mix or for other purposes. Another fairly obvious response would be to invest in stocks that have a history of paying dividends. One possible category of "winner" in this search could be utility stocks. Another possible beneficiary of the lower tax rates on dividends would be preferred stock, including convertible preferred and "discounted" preferred, which is treated for tax purposes much like a zero-coupon bond. Of course, the different risks associated with preferred stock, at least in comparison with bonds, must be assessed carefully.

Riding the downside, however, are those investors who have brought carryover losses into 2003 incurred during a time when losses were worth more in the sense of being able to offset income that was taxed at a higher rate. Those losses now can only be used within the framework of the new current income tax brackets and lower capital gains rate; no adjustment is made for this "devaluation" of carryover losses.

Other behavioral changes to look for include the impact on the municipal bond market. The future popularity of municipal bonds will probably be dependent on the tax situation and residence of taxpayers (see discussion of wealthy investors at ¶ 138, below). One caveat for investors to ponder as well concerns the fact that the lower rates on dividend income are only applicable to dividends paid by certain corporations. The House bill originally limited this provision to dividends paid by *domestic* corporations. However, the Conference agreement extends the benefits of the rate reduction to corporations incorporated within a U.S. possession, a corporation treated as a qualified foreign corporation under a comprehensive U.S. tax treaty or a foreign corporation whose stock is traded on an established U.S. equities market. Dividends received from a foreign investment company, a passive foreign investment company or a foreign personal holding company will not qualify for the reduced tax rate.

Finally, the reaction of the stock market itself will have at least some impact on the future behavior of investors. Although some commentators have suggested that a measurable rise in the markets will occur as a direct result of the change in the taxation of dividends, just as many say that the impact will be negligible, or that the change has already been factored into valuations in anticipation of the 2003 Act's passage.

¶ 130

PRACTICAL ANALYSIS. Tim Kochis of Kochis Fitz, San Francisco, California, finds that the 2003 Act will make investment leverage more attractive than before. While margin investing is not to everyone's taste, it has always been a very good theoretical proposition where the expected investment return would exceed the cost of the debt. The same principle is at work in the conventional proposition of financing real estate purchases, for example. Well, if leverage was attractive before, especially when the interest cost is deductible and the expected return is largely in the form of capital appreciation, tax features made the favorable differential even better: interest expense deductible against ordinary income rates, return taxable at capital gains rates. Now, that tax differential is even greater: ordinary income rates decline by 9.3 percent (from 38.6 percent to 35 percent) while long-term capital gains rates decline by 25 percent (from 20 percent to 15 percent). The benefits of leverage have gone way up.

All other things equal, investors will prefer dividend-paying stocks since the tax rate on dividends declines to 15 percent. Rarely, however, are other things equal. Investors will still invest for maximum "total return" (dividends AND appreciation). Both elements will now be taxed equivalently, so investors would presumably not have a tax-oriented preference, focusing rather on the largest sum of the two elements. However, since the dividend element is more immediate and seemingly more secure, many investors will prefer to receive dividends rather than rely on the more distant and more speculative appreciation. Consequently, it may be harder for corporations to now withstand shareholders' urgings about inaugurating/increasing dividend payouts. Further, since this low rate on dividends is scheduled to sunset, many corporations may be tempted to pay out artificially high dividends while this window is open. That potential distortion is likely to play at least a small role in the eventual debate about repealing the sunset and making this provision permanent. What we might also expect from this equating of dividend and gains tax rates is a fresh discourse about the proper role of dividend policy. In some companies, the best use of earnings is internal re-investment because the company has more attractive opportunities than those available to its shareholders in their individual capacities. In other cases, the internal opportunities may have been exhausted and the wisest course is simply to distribute earnings to the owners for them to redeploy as they see fit. Tax rates should never have played a role in this case-by-case decision. Now they won't be able to properly influence the result.

Reduced capital gains tax rates will free-up more entrenched capital. Even at rates as low as 20 percent, many people were reluctant to transact in existing holdings for reluctance to incur the tax. In a similar vein, many older individuals were willing to hold positions, awaiting basis step-up at death. The merits of these rationales were always weak; they have now become 25

¶ 130

percent weaker. At some low level—perhaps 15 percent is it—people will just shrug off tax burden as a reason for not taking action that is otherwise appropriate.

PRACTICAL ANALYSIS. Michael J. Grace of Jackson & Campbell, PC, Washington, D.C., observes that in the short run, the 2003 Act probably will stimulate some forms of investing. Enticed by 50 percent bonus depreciation or increased expensing under Code Sec. 179, some businesses will purchase new equipment. Attracted by reduced tax rates on dividends, some individuals will purchase stocks that pay healthy dividends.

The temporary nature of many of the provisions and their scheduled sunset dates, however, may skew some investment decisions. For example, accelerated investments in Code Sec. 179 property before 2006 may be offset by reduced investments after 2005. Compare the theory that automobile manufacturers' current rebates to purchase vehicles tend to "cannibalize" future sales. Lured by temporarily reduced rates on capital gains, an individual may buy or sell assets before the time at which the transaction economically makes sense for that individual. Similarly, motivated by temporarily reduced rates on dividends, an individual may invest funds in dividend-paying stocks instead of other assets that make more sense based on the individual's appropriate asset allocation and tolerance for risk.

There exist ample reasons for skepticism that reducing tax rates on capital gains and dividends will stimulate individuals to consume. Economic statistics indicate that approximately 50 percent of stocks are held in accounts that currently pay no tax on dividends they receive (e.g., 401(k) plans, IRAs and pension plans). Most stocks held in taxable accounts are owned by upper-income taxpayers. Economists report that such taxpayers tend to save and reinvest tax savings rather than consume them. The most significant reductions in rates (to five percent) have been granted to lower-income taxpayers who tend not to invest in stocks.

Possibly, reducing tax rates on dividends will benefit investors most significantly by increasing after-tax returns on stocks. Economic statistics indicate that, historically, dividends represent approximately 50 percent of the total return on stocks. Lower taxes on dividends will yield higher after-tax returns.

Effect on Retirement Investors

¶ 132

Individuals who are investing primarily for their retirement may, at first glance, be disappointed in the 2003 Act. Sweeping changes to retirement accounts that had been proposed by the President earlier in the year did not make their way into the final legislation. Considering the amount of debate that preceded passage of the 2003 Act and the apparent difficulty in crafting a bill that would pass both houses of Congress, the chances for radical reform of retirement accounts in the near future are probably slim. However, that is not to say that the 2003 Act leaves these investors without anything to think about.

A major consideration for retirement-oriented investors will be their asset allocation, particularly with respect to holdings inside versus outside of a retirement account. It has been estimated that approximately 50 percent of the total investment in stocks is currently held in retirement accounts. The negative point for such investors is that they will not see a direct benefit in the lower-income tax rates applicable to dividends because distributions from these retirement accounts will ultimately be subject to the rates applicable to ordinary income. Nevertheless, at least according to some commentators, the overall value of their holdings may rise based on the generally positive impact of the new dividend treatment on the value of the markets as a whole. However, particularly for those investors who are able to take full advantage of the current contribution limits on deferred retirement accounts, lowered rates on long-term capital gains (¶ 305) and dividends (¶ 325) will present an interesting planning opportunity for establishment of an additional retirement "side fund."

Another possible planning opportunity concerns the treatment of net unrealized appreciation (NUA) on a lump-sum distribution of employer stock from a retirement plan. The combination of decreased ordinary income tax rates applicable to the portion of the distribution taxable at the time of the distribution, along with lower capital gains rates on the subsequent appreciation, will make this strategy even more appealing.

PRACTICAL ANALYSIS. Vincent O'Brien, President of Vincent J. O'Brien, CPA, PC, Lynnbrook, New York, observes that individuals and their advisors must assess the effect of the change in tax rates (i.e., the changes in rates applicable to ordinary income, long-term capital gains, and dividends) when planning their contributions to retirement accounts and investments in non-retirement account vehicles.

As the individual income tax rates decline, there is also a decline in the effective tax savings when making contributions to a traditional IRA and/or an employer-sponsored retirement account, which reduce gross income for the current year. Although such contributions continue to provide significant tax savings in the current year, it is important to compare these savings to the future tax effects that will apply when an individual withdraws from these accounts.

Gains from the sale of investments that are not held in a retirement account may be eligible for the new lower rate applicable to long-term capital gains. This rate is now substantially lower than the top marginal income tax rate applicable to distributions from a traditional IRA and/or an employer-sponsored retirement account. (To the extent that investments generate dividends, those dividends will also be subject to the new lower rate.)

Individuals must carefully compare all of the tax consequences of investments held in retirement accounts to those held outside of retirement accounts. The immediate tax benefit of contributions to retirement accounts may still tip the scale in favor of such

¶ 132

vehicles; however, each time the rates substantially change, it is important to revisit the comparison.

PRACTICAL ANALYSIS. Robert Keebler of Virchow, Krause & Company, LLP, Green Bay, Wisconsin, notes that when an employee retires from a company that allows investment in the employer's stock, a substantial tax advantage exists when taking a lump sum retirement plan distribution. The rules are simple but the analysis is very complex. Under Code Sec. 402, the employee is taxed on the basis of the stock within the qualified plan. Later, when the stock is sold, the difference between the basis and sales price (subject to limited exception) is taxed at long-term capital gains tax rate. Under the new tax bill, a very powerful strategy just became a lot better.

With income tax brackets expanding and ordinary rates falling, the cost of a lump-sum distribution just decreased, while at the same time the later sale of stock will be taxed at only 15 percent. In fact, for some taxpayers in the 15-percent bracket, this rate will fall to five percent. To make matters even better, the dividends received in the meantime will be taxed at only 15 percent. Lastly, with the capital gain rate decreasing by more than the income tax rate, the strategy of using NUA stock to fund a charitable remainder trust will be even more viable.

Effect on Education Investors

¶ 134

Similar to the situation confronted by investors who are engaged in planning for retirement, those who are particularly concerned with education planning will have to read between the lines of the 2003 Act for their opportunities. The 2003 Act makes no direct changes to the provisions governing Code Sec. 529, Qualified Tuition Plans, or to Code Sec. 530, Coverdell Education Savings Accounts. Although these accounts remain valuable resources to help one save for educational needs, the acceleration of lower income tax rates (¶ 205), generally, and the addition of special rates on capital gains (¶ 305) and dividends (¶ 325) provide an additional incentive for education savers. The increased child tax credit (¶ 225) could also be thought of as another source of funds to save for a child's education. Gifts of appreciated or income-producing property to children over age 13 should also be considered (see "Effect on Estate Planning," below). Note that a provision in the Senate bill that would have increased the age for investment income being taxed at the parents' rates did not make its way into the final legislation.

Effect on Estate Planning

¶ 136

Those individuals who are concerned about estate planning may want to invoke the immortal words of Yogi Berra, "it's *deja vu* all over again," after they look at the way in which several of the provisions of the 2003 Act phase in and phase out over time. If you recall, EGTRRA was dubbed by some as the "Throw Momma From the Train Act" in reaction to the fact that it repealed the federal estate tax completely for only one year (2010) and then returns the tax, generally, to pre-EGTRRA law, in 2011. At least in the case of long-term capital gains (¶ 305) and dividends (¶ 325), the 2003 Act would return to the present law rates in 2009.

In conjunction with the repeal of the estate tax, EGTRRA considerably altered the rules governing the basis of property received from a decedent. Whereas prior law gave such assets a stepped-up basis to date-of-death value, EGTRRA restricts the increase in basis to only a limited amount ($3 million for assets going to a surviving spouse and $1.3 million for assets going to anyone). This could create difficult choices for estate planners and fiduciaries with respect to how to allocate assets to best take advantage of the revised basis rules. Assuming for the moment, however, that changes in the long-term capital gain rates (¶ 305) and the repeal of the estate tax are eventually made permanent (or at least to the extent that these two provisions coexist in the same year(s)), this would serve to soften considerably the blow otherwise felt by those heirs left holding appreciated assets without benefit of the step-up in basis.

Of more immediate concern is the impact of lower tax rates for capital gains and dividends on gifting. Gifts of appreciated long-term capital gain property and dividend-producing stock will be more valuable from a tax point of view. Opportunities to make such gifts to those parties subject to the five-percent (zero in 2008) rate applicable to taxpayers in the lowest income tax brackets (e.g., a child over 13 so as not to be subject to the kiddie tax rates) should also be explored. The corollary appears to be that charitable gifts of the same property would be less advantageous under these rate assumptions. However, there is at least one possible charitable strategy that is worth looking into that involves use of a charitable remainder trust (CRT). The tier system of taxation applicable to distributions from CRTs would seem to provide an opportunity to structure an investment portfolio using preferred stock to take advantage of the lower rates on dividends. The major caveat to this strategy is that preferred stock may present more of an interest rate and creditor priority risk than bonds.

PRACTICAL ANALYSIS. Robert Keebler of Virchow, Krause & Company, LLP, Green Bay, Wisconsin, observes that the charitable remainder trusts represent one of the more unique taxing regimes in the entire Internal Revenue Code. Code Sec. 664 provides the "tier" system of taxation, often called the "WIFO" system. You will recall from accounting that WIFO stands for "worst in, first out." Under the tier system, income of a charitable remainder trust is broken into either the ordinary income tier, capital gain tier, tax exempt income tier or corpus tier. These ordering provisions represent how distributions from charitable remainder trusts are taxed. For example, if a trust was invested in a 100-percent bond portfolio that earned an eight-percent return, and the trust payment was eight percent annually, 100 percent of the distribution would be taxable as ordinary income. Under current law, the same would hold true for a preferred stock portfolio earning a similar eight-percent return.

However, under the 2003 Act, dividends would be subject to tax in a manner similar to that of long-term capital gains. This will create an immediate need to review investment policy statements for charitable remainder trusts. Sophisticated investment advisors will attempt to devise plans in which they structure preferred stock portfolios, taking on a similar amount of risk that bond portfolios would bear. By carefully structuring such portfolios, assuming the risk can be managed, they will convert ordinary income perhaps taxed at 35 percent to capital gains taxed at 15 percent, a savings of 20 percentage points.

If the charitable remainder trust distributes $500,000 a year of income, this will result in a tax savings of $100,000. However, if a client is considering undertaking this strategy, it is very important to work closely with their investment advisors to manage the interest rate risk and the creditor priority risk. It is important to remember that preferred stock will have a lower bankruptcy priority than bonds. Further, it is important to remember that many preferred stocks are permanent equity in a corporation. Therefore, because they have an unlimited duration, when interest rates move back up, preferred stock will decrease in value, similar to bonds. Bonds, however, having a limited maturity, will not experience as severe price swings. The key will be to manage the investment risk while taking advantage of these tremendous tax savings opportunities.

Effect on Wealthy Investors

¶ 138

Intentionally or not, the 2003 Act will have significant impact, mostly positive, on wealthy investors. They are poised to receive the largest benefits from the sale of long-term appreciated assets (¶ 305) and from lowered rates on dividends received (¶ 325). They will also receive a major bonus in the immediate drop of the top income tax rate from 38.6 percent to 35 percent (¶ 205). Another little noticed change in the 2003 Act is the reduction in the personal holding company tax rate to 15 percent (¶ 370).

What are the potentially negative aspects of the 2003 Act on wealthy investors? For one, the lower capital gain rates are not applicable to all assets. Collectibles remain subject to a 28-percent rate and depreciable real estate having unrecaptured Code Sec. 1250 gain will be subject to a 25-percent rate. In addition, although the increased spread between the tax rates applicable to long-term and short-term capital gains should discourage short-term trading, it would seem to encourage schemes for taxpayers to "game" the system by converting short-term gain or ordinary income into long-term gain.

Other potential problems also exist. For example, § 311(e) of the Taxpayer Relief of 1997 (P.L. 105-34) gave taxpayers the opportunity to qualify for an 18-percent capital gains rate on property purchased before 2001. In order to do so, however, taxpayers had to make a "deemed-sale-and-repurchase election" and recognize gain on the sale. This election was irrevocable. Under the 2003 Act, the five-year holding period required in connection with the 18-percent capital gains rate has been eliminated, but the Act makes no provision for those taxpayers who made the § 311(e) election. Due to sunsets, the eight and 18-percent rates for five-year holding period property would return in 2009.

Other questions concerning taxpayer behavior remain open, such as what will become of municipal bonds? Early in the legislative process, when the President was calling for total elimination of individual taxes on dividends, there was concern that the municipal bond market would suffer greatly as a result of the 2003 Act. Because the Act ultimately did not totally exclude taxes on dividends, and for other reasons, municipal bonds should continue to prosper. Particularly, for wealthy investors in areas of the country with high state and local taxes, municipal bonds should prove to have lasting value. In addition, the generally lower risk associated with municipal bonds should also remain attractive to many wealthy taxpayers in evaluating their portfolios.

Finally, it has been suggested that wealthy investors will seek to enhance the results obtained as a result of lower taxes on dividends (¶ 325) by borrowing to buy dividend-paying stocks and deducting the interest paid. This strategy will only work to the extent the taxpayer has investment income from sources other than the dividends in an amount equal to the deduction being contemplated. For taxpayers who do not have such investment income from other sources, it will come down to a choice of either including the dividend in investment income for purposes of taking the deduction or taking advantage of the reduced rate on dividends.

JOBS AND GROWTH ACT IMPACT ON BUSINESSES

Overall Effect on Businesses

¶ 140

There are two significant provisions in the new legislation directed at business, both intended to encourage capital spending. For smaller businesses, the Code Sec. 179 expense limit is increasing from $25,000 to $100,000, while the phase-out based on total capital expenditures for the year will start at $400,000 rather than $200,000 (¶ 355). For all businesses, the first-year bonus depreciation enacted in the 2002 Tax Act is expanded from 30 percent to 50 percent (¶ 350).

The indirect impact of the new law on businesses, however, may prove to be even more significant than these two highly significant provisions to spark capital investment by small businesses. Individuals as the ultimate owner of all business, whether sole proprietors, partners, LLCs, S corporations or C corporations, will have their business decisions altered by the major changes in the 2003 Act directly applicable to them. These include primarily the reduction in marginal rates and the reduction in dividend and capital gain rates.

The portion of the Code Sec. 1202 exclusion for small business stock treated as a tax preference item is reduced (¶ 315). The familiar concept of the collapsible corporation disappears from the Code (¶ 360). As an indirect result of the reduction in dividend rates, the tax rates applicable to the accumulated earnings tax and the personal holding company tax are reduced (¶ 365 and ¶ 370). New rules clarify how dividends received from pass-through entities, as compared to regular corporations, will be treated (¶ 325 and ¶ 335).

Even more significant than the changes that are spelled out in the new law are the changes that must be read into the new law. What effect will the dividend and capital gain rate changes have on businesses making the choice between operating as a regular corporation or a pass-through entity? What effect will these rate changes have on the decision of a corporation to retain earnings or to pay earnings to shareholders as dividends?

Effect on Corporations Generally

¶ 145

Corporations, like other businesses, would potentially qualify for the Code Sec. 179 expense election, if they qualify as a small business, or for the expanded first-year bonus depreciation (¶ 355 and ¶ 350). The main impetus for accelerating a capital acquisition is likely to be the impending expiration of a tax benefit. The extension of the first-year bonus depreciation through 2004, therefore, may actually reduce expenditures that would have been made this year to take advantage of the expiring 30-percent first-year bonus depreciation provisions created under the tax legislation enacted in 2002.

Corporations have been in the spotlight for the last couple of years after Enron, World.com, and other disclosures of corporate malfeasance. The IRS has also been on a campaign to curtail the use of corporate tax shelters based on questionable interpretations of tax law to reduce taxes. Concerns have been raised about corporate inversions, i.e., corporations choosing to move their main holding corporation overseas for tax reasons. This focus on corporations led to the question of whether tax laws were creating distortions that encouraged unproductive, if not illegal, corporate behavior.

Have corporations been making excessive use of debt markets rather than capital markets because of the availability of the interest deduction while no similar tax benefit is available for dividends? The most obvious response to this proposition might be to provide business with a dividend-paid deduction similar to the interest deduction. However, giving corporations a tax break at a time when their public image was somewhat tarnished did not appear to be a good idea to the Administration. Accordingly, a dividend exclusion was proposed that, through compromise with the Congress, ended up as a significant reduction in the rates at which dividends are taxed to shareholders (¶ 325). With a large percentage of shareholders already paying no tax on dividends received due to their tax-exempt status (principally through qualified retirement plan investments), it is also less expensive to reduce the tax at the shareholder level rather than the corporate level. The new law leaves the reduction in place for six years—many provisions in the new law sunset after two years—in order to try to insure that the period would be at least long enough to have a positive effect on corporate behavior.

Will corporations respond by increasing dividend payments? It would appear likely that corporations will at least initiate or increase dividend payments in the hope of attracting capital, raising their stock price, and, therefore, making it easier to raise equity capital. Whether growth-oriented companies will feel that dividend payments still taint their growth-focused image remains to be seen. The six-year sunset may encourage many companies to proceed cautiously and respond to market pressures rather than taking bold action at the outset.

Will the dividend rate reductions reduce the attractiveness of corporate tax shelters? Corporate tax shelters have largely been marketed as a way of generating tax losses to offset what would otherwise be income taxed at the corporate level. Corporate tax rates have not been changed under the new law, and dividend payments will provide no corporate-level reduction in taxes. The package of corporate tax shelter restrictions that the Senate proposed were not included in this legislation although they may be revived to pay for legislation in the future. The dividend rate reductions are not tied to whether the corporation first paid tax on the earnings previously distributed (¶ 325). Far from avoiding double taxation of dividends, this law creates the possibility to plan for avoiding any tax on dividends except, at most, the 15-percent shareholder-level tax. Therefore, far from reducing the attractiveness of corporate tax shelters, this legislation is likely to stimulate the invention of new planning devices to reduce corporate-level taxes, whether the funds are retained or paid out as dividends. Of course, in order to pay out dividends, corporations need to have the cash to make the payment, rather than paper profits achieved through corporate devices to artificially enhance financial statements. However, borrowing to make the dividend payment produces an interest deduction for the corporation. In this respect, the new law might actually result in an increase in corporations going to the debt market for funds.

PRACTICAL ANALYSIS. Michael J. Grace of Jackson & Campbell, PC, Washington, D.C., finds that Congress' decision to reduce tax rates on long-term capital gains and dividends to the same level makes a great deal of sense. Economically, selling stocks at a gain and collecting dividends merely represent two different ways of earning returns on investments. The two events arguably should be taxed the same way. Equating the two rates also will enable corporations to choose between paying dividends and repurchasing stock based on the economic merits rather than the tax consequences of those alternatives. In recent years, commentators have observed that the rate differential between ordinary income (including dividends) and capital gains artificially influenced corporations to repurchase shares rather than pay cash dividends. One would hope that future Congresses and Administrations will perceive the merits of maintaining parity between the two rates.

Historically, increasing the differential between tax rates on ordinary income and tax rates on capital gains tends to encourage aggressive tax-sheltering activity. Reducing the rates applicable to dividends compared to ordinary income similarly may foster new techniques that may or may not prove abusive. Some corporations may choose to issue more stock to employees in order to "compensate" them with dividends compared to salaries taxable at regular rates. Before embarking on that course of action, however, the corporation should consider other factors such as the dilutive effects of stock options and other forms of awarding stock to employees, the taint of adverse publicity (post-Enron, etc.) associated with stock options, and the fact that corporations can deduct salaries but not dividends.

Some corporations may find it attractive to borrow money in order to pay increased dividends. Unlike individuals, corporations face relatively few restrictions on their ability to deduct interest expense. However, a corporation contemplating such a strategy also must consider the financial consequences of increasing its debt.

One budget provision in the law, that has also been used in prior tax legislation, delays 25 percent of any corporate estimated tax payment that is normally due on September 15, 2003, until October 1, 2003, the start of the new fiscal year (¶ 375).

¶ 145

Effect on Closely Held Corporations

¶ 147

Closely held corporations that have traditionally tried to extract funds in the form of compensation, rather than dividends, will now have some new options. Compensation will still receive a corporate-level deduction while dividends will not. But compensation is taxed at rates as high as 35 percent at the individual level, while dividends will only be taxed at a maximum of 15 percent (¶ 325). The best of both worlds might be to find some method other than compensation to reduce corporate-level tax—retirement plan contributions and interest deductions come to mind—while returning to a practice of paying dividends as a way of getting funds to shareholders.

The accumulated earnings tax penalty under Code Sec. 531 is reduced to 15 percent rather than the highest individual marginal rate (¶ 365). The accumulation of earnings penalty should, however, still be avoided.

Effect on Pass-through Entities Generally

¶ 150

With the rise of limited liability companies, IRS "check-the-box" regulations for non-corporate entities to elect to be taxed as pass-through entities, and increasingly flexible state statutes, corporations have ceased to become vehicles of choice for many except publicly held entities, entities planning public offerings, or entities that, through compensation or other devices, could regularly report minimal corporate-level tax. The key to the rise of pass-through entities was the avoidance of the corporate-level tax. The price to pay was having all entity-level income passed through to the owners for taxation.

Pass-through entities, like corporations, can potentially take advantage of the expanded Code Sec. 179 expensing election and the 50-percent first-year bonus depreciation (¶ 355 and ¶ 350). Again, as with corporations, the extension of first-year bonus depreciation through 2004 may actually serve to reduce any capital purchases that would otherwise have been accelerated into 2003 to take advantage of the expiring 30-percent first-year bonus depreciation.

PRACTICAL ANALYSIS. Michael J. Grace of Jackson & Campbell, PC, Washington, D.C., believes that it will be interesting to monitor the extent to which the 2003 Act affects the trend in recent years toward conducting business through passthrough entities (e.g., partnerships, LLCs, and S corporations) rather than regular corporations. The 2003 Act will change the dynamics of comparing regular corporations with passthrough entities concerning the taxation of both income from operations and gain upon selling an interest in an entity.

Other than accelerating the Economic Growth and Tax Relief Reconciliation Act of 2001's reduction of marginal rates, the 2003 Act does not change the rates at which owners of passthrough entities are subject to tax on their shares of the net income from the underlying businesses. Partners and shareholders of S corporations are subject to tax on such income (other than the entity's dividends and capital gains) at the rates applicable to ordinary income. Even after their reduction by the Act, those rates can range as high as 35 percent. (Dividends and capital gains of the entity that flow through to partners and S corporation shareholders will qualify to be taxed at 15 percent or 5 percent, as the case may be.) See Code Secs. 702 and 1366. Before the 2003 Act, the net income from a regular corporation's business, paid out to shareholders as dividends, also was taxable as ordinary income. Under the 2003 Act, by comparison, shareholders of regular corporations will pay tax on their dividends at 15 percent or five percent, as the case may be.

Similarly, when a partner or a member of an LLC taxable as a partnership sells an interest in the entity, some of the gain may be taxable as ordinary income rather than capital gain. See Code Sec. 751(a). By contrast, a shareholder of a regular corporation has capital gain upon selling stock in the corporation. Now, that gain will be taxable at five percent or 15 percent, as the case may be.

Numerous factors, however, should continue to render passthrough entities attractive compared to regular corporations. The 2003 Act's reduced rates on dividends and capital gains are scheduled to sunset after 2008. While passthrough entities continue to offer the benefit of a single level of tax, the Act did not completely eliminate the "double" taxation of a regular corporation's profits; it merely reduced the rates applicable at the second level (i.e., to dividends). Many taxpayers value the flexibility of entities taxable as partnerships (e.g., LLCs classified as partnerships for tax purposes). Finally, the potential tax consequences of "exiting" different types of entities must be considered. When a corporation distributes appreciated property in liquidation to its shareholders, tax will continue to be payable at both the corporate level and the shareholder level. See Code Secs. 311 and 331. Entities taxable as partnerships, by contrast, generally can distribute property to partners without paying tax at the entity level. See Code Sec. 731.

Effect on Partnerships and LLCs

¶ 152

What effect will the new law have on the attractiveness of partnerships and LLCs? The reduction of individual marginal rates (¶ 205), while corporate rates remain the same, will tend to make partnerships and LLCs even more attractive. The reduction in the individual dividend rates to a maximum of 15 percent when the top corporate rate remains at 35 percent still leaves a potential 50-percent tax on income earned at the corporate level (¶ 325). With the 15-percent rate potentially applicable even if no corporate-level tax has been paid, however, it is possible that corporate earnings could be taxed at only 15 percent, at the shareholder level, while earnings of pass-through entities are taxed at up to 35 percent at the shareholder level. The continuing attractiveness of pass-through entities may depend in part, therefore, on the future success corporations have in passing dividends through to shareholders that have not been taxed at the corporate level. If this becomes an established practice, the attractiveness of the corporate format will see a renaissance. As long as a sunset hangs over the favorable treatment of dividends, however, it is likely to put a damper on such long-term planning considerations.

¶ 152

Effect on S Corporations

¶ 154

The new tax law is likely to make S corporations relatively less attractive. Already viewed as less flexible than partnerships and LLCs in the pass-through world, their attraction has often been their similarity to the corporate structure while offering the advantages of pass-through treatment. With the relative advantage of pass-through treatment somewhat reduced by this legislation, the S corporation election might be made with more caution than in the past. S corporation status would be enhanced by the reduction in individual marginal rates as compared to the static corporate tax rates.

Effect on REITs

¶ 156

With a focus on real estate, many capital acquisitions of Real Estate Investment Trusts (REITs) will not qualify for first-year bonus depreciation because the depreciable life exceeds 20 years. Also, real estate would generally not qualify for Code Sec. 179 expensing. Further, REIT distributions will generally not qualify for the reduced tax rate on dividends unless the distributions represent previously taxed undistributed income or are being passed through by the REIT from corporations in which the REIT is a shareholder (¶ 335).

Effect on Small Businesses

¶ 160

Small business, whether incorporated, or operating as a pass-through entity or sole proprietorship, will get a significant benefit from the four-fold increase in the Code Sec. 179 expensing election as well as the doubling of the size of capital purchases allowed before the phase-out kicks in (¶ 355). The bonus depreciation increase will also assist on acquisitions of new equipment (¶ 350). Small business owners will tend to achieve the maximum benefit by using the Code Sec. 179 expensing provision first on purchases of used assets and assets with longer depreciable lives, while saving the bonus depreciation for any qualifying purchases not picked up by Code Sec. 179. While the extension of the bonus depreciation sunset might encourage businesses to delay purchases that they would have made in 2003 until 2004, the new $100,000 Code Sec. 179 expense limit renews each year, and the 2003 limit will be lost if not fully utilized in 2003.

One tax benefit increasingly being used by small businesses is the acquisition of a vehicle weighing over 6,000 pounds, such as a heavy SUV, for use in the business. Although the luxury automobile first-year depreciation limits are being raised by this legislation to $7,650 to accommodate the increase in bonus depreciation (¶ 350), heavy SUVs escape the depreciation limits completely and can qualify for full use of the Code Sec. 179 and bonus depreciation limits. Federal legislation to curtail this practice was considered as part of a package of revenue raisers in the Senate, but it was not enacted as part of this legislation. States that have been decoupling their tax treatment of depreciation from the federal tax treatment of bonus depreciation may be less generous to taxpayers in the state tax treatment of acquisitions of heavy SUVs.

Unincorporated small business owners will also, of course, be entitled to the benefit of the individual marginal rate reductions (¶ 205). The Treasury has estimated that, for 2003, 23 million small business owners will receive tax cuts averaging $2,209 from the overall effects of this legislation (Treasury Department, Office of Public Affairs Release (May 22, 2003), Effects of Major Individual Income Tax Relief Provisions in Jobs and Growth Tax Relief Reconciliation Act of 2003).

PRACTICAL ANALYSIS. George Jones, of CCH INCORPORATED, Washington, D.C., observes that pencils need to be sharpened in evaluating how a small business should time the purchases of equipment, and how elections should be taken, in light of the new law. The interaction of the capitalization-versus-expensing rules, the section 179 expensing limitations, bonus first-year depreciation restrictions, and their interrelationship with the regular accelerated depreciation rules create the need for spreadsheet precision. (The timing of purchases toward the end of 2004 involves another, entirely separate set of considerations since bonus depreciation is scheduled to end at the end of 2004, while enhanced section 179 expensing continues on for another year.) For now, however, a small business's timing and treatment of purchases should take into account three primary considerations:

First, the cost of the asset may be immediately and fully deductible as a business expense under Code Sec. 162, thus avoiding any requirement to capitalize and depreciation it altogether. There is some risk, however, in being too aggressive on the side of claiming an immediate deduction. If, on audit, the IRS concludes that the asset must be capitalized, the IRS could deny a late election at that time to use either section 179 expensing or bonus depreciation advantageously. Nevertheless, if a purchase can safely fit under the section 162 business expense rules, that deduction generally should be taken without hesitation since it does not count against the section 179 expensing limitation at all.

Second, once a business decides that an asset must be capitalized, it must decide whether it qualifies for either section 179 expensing or bonus depreciation on that asset and, if so, which one to take first. Fortunately, the final decision does not need to be made until after year-end when the return for the tax year is filed. Nevertheless, knowing what immediate first-year write-off will be available is critical to many small businesses' upfront purchasing decisions.

If the asset is used property, the decision to expense or take bonus depreciation is easier to make since, as used property, the asset automatically cannot qualify for bonus depreciation. The decision then comes down to which qualifying section 179 assets should be designated to count toward the new $100,000 annual expensing limit. Initially, compute whether all qualifying section 179 property for the tax year comes within the new $400,000 limit on purchases; otherwise, the deduction will be phased out quickly, dollar for dollar, on the excess. Assuming that limit is not reached,

¶ 160

however, the section 179 $100,000 deduction generally should be taken on assets in reverse order of useful life, since property with a shorter useful life will be subject to faster depreciation.

Third, if qualifying section 179 property is also new, the alternative option of taking the 50-percent bonus depreciation must be factored into the decision. If a single asset is involved, it is generally more advantageous to take a full first-year deduction than one for 50 percent. If multiple assets are under consideration, first using up the section 179 expensing limitation on the assets with the longest depreciation period generally makes the most sense.

Finally, an asset may be able to support both an expensing deduction and bonus depreciation. For example, as new asset purchased for $330,000 could be entitled to $100,000 expensing, $115,000 bonus depreciation on the remaining $230,000 basis, and regular first-year depreciation on the reduced $115,000 basis.

Effect on Capital-Intensive Businesses

¶ 165

Capital-intensive businesses, often hardest hit by overseas competition and the weak economy, are clear beneficiaries of the increased bonus depreciation provided that they have taxes to reduce and equipment to buy (¶ 350). With the increase in the Code Sec. 179 phase-out limits to $400,000 per year, many more businesses making significant capital acquisitions would also be able to take advantage of that expensing option (¶ 355).

Effect on Labor-Intensive Businesses

¶ 167

Even relatively large labor-intensive businesses may find that they are able to take advantage of the Code Sec. 179 expensing provision if their capital acquisitions do not routinely exceed $500,000 per year (¶ 355). Increased bonus depreciation would be available as well (¶ 350).

Forms of employee compensation are always critical to labor-intensive businesses. The reduction in marginal tax rates will tend to make traditional forms of cash compensation more attractive (¶ 205). The trend toward expensing stock options for accounting purposes will reduce the attractiveness of stock options from an accounting point of view, but stock options will remain an important vehicle for cash-strapped companies seeking to acquire talent. The dividend rate reduction will make the holding of dividend-paying company stock by employees relatively more attractive, but will make phantom stock plans or other stock equivalent forms of compensation relatively less attractive (¶ 325).

Effect on Technology Businesses

¶ 170

Technology companies led the way in the growing popularity of using stock options as a key form of compensation. It appeared to be a mutually beneficial arrangement. The companies did not have a lot of spare cash, and the employees were enticed by the growth potential of the stock. The trend toward expensing stock options for accounting purposes will make options somewhat less attractive from the company's point of view, but still important if cash is in short supply. The tech bust has tarnished the rose of stock options as compensation from the employee point of view. With reduced marginal rates, cash compensation will look even better (¶ 205). On the other hand, lower dividend and capital gain rates will make stock ownership also seem attractive (¶ 325 and ¶ 305). One clear advantage for technology companies in the new legislation is that off-the-shelf computer software now qualifies for the Code Sec. 179 business expensing election (¶ 355).

Effect on Multi-National Businesses

¶ 175

Multi-national businesses may be pleased as much by what did not make it into this legislation as what made it in. A proposal to repeal the Code Sec. 911 foreign earned income exclusion was dropped, as were provisions attacking corporate inversions. The final version of the dividend rate reduction provision extends the benefits of the rate reduction to corporations incorporated within a U.S. possession, a corporation treated as a qualified foreign corporation under a comprehensive U.S. tax treaty, or a foreign corporation whose stock is traded on an established U.S. equities market (¶ 325). In order to be viewed as comprehensive, the tax treaty must generally include an exchange of information program.

Dividends received from a foreign investment company, a passive foreign investment company or a foreign personal holding company will not qualify for the reduced tax rate (¶ 325).

Effect on Financial Entities

¶ 180

Amounts paid by mutual savings banks, cooperative banks, domestic building and loan associations, and other savings institutions chartered and supervised as savings and loan or similar associations under federal or state law, even if labeled a dividend, will not qualify for the reduced tax rate on dividends if the distribution qualified for a deduction under Code Sec. 591 (¶ 325).

Effect on Personal Holding Companies

¶ 182

Personal holding companies will have the penalty imposed on personal holding company income lowered to 15 percent rather than the highest marginal rate (¶ 370). Since this penalty rate would still be imposed in addition to the corporate tax rate, it would remain unattractive to retain undistributed earnings in a personal holding company. Dividends received from a foreign personal holding company will not qualify for the reduced dividend tax rate (¶ 325).

Effect on Collapsible Corporations

¶ 184

Code Sec. 341 is something of a relic following the repeal of the General Utilities doctrine that made it generally difficult to get assets out of corporate form without paying a corporate-level tax. However, it still remained as something of a trap for the unwary and the subject of several recommendations for repeal. Although not directly related to the issue of reduction in dividend rates, buried in that provision is the repeal of the collapsible corporation provisions of the Code (¶ 360).

Effect on Regulated Investment Companies

¶ 186

Dividends generated by regulated investment companies will be taxed at the maximum rate for individuals. Dividends passed through regulated investment companies from corporations will qualify for the reduced tax rate on dividends provided that the gross-income test under the regulated investment company rules is met (¶ 335). Interest earned on money market mutual funds and bond mutual funds, although traditionally labeled dividend distributions by regulated investment companies, appears likely, when passed through to mutual fund investors, to not qualify for the reduced rates on dividend taxation.

Effect on Not-for-Profit Entities

¶ 190

Dividends paid by tax-exempt corporations and tax-exempt farmers cooperatives would not qualify for the reduced dividend tax rate (¶ 325).

Employee Stock Ownership Plans

¶ 192

Dividends paid by corporations to their employee stock ownership plans would not qualify for the reduced dividend tax rate (¶ 325).

Effect on Governmental Entities

¶ 195

The reduced dividend rate, reduced capital gain rates, and lower individual marginal rates will all serve to make taxable investments relatively more attractive than tax-free bond investments (¶ 325, ¶ 305 and ¶ 205). To compensate, states and municipalities will likely have to make returns on bonds relatively more attractive to compete with taxable investments. This change comes at a time when states are already burdened by deficits in their budgets. One non-tax provision in the new legislation sets aside a $20 billion dollar fund to be distributed to the states, half to assist with Medicaid payments and half for discretionary spending (¶ 240). Although bonds will still be an attractive portion of an investment portfolio due to their relative stability compared to stocks, tax-free bonds also have to compete with U.S. government bonds, which are likely to rise in prominence again as the deficit grows, and corporate bonds in maintaining a place in the investment portfolio. Taxable bond interest will be relatively more attractive due to the reduction in marginal rates.

JOBS AND GROWTH ACT SAMPLE SCENARIOS

Sample Scenarios for Individuals

¶ 198

The following are sample scenarios illustrating the impact of the 2003 Act on various hypothetical individual taxpayers.

Single taxpayer—age 65, $30,000 of AGI, which includes $3,000 in dividend income

	Proposal	Present Law	Savings	% of AGI
Adjusted Gross Income	$30,000	$30,000		
Std. Deduction	5,900	5,900		
Personal Exemptions	3,050	3,050		
Taxable Income	$21,050	$21,050		
Tax	$ 2,508	$ 2,858	$350	1.17%

Head of household—one child under age 17, $30,000 of income

	Proposal	Present Law	Savings	% of AGI
Adjusted Gross Income	$30,000	$30,000		
Std. Deduction	7,000	7,000		
Personal Exemptions	6,100	6,100		
Taxable Income	$16,900	$16,900		
Tax	2,035	2,035		
Child Credit	(1,000)	(600)	400	
Tax After Credits	$ 1,035	$ 1,435	$400	1.33%

Married couple—two children under age 17, $50,000 of income

	Proposal	Present Law	Savings	% of AGI
Adjusted Gross Income	$50,000	$50,000		
Std. Deduction	9,500	7,950		
Personal Exemptions	12,200	12,200		
Taxable Income	$28,300	$29,850		
Tax	3,545	3,878	333	
Child Credit	(2,000)	(1,200)	800	
Tax After Credits	$ 1,545	$ 2,678	$1,133	2.27%

Jobs and Growth Tax Relief Reconciliation Act of 2003

Married couple—two children under age 17, $50,000 of income, which includes $2,000 in capital gains

	Proposal	Present Law	Savings	% of AGI
Adjusted Gross Income	$50,000	$50,000		
Std. Deduction	9,500	7,950		
Personal Exemptions	12,200	12,200		
Taxable Income	$28,300	$29,850		
Tax	3,345	3,778	433	
Child Credit	(2,000)	(1,200)	800	
Tax After Credits	$ 1,345	$ 2,578	$1,233	2.47%

Single taxpayer—no children, $50,000 of income

	Proposal	Present Law	Savings	% of AGI
Adjusted Gross Income	$50,000	$50,000		
Std. Deduction	4,750	4,750		
Personal Exemptions	3,050	3,050		
Taxable Income	$42,200	$42,200		
Tax	$ 7,360	$ 7,686	$326	.65%

Single taxpayer—no children, $50,000 of income, which includes $3,000 in capital gains

	Proposal	Present Law	Savings	% of AGI
Adjusted Gross Income	$50,000	$50,000		
Std. Deduction	4,750	4,750		
Personal Exemptions	3,050	3,050		
Taxable Income	$42,200	$42,200		
Tax	$ 7,060	$ 7,476	$416	.83%

Married couple—two children under age 17, $100,000 of income, $15,000 in itemized deductions

	Proposal	Present Law	Savings	% of AGI
Adjusted Gross Income	$100,000	$100,000		
Itemized Deductions	15,000	15,000		
Personal Exemptions	12,200	12,200		
Taxable Income	$ 72,800	$ 72,800		
Tax	11,820	13,362	1,542	
Child Credit	(2,000)	(1,200)	800	
Tax After Credits	$ 9,820	$ 12,162	$2,342	2.34%

¶ 198

Explanation

Married couple—two children under age 17, $100,000 of income, which includes $5,000 in capital gains, $15,000 in itemized deductions

	Proposal	Present Law	Savings	% of AGI
Adjusted Gross Income	$100,000	$100,000		
Itemized Deductions	15,000	15,000		
Personal Exemptions	12,200	12,200		
Taxable Income	$ 72,800	$ 72,800		
Tax	11,320	13,012	1,692	
Child Credit	(2,000)	(1,200)	800	
Tax After Credits	$ 9,320	$ 11,812	$2,492	2.49%

Married couple—two children under age 17, $100,000 of income, which includes $5,000 in dividend income, $15,000 in itemized deductions

	Proposal	Present Law	Savings	% of AGI
Adjusted Gross Income	$100,000	$100,000		
Itemized Deductions	15,000	15,000		
Personal Exemptions	12,200	12,200		
Taxable Income	$ 72,800	$ 72,800		
Tax	11,320	13,362	2,042	
Child Credit	(2,000)	(1,200)	800	
Tax After Credits	$ 9,320	$ 12,162	$2,842	2.84%

Single taxpayer—$100,000 of income, which includes $3,000 in dividend income, $15,000 in itemized deductions

	Proposal	Present Law	Savings	% of AGI
Adjusted Gross Income	$100,000	$100,000		
Itemized Deductions	15,000	15,000		
Personal Exemptions	3,050	3,050		
Taxable Income	$ 81,950	$ 81,950		
Tax	$ 17,302	$ 18,813	$1,511	1.51%

Married couple—two children under age 17, $300,000 of income, which includes $10,000 in dividend income, $50,000 in itemized deductions

	Proposal	Present Law	Savings	% of AGI
Adjusted Gross Income	$300,000	$300,000		
Itemized Deductions	45,185	45,185		
Personal Exemptions	3,172	3,172		
Taxable Income	$251,643	$251,643		
Tax	62,688	69,607	6,919	
Child Credit	(0)	(0)	0	
Tax After Credits	$ 62,688	$ 69,607	$6,919	2.31%

¶ 198

Chapter 2

Individuals

RATE REDUCTIONS
Acceleration in individual income tax rate cuts .... ¶ 205
10-percent tax bracket expanded ... ¶ 210

MARRIAGE PENALTY RELIEF
15-percent tax bracket of joint filers expanded .... ¶ 215
Standard deduction of joint filers increased .... ¶ 220

CREDITS
Acceleration and advance payment of child tax credit increase .... ¶ 225

ALTERNATIVE MINIMUM TAX
Minimum tax relief for individuals .. ¶ 230

CAPITAL GAINS AND DIVIDENDS
Reduction in capital gains rates (see ¶ 305 and following)

Dividends taxed at capital gain rates (see ¶ 325 and following)

STATE AID
Temporary state fiscal relief .... ¶ 240

RATE REDUCTIONS

Acceleration in Individual Income Tax Rate Cuts

¶ 205

Background

The Economic Growth and Tax Relief Reconciliation Act of 2001 (EGTRRA) (P.L. 107-16) scheduled a phased-in reduction of the tax rates in excess of the 15-percent rate that are applicable to individuals and estates and trusts. Prior to enactment of EGTRRA, these tax rates were 39.6 percent, 36 percent, 31 percent and 28 percent. These rates were scheduled to be reduced in four steps as follows (Code Sec. 1(i)(2), as amended by P.L. 107-16):

Tax year beginning during calendar year:	28% rate is reduced to:	31% rate is reduced to:	36% rate is reduced to:	39.6% rate is reduced to:
2001*	27.5%	30.5%	35.5%	39.1%
2002 and 2003	27%	30%	35%	38.6%
2004 and 2005	26%	29%	34%	37.6%
2006–2010	25%	28%	33%	35%
2011 and after	28%	31%	36%	39.6%

* Each 2001 rate is a blended rate, reflecting the 27%, 30%, 35% and 38.6% rates that did not go into effect until after June 30, 2001.

Under the EGTRRA sunset provision (Act Sec. 901(a) of P.L. 107-16), these reductions do not apply to tax years beginning after December 31, 2010. Thus, these tax rates are scheduled to return to the former 39.6-percent, 36-percent, 31-percent and 28-percent rates at that time.

Prior to enactment of the tax rate reductions in the Jobs and Growth Tax Relief Reconciliation Act of 2003 as explained below, the following individual and estate and trust tax rate schedules would have applied in 2003.

¶ 205

Jobs and Growth Tax Relief Reconciliation Act of 2003

Background

Caution: The following 2003 tax rate schedules applied prior to enactment of the Jobs and Growth Tax Relief Reconciliation Act. They are reproduced for informational purposes only and are no longer valid.

Pre-2003 Act—Single Individuals
2003

Taxable Income Over	But Not Over	Pay	+	% on Excess	of the amount over—
$ 0—	$ 6,000	$ 0		10 %	$ 0
6,000—	28,400	600.00		15	6,000
28,400—	68,800	3,960.00		27	28,400
68,800—	143,500	14,868.00		30	68,800
143,500—	311,950	37,278.00		35	143,500
311,950—	......	96,235.50		38.6	311,950

Pre-2003 Act—Married Filing Jointly and Surviving Spouses
2003

Taxable Income Over	But Not Over	Pay	+	% on Excess	of the amount over—
$ 0—	$ 12,000	$ 0		10 %	$ 0
12,000—	47,450	1,200.00		15	12,000
47,450—	114,650	6,517.50		27	47,450
114,650—	174,700	24,661.50		30	114,650
174,700—	311,950	42,676.50		35	174,700
311,950—	......	90,714.00		38.6	311,950

Pre-2003 Act—Married Filing Separately
2003

Taxable Income Over	But Not Over	Pay	+	% on Excess	of the amount over—
$ 0—	$ 6,000	$ 0		10 %	$ 0
6,000—	23,725	600.00		15	6,000
23,725—	57,325	3,258.75		27	23,725
57,325—	87,350	12,330.75		30	57,325
87,350—	155,975	21,338.25		35	87,350
155,975—	......	45,357.00		38.6	155,975

Pre-2003 Act—Heads of Households
2003

Taxable Income Over	But Not Over	Pay	+	% on Excess	of the amount over—
$ 0—	$ 10,000	$ 0		10 %	$ 0
10,000—	38,050	1,000.00		15	10,000
38,050—	98,250	5,207.50		27	38,050
98,250—	159,100	21,461.50		30	98,250
159,100—	311,950	39,716.50		35	159,100
311,950—	....	93,214.00		38.6	311,950

¶ 205

Explanation

Background

Pre-2003 Act—Estates and Nongrantor Trusts
2003

Taxable Income Over	But Not Over	Pay	+	% on Excess	of the amount over—
$ 0—	$ 1,900	$ 0		15 %	$ 0
1,900—	4,500	285.00		27	1,900
4,500—	6,850	987.00		30	4,500
6,850—	9,350	1,692.00		35	6,850
9,350—	......	2,567.00		38.6	9,350

10-percent bracket. In addition to the phased-in reduction of the 28-percent, 31-percent, 36-percent and 39.6-percent tax rates, EGTRRA created a new 10-percent tax bracket, effective beginning in 2001. The 10-percent bracket applies only to individuals, not to estates and trusts. In tax years beginning after December 31, 2007, the end point of the 10-percent bracket was scheduled to increase an additional $2,000 for joint filers and an additional $1,000 for single filers and married taxpayers filing separately (Code Sec. 1(i)(1), as added by P.L. 107-16).

Marriage penalty relief. EGTRRA also scheduled a phased-in increase in the top end of the 15-percent tax bracket for married taxpayers filing jointly over a four-year period beginning in 2005 (Code Sec. 1(f)(8), as added by P.L. 107-16). Upon completion of the phase-in, the amount of a joint filer's taxable income subject to the 15-percent rate would equal twice the amount of single filer's taxable income subject to the 15-percent rate.

Another EGTRRA provision increased the standard deduction for joint filers to twice the amount of a single filer's standard deduction over a five-year phase-in period that is scheduled to begin in 2005 (Code Sec. 63(c)(7), as added by P.L. 107-16).

These two provisions were intended to substantially reduce the so-called "marriage penalty."

Jobs and Growth Act Impact

Reduction in top tax rates accelerated to 2003.—Under the new law, the 25-percent, 28-percent, 33-percent and 35-percent tax rates which were scheduled by EGTRRA to take effect in 2006 are set to apply to tax years beginning in 2003 through 2010 (Code Sec. 1(i)(2), as amended by the Jobs and Growth Tax Relief Reconciliation Act of 2003).

The 15-percent tax bracket of married taxpayers filing jointly is also immediately increased to twice the size of a single filer's 15-percent bracket, effective for tax years beginning in 2003 and 2004. See ¶ 215. The increase in the standard deduction for joint filers to twice the amount of a single filer's standard deduction is likewise immediately effective for the 2003 and 2004 tax years. See ¶ 220.

Comment. In tax years beginning after 2004, the size of the 15-percent bracket and standard deduction for married persons will be based on the applicable phase-in percentage that would otherwise have applied under EGTRRA for the tax year.

¶ 205

Jobs and Growth Tax Relief Reconciliation Act of 2003

The $2,000 and $1,000 increases for the 10-percent tax bracket for individuals other than those filing as head of household are accelerated from tax years beginning after 2007 to tax years beginning after 2002. See ¶ 210.

Top tax rates reduced. The following chart indicates the applicable rates under the new law (Code Sec. 1(i)(2), as amended by the 2003 Act).

Tax year beginning during calendar year:	28% rate is reduced to:	31% rate is reduced to:	36% rate is reduced to:	39.6% rate is reduced to:
2002	27%	30%	35%	38.6%
2003–2010	25%	28%	33%	35%
2011 and after	28%	31%	36%	39.6%

Comment. The accelerated rate reduction is subject to the same sunset rule that applied under EGTRRA (Act Sec. 107 of the 2003 Act). Consequently, the pre-EGTRRA rates (39.6 percent, 36 percent, 31 percent and 28 percent) will go back into effect in tax years beginning after 2010 unless Congress takes legislative action.

Comment. Each 2002 rate above the 15-percent rate is reduced by 2 percentage points for tax year 2003 and subsequent years, except the 38.6-percent rate (i.e., the highest rate), which is reduced by 3.6 percentage points.

The following unofficial tax rate schedules for 2003 reflect the tax rate reductions enacted by the 2003 Act that are effective for tax years that begin in calendar year 2003. These reductions include:

(1) the acceleration of the reduction of the pre-EGTRRA 39.6-percent, 36-percent, 31-percent and 28-percent rates to 35 percent, 33 percent, 28 percent and 25 percent, respectively, effective for 2003 through 2010;

(2) an increase in the size of the 15-percent tax bracket for married taxpayers filing jointly to an amount that is equal to twice the limit for the 15-percent tax bracket for single individuals, effective for 2003 and 2004 (¶ 215); and

(3) a $2,000 increase in the 10-percent bracket of married taxpayers filing jointly and a similar $1,000 increase for single taxpayers and married taxpayers filing separately for 2003 and 2004 (see ¶ 210).

Comment. Due to the fact that the dollar ranges within certain brackets are adjusted annually for inflation, CCH cannot project tax rate schedules for 2004 and later tax years.

Caution: The following 2003 tax rate schedules are unofficial.

Post-2003 Act—Single Individuals
2003

Taxable Income Over	But Not Over	Pay	+	% on Excess	of the amount over—
$ 0—	$ 7,000	$ 0		10 %	$ 0
7,000—	28,400	700.00		15	7,000
28,400—	68,800	3,910.00		25	28,400
68,800—	143,500	14,010.00		28	68,800
143,500—	311,950	34,926.00		33	143,500
311,950—	....	90,514.50		35	311,950

¶ 205

Explanation

Post-2003 Act—Married Filing Jointly and Surviving Spouses
2003

Taxable Income Over	But Not Over	Pay	+	% on Excess	of the amount over—
$ 0—	$ 14,000	$ 0		10 %	$ 0
14,000—	56,800	1,400.00		15	14,000
56,800—	114,650	7,820.00		25	56,800
114,650—	174,700	22,282.50		28	114,650
174,700—	311,950	39,096.50		33	174,700
311,950—	......	84,389.00		35	311,950

Post-2003 Act—Married Filing Separately
2003

Taxable Income Over	But Not Over	Pay	+	% on Excess	of the amount over—
$ 0—	$ 7,000	$ 0		10 %	$ 0
7,000—	28,400	700.00		15	7,000
28,400—	57,325	3,910.00		25	28,400
57,325—	87,350	11,141.25		28	57,325
87,350—	155,975	19,548.25		33	87,350
155,975—	......	42,194.50		35	155,975

Post-2003 Act—Heads of Households
2003

Taxable Income Over	But Not Over	Pay	+	% on Excess	of the amount over—
$ 0—	$ 10,000	$ 0		10 %	$ 0
10,000—	38,050	1,000.00		15	10,000
38,050—	98,250	5,207.50		25	38,050
98,250—	159,100	20,257.50		28	98,250
159,100—	311,950	37,295.50		33	159,100
311,950—	......	87,736.00		35	311,950

Post-2003 Act—Estates and Nongrantor Trusts
2003

Taxable Income Over	But Not Over	Pay	+	% on Excess	of the amount over—
$ 0—	$ 1,900	$ 0		15 %	$ 0
1,900—	4,500	285.00		25	1,900
4,500—	6,850	935.00		28	4,500
6,850—	9,350	1,593.00		33	6,850
9,350—	......	2,418.00		35	9,350

Withholding adjustments. Since the reduced tax rates are effective as of the beginning of 2003, many taxpayers have had too much tax withheld. The Conference Committee Report indicates that the conferees intend that taxpayers who have had their taxes overwithheld should obtain a refund through the normal process of filing an income tax return. Reimbursement should not be sought directly through the payor (e.g., the payor of interest, dividends and other amounts

¶ 205

subject to backup withholding), that is, the person or entity responsible for the withholding.

Comment. The IRS is expected to issue updated wage withholding tables that reflect the tax rate cuts. Presumably, the revised withholding tables will not reduce withholding rates to take the retroactive nature of the tax cuts into account. Thus, unless an employee claims additional withholding exemptions on Form W-4 for the 2003 tax year, the benefit of the tax cut attributable to the period from January 1, 2003, to the time that employers start withholding under revised tables will not be received until after 2003 returns are filed and refunds obtained. Taxpayers who pay estimated tax should consider reestimating their remaining required payments for 2003.

Comment. A release by the Department of Treasury, Office of Public Affairs (May 22, 2003), indicates that the IRS will post revised withholding information on its website (www.irs.gov) on the date of enactment (i.e., the date the bill is signed by President Bush). It will also mail revised withholding information to employers by mid-June. Employers are expected to implement withholding reductions as soon as they receive these new withholding materials.

With respect to withholding that is set by reference to statutorily mandated withholding rates that are affected by a change in tax rates, the Committee expects the IRS to provide a "brief, reasonable period of transition" for payors to adjust their withholding rates.

Comment. Under EGTRRA, a number of statutory withholding provisions were amended to reflect the creation of the new 10-percent bracket and the phased-in reduction of the top rates. No similar amendments are needed under the 2003 Act due principally to the "generic" wording of the statutes. Examples of withholding rates that are statutorily set and affected by the acceleration of the EGTRRA tax cuts include:

(1) voluntary withholding agreements from specified federal payments, such as social security, under which the withholding rate requested may be based on "any of the lowest income tax brackets" applicable to single individuals (Code Sec. 3402(p)(1)(B));

(2) withholding on gambling winnings in an amount equal to the product of the winnings and the "third lowest rate of tax" applicable to single individuals (Code Sec. 3402(q)); and

(3) backup withholding on interest, dividend, and certain other payments in an amount equal to the product of the payment and the "fourth lowest rate of tax" applicable to single individuals (Code Sec. 3406(a)(1)).

Further, supplemental wage payments on which withholding is 27 percent during 2003 will also need to be reduced to 25 percent in 2004 as a result of the accelerated cuts.

Rate proration. Changes in rates under Code Sec. 1(i) are not subject to the rule for prorating taxes under Code Sec. 15 (Code Sec. 15(f), which states: "This section shall not apply to any change in rates under subsection (i) of section 1, (relating to rate changes after 2000)"). The changes to all rate brackets, including the size of such brackets, made by the 2003 Act are made under Code Sec. 1(i). Thus, the proration rule apparently does not apply. For example, estates and trusts with fiscal years should not be subject to the proration rule. The proration issue is only significant to fiscal-year taxpayers since the tax cuts are effective as of January 1, 2003.

¶ 205

Explanation

Caution. The heading for Code Sec. 15(f) refers to "Rate Reductions Enacted by the Economic Growth and Tax Relief Reconciliation Act." Any significance that the heading might have could be negated, however, if the 2003 rate reductions are considered an acceleration of those reductions.

Accumulated earnings and personal holding company tax rates reduced. Under prior law, the accumulated earnings tax was equal to the product of the highest rate of tax under Code Sec. 1(c) (i.e., the highest rate applicable to single filers) and a corporation's accumulated taxable income (Code Sec. 531, prior to amendment by the 2003 Act). The personal holding company tax was computed by multiplying undistributed personal holding company income by the highest rate of tax on single filers (Code Sec. 541, prior to amendment by the 2003 Act).

The new law, however, reduces the tax rate for the accumulated earnings tax and personal holding company tax to 15 percent effective for tax years beginning after December 31, 2002, and beginning before January 1, 2009. See ¶ 365 (accumulated earnings tax) and ¶ 370 (personal holding company tax).

The following table compares tax liabilities of single filers at $10,000 increments of taxable income using the old 2003 rate schedules and the new 2003 rate schedules.

Single Filers

Taxable Income	Old 2003 Rates	New 2003 Rates	Tax Savings
$ 10,000	$ 1,200	$ 1,150	$ 50
$ 20,000	$ 2,700	$ 2,650	$ 50
$ 30,000	$ 4,392	$ 4,310	$ 82
$ 40,000	$ 7,092	$ 6,810	$ 282
$ 50,000	$ 9,792	$ 9,310	$ 482
$ 60,000	$12,492	$11,810	$ 682
$ 70,000	$15,228	$14,346	$ 882
$ 80,000	$18,228	$17,146	$1,082
$ 90,000	$21,228	$19,946	$1,282
$100,000	$24,228	$22,746	$1,482
$110,000	$27,228	$25,546	$1,682
$120,000	$30,228	$28,346	$1,882
$130,000	$33,228	$31,146	$2,082
$140,000	$36,228	$33,946	$2,282
$150,000	$39,553	$37,071	$2,482
$160,000	$43,053	$40,371	$2,682
$170,000	$46,553	$43,671	$2,882
$180,000	$50,053	$46,971	$3,082
$190,000	$53,553	$50,271	$3,282
$200,000	$57,053	$53,571	$3,482

Jobs and Growth Tax Relief Reconciliation Act of 2003

The following table compares tax liabilities of joint filers at $10,000 increments of taxable income using the old 2003 rate schedules and the new 2003 rate schedules.

Married Filing Jointly

Taxable Income	Old 2003 Rates	New 2003 Rates	Tax Savings
$ 10,000	$ 1,000	$ 1,000	$ 0
$ 20,000	$ 2,400	$ 2,300	$ 100
$ 30,000	$ 3,900	$ 3,800	$ 100
$ 40,000	$ 5,400	$ 5,300	$ 100
$ 50,000	$ 7,206	$ 6,800	$ 406
$ 60,000	$ 9,906	$ 8,620	$1,286
$ 70,000	$12,606	$11,120	$1,486
$ 80,000	$15,306	$13,620	$1,686
$ 90,000	$18,006	$16,120	$1,886
$100,000	$20,706	$18,620	$2,086
$110,000	$23,406	$21,120	$2,286
$120,000	$26,267	$23,781	$2,486
$130,000	$29,267	$26,581	$2,686
$140,000	$32,267	$29,381	$2,886
$150,000	$35,267	$32,181	$3,086
$160,000	$38,267	$34,981	$3,286
$170,000	$41,267	$37,781	$3,486
$180,000	$44,532	$40,846	$3,686
$190,000	$48,032	$44,146	$3,886
$200,000	$51,532	$47,446	$4,086

PRACTICAL ANALYSIS. Sidney Kess, New York, CCH consulting editor, author and lecturer, observes that not all taxpayers will see a cut in their taxes. For example, the expansion of the 10-percent tax bracket applies only to married persons and singles; it does not affect heads of households. The expansion of the 15-percent tax bracket applies only to married persons filing joint returns or married filing separately. Heads of households must be in a tax bracket of at least 25 percent to see any reduction in their taxes from the reductions in the marginal rates and expansion of brackets.

For further information about the income tax rates for individuals, see 2003FED ¶ 3270.01, FTS § A:1.42, or 2003FTG ¶ 1010.

★ *Effective date.* The provision applies to tax years beginning after December 31, 2002 (Act Sec. 105(b) of the Jobs and Growth Tax Relief Reconciliation Act of 2003).

EGTRRA sunset provision. Amendments made by Title I of the 2003 Act are subject to the sunset provision found in Title IX of the Economic Growth and Tax Relief Reconciliation Act of 2001 (P.L. 107-16). These 2003 amendments are subject to the EGTRRA sunset provision in the same manner as the provision of

¶ 205

Explanation

EGTRRA to which the amendment relates (Act Sec. 107). See ¶ 29,001 for CCH Explanation and ¶ 10,070 for related committee report.

Act Sec. 105(a) of the Jobs and Growth Tax Relief Reconciliation Act of 2003, amending Code Sec. 1(i)(2); Act Sec. 105(b). Law at ¶ 5005. Committee Report at ¶ 10,050.

10-Percent Tax Bracket Expanded

¶ 210

Background

The Economic Growth and Tax Relief Reconciliation Act of 2001 (EGTRRA) (P.L. 107-16) was enacted on June 7, 2001. The centerpiece of EGTRRA was a two-pronged tax cut.

The first part of the tax cut was a phased-in reduction of the 28-percent, 31-percent, 36-percent and 39.6-percent tax rates to 25 percent, 28 percent, 33 percent and 35 percent, respectively (Code Sec. 1(i)(2), as added by P.L. 107-16). As explained at ¶ 205, the Jobs and Growth Tax Relief Reconciliation Act of 2003 eliminates the remaining phase-in period and puts these rates into effect beginning with the 2003 tax year. The second part of the tax cut, which benefited all taxpayers, carved out a new 10-percent income tax bracket from a portion of the existing 15-percent tax bracket (Code Sec. 1(i)(1), as added by P.L. 107-16). The new 10-percent bracket is also called the "initial bracket amount."

The creation of the 10-percent tax bracket by splitting the 15-percent bracket was effective for tax years beginning after December 31, 2000.

Comment. The tax savings attributable to the new 10-percent bracket in the 2001 tax year were received through a rate-reduction credit that was paid in advance by issuing checks to qualifying taxpayers shortly after enactment of EGTRRA. Advance payment was intended to immediately stimulate the economy. The checks were generally issued in the amount of $600 for joint filers, $500 for heads-of-households, and $300 for single filers and married taxpayers filing separately.

Under EGTRRA, the 10-percent tax bracket applied to the following amounts of taxable income in the case of tax years beginning after 2000 and before 2008 (Code Sec. 1(i)(1), as added by P.L. 107-16):

Pre-2003 Act—Tax years beginning in 2001 through 2007

Filing status	Taxable income subject to 10% bracket
Married filing jointly	$0–$12,000
Single	$0–$ 6,000
Head of household	$0–$10,000
Married filing separately	$0–$ 6,000

In tax years beginning after December 31, 2007, the 10-percent bracket is scheduled to increase by $2,000 for joint filers and by $1,000 for single filers and married taxpayers filing separately (Code Sec. 1(i)(1)(B), as added by P.L. 107-16). No increase is scheduled for heads of households. Thus, the taxable income subject to the 10-percent bracket for each filing status under EGTRRA for this period is as follows:

Background

Pre-2003 Act—Tax years beginning in 2008 through 2010

Filing status	Taxable income subject to 10% bracket
Married filing jointly	$0–$14,000
Single	$0–$ 7,000
Head of household	$0–$10,000
Married filing separately	$0–$ 7,000

Under EGTRRA, the 10-percent bracket amount is not adjusted for inflation until tax years beginning after December 31, 2008 (Code Sec. 1(i)(1)(C)).

Comment. The income limit for the 10-percent tax bracket for joint filers is twice the limit for the 10-percent tax bracket for single filers and married taxpayers filing separately. EGTRRA also contains a provision that gradually increases the income limit for the 15-percent tax bracket for joint filers to twice the limit for the 15-percent tax bracket for single filers over a four-year period beginning in 2005 (Code Sec. 63(c)(7), as added by P.L. 107-16). See ¶ 215.

The income limit for the 10-percent bracket for head-of-household filers is not scheduled under EGTRRA to increase in tax years beginning in 2008 through 2010.

As the result of the EGTRRA sunset provision, the 10-percent tax bracket is scheduled to terminate in tax years beginning after December 31, 2010. At that time, income falling within the 10-percent bracket will fall under the 15-percent tax bracket.

Comment. The 10-percent tax bracket does not apply to estates and trusts (Code Sec. 1(i)(1)(A)(i)).

Jobs and Growth Act Impact

10-percent individual bracket temporarily expanded in 2003 and 2004.—The new law makes the expansion of the 10-percent bracket (also referred to as the initial bracket amount) scheduled by EGTRRA for 2008, 2009 and 2010 also effective in 2003 and 2004 (Code Sec. 1(i)(1)(B)(i), as amended by the Jobs and Growth Tax Relief Reconciliation Act of 2003). In tax years beginning after December 31, 2004, the taxable income levels for the 10-percent tax bracket will revert to the levels allowed under EGTRRA.

Thus, for 2003 and 2004, the 10-percent bracket for married taxpayers filing jointly will increase by $2,000 (from $12,000 to $14,000), and the 10-percent bracket of single filers and married taxpayers filing separately will increase by $1,000 (from $6,000 to $7,000).

Caution. The Conference Committee Report states that the 10-percent bracket amounts will be adjusted for inflation for tax years beginning after December 31, 2003. However, the law provides that the 10-percent bracket will be adjusted for inflation in 2004 and also in tax years beginning after 2008 (i.e., 2009 and 2010 due to the sunset provision) (Code Sec. 1(i)(1)(C), as amended by the 2003 Act).

Comment. EGTRRA had provided for inflation adjustments to the 10-percent bracket only in tax years beginning after December 31, 2008.

¶ 210

Explanation

Comment. The 10-percent bracket amount for married taxpayers filing separately and single filers is equal to one-half of the inflation-adjusted bracket amount for married taxpayers filing jointly (Code Sec. 1(i)(1)(B)(iii), as added by EGTRRA). Thus, the inflation adjustment for married taxpayers who file separate returns and for taxpayers who file as single is achieved indirectly.

Under the new law, and without regard to the inflation adjustments that will apply in 2004, 2009 and 2010, the 10-percent tax brackets for tax years beginning after December 31, 2002, and ending before January 1, 2011, will be as follows:

Post-2003 Act—Tax years beginning in 2003 and 2004

Filing status	Taxable income subject to 10% bracket
Married filing jointly	$0–$14,000
Single	$0–$ 7,000
Head of household	$0–$10,000
Married filing separately	$0–$ 7,000

Post-2003 Act—Tax years beginning in 2005, 2006 and 2007

Filing status	Taxable income subject to 10% bracket
Married filing jointly	$0–$12,000
Single	$0–$ 6,000
Head of household	$0–$10,000
Married filing separately	$0–$ 6,000

Post-2003 Act—Tax years beginning in 2008, 2009 and 2010

Filing status	Taxable income subject to 10% bracket
Married filing jointly	$0–$14,000
Single	$0–$ 7,000
Head of household	$0–$10,000
Married filing separately	$0–$ 7,000

The expansion of the 10-percent tax bracket for 2003 and 2004 has no effect on head-of-household filers. Taxable income subject to the 10-percent bracket for these taxpayers remains $10,000.

Comment. The acceleration of the $2,000 increase in the 10-percent tax bracket for joint filers results in a tax savings of up to $100 (($2,000 × 15%) − ($2,000 × 10%)). The $1,000 increase in the 10-percent bracket for single and married filing separately filers results in a $50 tax savings (($1,000 × 15%) − ($1,000 × 10%)). Married taxpayers filing jointly will receive additional tax savings as a result of the acceleration of the expansion of their 15-percent tax bracket and standard deduction amounts. See ¶ 215 and ¶ 220.

Tables to be modified. The IRS is required to modify 2003 tax tables which have been prescribed to reflect the increase in the 10-percent bracket amount (Act Sec. 104(c)(2) of the 2003 Act).

Comment. Technically, this provision only requires the IRS to revise and reissue previously issued tax tables to reflect the increase in the 10-percent bracket. Clearly, however, any reissued tables will also reflect the other applicable rate cuts contained in the new law (i.e., the increased 15 percent bracket for joint filers (¶ 215) and the reduction in the tax rates (¶ 205)).

¶ 210

PRACTICAL ANALYSIS. Vincent O'Brien, President of Vincent J. O'Brien, CPA, PC, Lynnbrook, New York, observes that the increase in the threshold for the lowest tax rate (although by a modest amount) continues to encourage tax planning among members of the same family. To the extent that an individual has a child (or children) age 14 or older, income earned by such a child will first be sheltered by the child's standard deduction. Then, the first $7,000 of income (for an unmarried child) will be subject to the 10-percent rate, which may represent a substantial savings when compared to the rate of the child's parents.

The top marginal income tax rate has declined in recent years; yet, the difference between the top rate and the lower rates still remains substantial, and tax planning among family members can still reap savings.

It is important to note that the kiddie tax (under which the child's 2003 unearned income in excess of $1,500 is taxed at the parent's marginal tax rate) continues to apply to children under the age of 14. Thus, transfers of assets to children who have not reached that age continue to provide only small amounts of tax savings.

For further information about the tax brackets for individuals, see 2003FED ¶ 3270.01, FTS § A:1.42[1], or 2003FTG ¶ 1010.

★ *Effective date.* The provision applies to tax years beginning after December 31, 2002 (Act Sec. 104(c) of the Jobs and Growth Tax Relief Reconciliation Act of 2003).

EGTRRA sunset provision. Amendments made by Title I of the 2003 Act are subject to the sunset provision found in Title IX of the Economic Growth and Tax Relief Reconciliation Act of 2001 (P.L. 107-16). These 2003 amendments are subject to the EGTRRA sunset provision in the same manner as the provision of EGTRRA to which the amendment relates (Act Sec. 107). See ¶ 29,001 for CCH Explanation and ¶ 10,070 for related committee report.

Act Sec. 104(a) and (b) of the Jobs and Growth Tax Relief Reconciliation Act of 2003, amending Code Sec. 1(i)(1); Act Sec. 104(c). Law at ¶ 5005. Committee Report at ¶ 10,040.

MARRIAGE PENALTY RELIEF

15-Percent Tax Bracket of Joint Filers Expanded

¶ 215

Background

A marriage penalty exists when the tax on the combined income of a married couple exceeds the sum of the taxes that would be imposed if each spouse filed a separate return as a single person. This situation exists most often when both spouses have income. If one spouse does not work or has a small amount of income, a marriage bonus may occur—that is, the couple pays less tax by filing a joint return than they would have if each spouse filed his or her own return.

Although many factors can contribute to a marriage penalty, the two most significant are the disparity in the size of a married and single person's standard

Background

deduction and the income levels at which the various tax brackets are applied. Parity with respect to these two factors would require that the standard deduction of a married couple be twice as large as that of a single person and that the tax brackets of a married person be applied to an amount of taxable income that is twice the amount of taxable income to which the same tax brackets of a single person apply.

The Economic Growth and Tax Relief Reconciliation Act of 2001 (EGTRRA) (P.L. 107-16) included provisions that address these two issues. First, EGTRRA included a provision that would increase the size of the standard deduction for joint filers to twice the size (i.e., 200 percent) of the standard deduction for a single filer. Under EGTRRA, the standard deduction of joint filers is scheduled to increase beginning in 2005, with the phase-in period completed in 2009. See ¶ 220.

EGTRRA also provided a phased-in increase in the top end of the 15-percent tax bracket for married taxpayers filing jointly (Code Sec. 1(f)(8), as added by P.L. 107-16).

The phase-in period, which was scheduled to start in 2005 and be completed in 2008, would cause the amount of taxable income that falls within a joint filer's 15-percent tax bracket to be exactly twice the amount (i.e., 200 percent) of the taxable income that falls within the 15-percent tax bracket of a single filer. For example, if taxable income over $7,000 but not over $31,700 of a single filer is subject to a 15-percent rate in 2008, then the maximum taxable income in the 15-percent bracket of a joint filer would be $63,400 ($31,700 × 200%). (These figures are hypothetical and used for illustrative purposes only.)

Comment. To the extent that the size of the 15-percent tax bracket increases, the amount of taxable income subject to the next highest tax bracket is reduced. In 2003 through 2010, the next highest bracket is 25 percent. See ¶ 205.

Comment. In general, the end points of the tax brackets for single filers are approximately 60 percent of the end points for married persons filing a joint return. However, the end point of the highest tax bracket is the same for single and joint filers.

The following chart shows the rate at which the amount of the 15-percent tax bracket for joint filers is scheduled to increase under EGTRRA relative to the 15-percent tax bracket for single filers. The end point of the 15-percent tax bracket is multiplied by the applicable percentage to determine the end point of a joint filer's 15-percent tax bracket.

For tax years beginning in calendar year—	The applicable percentage is—
2005	180
2006	187
2007	193
2008–2010	200

After 2010, pre-EGTRRA law will be reinstated pursuant to the EGTRRA sunset provision.

The scheduled increase in the 15-percent tax bracket for married taxpayers filing jointly also results in an increase in the size of the 15-percent tax bracket for married taxpayers filing separately. This is because the amount which falls within each tax bracket of a married person filing separately is equal to one-half of the amount which falls within each of a joint filer's tax brackets.

¶ 215

Jobs and Growth Act Impact

15-percent tax bracket of joint filers increased in 2003 and 2004.—The new law increases the size of a joint filer's 15-percent tax bracket to twice the size of a single person's tax bracket in 2003 and 2004. Beginning in 2005, the size of a joint filer's 15-percent tax bracket will be determined in accordance with the phase-in schedule enacted by the Economic Growth and Tax Reconciliation Act of 2001 (EGTRRA) (P.L. 107-16) (Code Sec. 1(f)(8), as amended by the Jobs and Growth Tax Relief Reconciliation Act of 2003).

Comment. The new law also increases a joint filer's standard deduction to 200 percent of an individual filer's standard deduction in 2003 and 2004. See ¶ 220.

The following chart shows the rate at which the 15-percent tax bracket for joint filers is scheduled to increase relative to the 15-percent tax bracket for single filers. The end point of a single taxpayer's tax bracket is multiplied by the applicable percentage to determine the end point of a joint filer's 15-percent tax bracket.

Post-2003 Act

For tax years beginning in calendar year—	The applicable percentage is—
2003	200
2004	200
2005	180
2006	187
2007	193
2008–2010	200

Comment. In 2003, a joint filer with at least $56,800 of taxable income will save $935 in taxes as a result of this provision. In 2003, the end point of the 15-percent tax bracket of a single individual is $28,400. Under the new law, the end point of the 15-percent tax bracket for a joint filer will be set at $56,800 ($28,400 × 2). If this change had not been enacted, the end point of a joint filer's 15-percent tax bracket would have been $47,450 in 2003. Thus, $9,350 ($56,800 − $47,450) that would have been taxed in the next highest bracket (25% under the new law) is taxed at a 15-percent rate instead. The potential 2003 tax savings due solely to the expansion of the 15-percent bracket is $935 ($9,350 × (25% − 15%)).

The following 2003 tax rate schedules are for taxpayers who are married filing jointly. The first schedule was in effect prior to enactment of the new law. The second unofficial schedule, prepared by CCH, reflects (1) the increase in the size of the 15-percent tax bracket; (2) a $2,000 increase in the 10-percent bracket for married taxpayers (see ¶ 210); and (3) a reduction in the income tax rates in excess of 15 percent from 27, 30, 35 and 38.6 percent to 25, 28, 33 and 35 percent, respectively (see ¶ 205).

A complete set of unofficial CCH-projected 2003 Tax Rate Schedules that reflect the tax rate reductions enacted by the 2003 Act are reproduced at ¶ 205.

Explanation

Caution: The following 2003 tax rate schedule for married taxpayers filing jointly applied prior to enactment of the Jobs and Growth Tax Relief Reconciliation Act of 2003. It is reproduced for comparative purposes only and is no longer valid.

Pre-2003 Act—Married Filing Jointly and Surviving Spouses
2003

Taxable Income Over	But Not Over	Pay	+	% on Excess	of the amount over—
$ 0—	$ 12,000	$ 0		10 %	$ 0
12,000—	47,450	1,200.00		15	12,000
47,450—	114,650	6,517.50		27	47,450
114,650—	174,700	24,661.50		30	114,650
174,700—	311,950	42,676.50		35	174,700
311,950—	....	90,714.00		38.6	311,950

Caution: The following 2003 tax rate schedule for married taxpayers filing jointly is unofficial.

Post-2003 Act—Married Filing Jointly and Surviving Spouses
2003

Taxable Income Over	But Not Over	Pay	+	% on Excess	of the amount over—
$ 0—	$ 14,000	$ 0		10 %	$ 0
14,000—	56,800	1,400.00		15	14,000
56,800—	114,650	7,820.00		25	56,800
114,650—	174,700	22,282.50		28	114,650
174,700—	311,950	39,096.50		33	174,700
311,950—	....	84,389.00		35	311,950

Inflation adjustments. The end point of the 15-percent tax bracket of a married taxpayer filing jointly is rounded to the next lowest multiple of $50 (Code Sec. 1(f)(8)(C), as added by EGTRRA). This rounding convention should only have an impact in 2005, 2006 and 2007 when the applicable percentages are 180, 187, and 193 percent, respectively. In tax years when the applicable percentage is 200 percent (i.e., 2003, 2004, 2008, 2009 and 2010), the end point of a joint filer's 15-percent tax bracket will always be a multiple of $50. This is because the end point of the 15-percent tax bracket of a single person is first rounded to the next lowest multiple of $50 before multiplying it by the applicable percentage (Code Sec. 1(f)(6)(A)).

Example. Assume that for 2003 the inflation-adjusted end point of a single taxpayer's 15% tax bracket before rounding is $28,413. This amount is rounded down to the next lowest multiple of $50 to $28,400. The end point of a joint filer's 15% tax bracket is determined by multiplying $28,400 by 200% (the applicable percentage for 2003). The end point of a joint filer's bracket, before rounding, is $56,800 ($28,400 × 200%). Since $56,800 is a multiple of $50, no additional rounding is required. If the applicable percentage had been 180%, the endpoint of a joint filer's bracket, before rounding, would have been $51,120 ($28,400 × 180%). Since $51,120 is not a multiple of $50, the 15% bracket would have been rounded down to $51,100.

¶ 215

Married taxpayers filing separately. The end point of the 15-percent tax bracket for a married taxpayer filing separately is equal to one-half of the inflation-adjusted end point of a joint filer's 15-percent tax bracket (Code Sec. 1(f)(8)(A)(ii)). In 2003, this is $28,400 ($56,800 × 50%). Thus, the increased 15-percent tax bracket for married persons filing jointly will also result in an increased 15-percent tax bracket for separate filers. Prior to the 2003 Act, the end point of the 15-percent tax bracket for married taxpayers filing separately was set at $23,725 for 2003. Thus, the 2003 tax savings attributable to the $4,675 difference ($28,400 − $23,725) which is taxed at a 15-percent rate rather than a 25-percent rate is $467.50 ($4,675 × (25% − 15%)). This is exactly one-half of the $9,350 tax savings of a joint filer, as computed in the Comment above.

PRACTICAL ANALYSIS. Martin Nissenbaum of Ernst & Young, New York, New York, observes that the widening of the 15-percent bracket for married filing jointly to twice that of single taxpayers will benefit all joint filers. Taxpayers may wish to determine whether items of income and deduction should be recognized in 2004 or in 2005, when the 15-percent bracket size will revert to 180 percent of the single 15-percent bracket.

For further information about the tax brackets for joint filers, see 2003FED ¶ 3270.01, FTS § A:1.42, or 2003FTG ¶ 1010.

★ *Effective date.* The provision is effective for tax years beginning after December 31, 2002 (Act Secs. 102(b)(2) and (c) of the Jobs and Growth Tax Relief Reconciliation Act of 2003).

EGTRRA sunset provision. Amendments made by Title I of the 2003 Act are subject to the sunset provision found in Title IX of the Economic Growth and Tax Relief Reconciliation Act of 2001 (P.L. 107-16). These 2003 amendments are subject to the EGTRRA sunset provision in the same manner as the provision of EGTRRA to which the amendment relates (Act Sec. 107). See ¶ 29,001 for CCH Explanation and ¶ 10,070 for related committee report.

Act Sec. 102(a) and (b)(1) of the Jobs and Growth Tax Relief Reconciliation Act of 2003, amending Code Sec. 1(f)(8); Act Sec. 102(b)(2), amending Act Sec. 302(c) of the Economic Growth and Tax Relief Reconciliation Act of 2001; Act Sec. 102(c). Law at ¶ 5005 and ¶ 7010. Committee Report at ¶ 10,020.

Standard Deduction of Joint Filers Increased

¶ 220

Background

A marriage penalty exists when the tax on the combined income of a married couple exceeds the sum of the taxes that would be imposed if each spouse filed a separate return as a single person. This situation exists most often when both spouses have income. If one spouse does not work or has a small amount of income a marriage bonus may occur—that is, the couple pays less tax by filing a joint return than they would have if each spouse filed his or her own return.

Although many factors can contribute to a marriage penalty, the two most significant are the disparity in the size of a married and single person's standard deduction and the income levels at which the various tax brackets are applied.

Background

Parity with respect to the first factor would require that the standard deduction of a married couple be twice as large as that of a single person. Parity with respect to the tax bracket factor would require that the tax brackets of a married person be applied to an amount of taxable income that is twice the amount of taxable income to which the same tax brackets of a single person apply.

The Economic Growth and Tax Relief Reconciliation Act of 2001 (EGTRRA) (P.L. 107-16) included provisions that address these two issues.

First, EGTRRA included a provision that increases the size of a joint filer's 15-percent tax bracket over four years beginning in 2005 to an amount equal to twice the size of a single person's 15-percent tax bracket. This rule is discussed in detail at ¶ 215.

EGTRRA also included a provision that increased the size of the standard deduction for joint filers to twice the size (i.e., 200 percent) of the standard deduction for a single filer. The standard deduction for joint filers is scheduled to increase beginning in 2005, with a phase-in completed in 2009. The EGTRRA sunset provision, however, will reinstate prior law after 2010.

The EGTRRA phase-in of the higher standard deduction for married taxpayers filing jointly is illustrated in the following chart:

For tax years beginning in calendar year—	The applicable percentage is—
2005	174
2006	184
2007	187
2008	190
2009 and 2010	200
2011	Pre-EGTRRA rules reinstated

The percentages are applied to the inflation-adjusted standard deduction that applies to single filers for the particular year.

Jobs and Growth Act Impact

Standard deduction of joint filers temporarily increased to twice that of single filers.—The new law increases the basic standard deduction of a married taxpayer filing jointly (and surviving spouses) to twice the amount of the inflation-adjusted standard deduction of a single filer for tax years beginning in 2003 and 2004 (Code Sec. 63(c)(7), as amended by the Jobs and Growth Tax Relief Reconciliation Act of 2003). In later tax years, the basic standard deduction of married taxpayers will be based on the same applicable percentages that are scheduled to go into effect under the Economic Growth and Tax Relief Reconciliation Act of 2001 (EGTRRA) (P.L. 107-16).

The basic standard deduction of joint filers will be determined by applying the following applicable percentages to the inflation-adjusted basic standard deduction of single filers:

¶ 220

Post-2003 Act

For tax years beginning in calendar year—	The applicable percentage is—
2003	200
2004	200
2005	174
2006	184
2007	187
2008	190
2009 and 2010	200

If the basic standard deduction of a married taxpayer filing jointly (i.e., the inflation-adjusted standard deduction of a single taxpayer multiplied by the applicable percentage) is not a multiple of $50, it is rounded to the next lowest $50. (Code Sec. 63(c)(2), as amended by P.L. 107-16).

Comment. The 2003 basic standard deduction for single filers is $4,750. Consequently, the basic standard deduction for married taxpayers filing jointly will be $9,500 in 2003 ($4,750 × 200%). Prior to enactment of the new law, the basic standard deduction for joint filers had been set at $7,950 for 2003. This represents a $1,550 increase ($9,500 − $7,950). The tax savings will depend upon the taxpayer's applicable tax bracket.

2003 Tax Bracket	2003 Tax Savings
10%	$155.00 ($1,550 × 10%)
15%	$232.50 ($1,550 × 15%)
25%	$387.50 ($1,550 × 25%)
28%	$434.00 ($1,550 × 28%)
33%	$511.50 ($1,550 × 33%)
35%	$542.50 ($1,550 × 35%)

These tax savings figures assume that the additional $1,550 standard deduction amount reduces taxable income that falls entirely within the same bracket. As explained at ¶ 205, the new law has reduced the 27-, 30-, 35- and 38.6-percent tax brackets to 25, 28, 33 and 35 percent, respectively, beginning in 2003.

Comment. A married taxpayer who itemizes will not benefit from the increased standard deduction. However, as a result of the increase, fewer married taxpayers will need to itemize since their basic standard deduction could exceed their itemized deductions.

Planning Note. Some states permit itemization only if the taxpayer also itemizes on the federal return. Taxpayers from these states may save more taxes overall by itemizing on the federal return even though their itemized deductions are less than their federal basic standard deduction.

PRACTICAL ANALYSIS. Harley T. Duncan of the Federation of Tax Administrators, Washington, D.C., notes that the increased standard deduction that is part of the marriage penalty relief provisions could affect those states that conform to federal taxable income as a starting point. They include Colorado, Hawaii, Idaho, Minnesota, North Carolina, North Dakota, Oregon, South Carolina, Utah and Vermont. Of these, Colorado, North Dakota, Oregon, Utah and Vermont conform to the federal code on an automatic or rolling basis.

¶ 220

Standard deduction of married taxpayers filing separately. Beginning in 2003, the basic standard deduction of a married taxpayer filing separately is equal to one-half of the inflation-adjusted standard deduction of a joint filer (Code Sec. 63(c)(2)(C), as amended by P.L. 107-16 and P.L. 107-147). Thus, the standard deduction for a married taxpayer filing separately in 2003 will be $4,750 ($9,500 × 50%). Prior to enactment of the new law, the inflation-adjusted basic standard deduction for a married person filing separately for 2003 was announced as $3,975.

Comment. In any year that the applicable percentage is 200 percent, the basic standard deduction for married taxpayers filing separately and single taxpayers will be identical. If the applicable percentage is less than 200 percent, the basic standard deduction of a married taxpayer filing separately will be less than that of a single taxpayer.

Example. Assume that the inflation-adjusted basic standard deduction for single filers is $5,000 in 2005. (This is a hypothetical figure.) The applicable percentage for 2005 is 174%. The basic standard deduction for a joint filer in 2005 would be $8,700 ($5,000 × 174%). The basic standard deduction of a married taxpayer filing separately would be $4,350 ($8,700 × 50%).

PRACTICAL ANALYSIS. Martin Nissenbaum of Ernst & Young, New York, New York, notes that the increase in the standard deduction intended to offset the "marriage penalty" will obviously not benefit married taxpayers claiming itemized deductions. Nevertheless, many taxpayers who would have otherwise itemized may instead claim the standard deduction in 2003 and 2004. (In 2003 the standard deduction will be $9,500 instead of $7,950.) In 2004, such taxpayers may wish to defer itemized deductions into 2005 when the standard deduction will revert to 174 percent of the single standard deduction.

For further information about the standard deduction for joint filers, see 2003FED ¶ 6023.023, FTS § A:12.61[2], or 2003FTG ¶ 6020.

★ *Effective date.* The provision applies to tax years beginning after December 31, 2002 (Act Sec. 103(c) of the Jobs and Growth Tax Relief Reconciliation Act of 2003).

EGTRRA sunset provision. Amendments made by Title I of the 2003 Act are subject to the sunset provision found in Title IX of the Economic Growth and Tax Relief Reconciliation Act of 2001 (P.L. 107-16). These 2003 amendments are subject to the EGTRRA sunset provision in the same manner as the provision of EGTRRA to which the amendment relates (Act Sec. 107). See ¶ 29,001 for CCH Explanation and ¶ 10,070 for related committee report.

Act Sec. 103(a) of the Jobs and Growth Tax Relief Reconciliation Act of 2003, amending Code Sec. 63(c)(7); Act Sec. 103(b), amending Act Sec. 301(d) of the Economic Growth and Tax Relief Reconciliation Act of 2001; Act Sec. 103(c). Law at ¶ 5025 and ¶ 7015. Committee Report at ¶ 10,030.

¶ 220

CREDITS

Acceleration and Advance Payment of Child Tax Credit Increase

¶ 225

Background

Taxpayers who have a qualifying child are eligible for the child tax credit (CTC). A qualifying child must be the taxpayer's child, stepchild, sibling, stepsibling or a descendent of any of these, or an eligible foster child, who is under age 17 at the close of the calendar year, who is a U.S. citizen or resident alien, and for whom the taxpayer is allowed a dependency exemption (Code Sec. 24(c), Code Sec. 32(c)(3)(B)(i), Code Sec. 151, and Code Sec. 152(b)(3)). The credit for 2003 and 2004 is $600 per qualifying child and this amount increases to $700 for tax years 2005 through 2008, $800 for tax year 2009 and $1,000 for tax year 2010 (Code Sec. 24(a)).

The CTC begins to phase out when modified adjusted gross income (AGI) reaches $110,000 for joint filers, $55,000 for married individuals filing separately, and $75,000 for unmarried individuals (Code Sec. 24(b)(2)). The credit is reduced by $50 for each $1,000, or fraction thereof, of modified AGI above the thresholds (Code Sec. 24(b)(1)). The CTC offsets the taxpayer's regular and alternative minimum tax liability (Code Sec. 26(a)(2)).

For tax years beginning in 2001 through 2004, the CTC may be refundable to the extent of 10 percent of the taxpayer's earned income (as defined by Code Sec. 32) in excess of $10,000, up to the per child credit amount, if the taxpayer has a total tax liability, minus nonrefundable credits previously taken, of less than his or her allowable CTC (Code Sec. 24(d)(1)). For 2005 and thereafter, the rate is increased to 15 percent. Beginning in 2002, the $10,000 base income amount is indexed for inflation ($10,350 in 2002 and $10,500 in 2003). Taxpayers with three or more children may calculate the refundable portion of the credit using the excess of their social security taxes over the earned income credit (additional credit for families with three or more children) if it produces a greater refundable credit than the 10 percent of income method (Code Sec. 24(d)(1)).

Comment. Any payment made to a taxpayer pursuant to the refundable portion of the CTC is not income. Furthermore, for purposes of determining a taxpayer's eligibility for any benefits, assistance or supportive services having income limitations on eligibility under any federal program or federally financed program, the refundable portion of the CTC is not taken into account as a resource for the month of receipt or the following month (Act Sec. 203 of the Economic Growth and Tax Relief Reconciliation Act of 2001 (EGTRRA) (P.L. 107-16)).

Because of a sunset provision in P.L. 107-16, the CTC would revert to $500 in 2011. In addition, the CTC would no longer be able to be used against the alternative minimum tax liability. The CTC would be limited to the amount by which the regular tax exceeds the alternative minimum tax beginning in 2011. Finally, the CTC also would become nonrefundable unless the taxpayer had three or more children and social security taxes in excess of the earned income credit (additional credit for families with three or more children) (Act Sec. 901 of P.L. 107-16).

Explanation

Jobs and Growth Act Impact

$400 increase in child tax credit.—The child tax credit (CTC) increases from $600 to $1,000 per qualifying child, effective for tax years 2003 and 2004 (Code Sec. 24(a)(2), as amended by the Jobs and Growth Tax Relief Reconciliation Act of 2003). However, the CTC will decrease to $700 per qualifying child for tax years 2005 through 2008, then rise to $800 for tax year 2009, and return to $1,000 for tax year 2010 (Code Sec. 24(a)(2)). These amounts sunset for tax years beginning after December 31, 2010; therefore, in tax year 2011 and thereafter, the CTC will return to $500 per qualifying child.

Comment. Since taxpayers required to make estimated tax payments in 2003 are directly affected by the increase in the CTC, the IRS will advise these taxpayers on how to adjust their estimated tax payments to reflect the CTC increase, including the effect of the refundable portion and any advance payment (Tax Complexity Analysis, Comments of the IRS and Treasury Department, Conference Committee Report).

Advance payment of CTC increase. In 2003, the increase in the CTC will be paid or credited in advance using the taxpayer's 2002 tax return as the basis of information (Code Sec. 6429, as added by the 2003 Act). There are two prerequisites for receiving the CTC refund amount:

(1) the taxpayer was allowed a CTC in 2002, as reflected on the 2002 tax return (Code Sec. 6429(a), as added by the 2003 Act); *and*

(2) the taxpayer had a qualifying child (or children) in 2002 who is under age 17 as of December 31, 2003 (Code Sec. 6429(b)(2), as added by the 2003 Act).

The additional credit for families with three or more children is disregarded for purposes of arriving at the CTC refund amount (Code Sec. 6429(b)(3), as added by the 2003 Act).

Comment. Generally, taxpayers who qualify for the advance payment of the CTC increase will receive $400 per qualifying child. However, the Conference Committee Report states that the advance payment is to be made based on the taxpayer's 2002 tax return information, as was done in 2001 with the rate reduction advance payment (Tax Complexity Analysis, Conference Committee Report). Therefore, taxpayers at the higher and lower ends of the income spectrum will probably receive only a portion of the $400 per qualifying child increase as an advance payment based on the amount of the CTC allowed on their 2002 tax returns. This directly affects taxpayers who were allowed less than the full amount of the CTC due to application of the CTC income phase-out provision or because they were subject to the tax liability and 10-percent-of-income limitations on their 2002 tax returns.

Example (1). Peter and Kathy Miller were allowed a $600 child tax credit for their daughter Amy (age 3) on their 2002 tax return. Their son Patrick was born on January 13, 2003. Since Patrick was not a qualifying child in 2002, the Millers will receive a CTC advance payment check in the amount of $400 only for Amy.

Example (2). Jim and Katie Murphy were allowed a $1,200 child tax credit for their children Colleen (age 16) and Kevin (age 12) on their 2002 tax return. Since Colleen's 17th birthday is December 28, 2003, the Murphys will receive a CTC advance payment check in the amount of $400 only for Kevin.

¶ 225

64   Jobs and Growth Tax Relief Reconciliation Act of 2003

Caution. Since the CTC advance payment is predicated on allowance of a CTC on the taxpayer's 2002 tax return, it is anticipated that no advance payment checks will be issued to taxpayers who did not claim the CTC for 2002.

Example (3). John Brown was born to Frank and Pam Brown on May 10, 2003. Since John is their first child, the Browns claimed no child tax credit on their 2002 tax return. The Browns will not receive a CTC advance payment check in 2003. However, they will be able to claim a CTC in the amount of $1,000 on their 2003 tax return, assuming they are not subject to the income phase-out provision or the tax liability and 10-percent-of-income limitations.

The CTC refund amount is applied per qualifying child as long as the prerequisites, a CTC allowed on the 2002 tax return and a qualifying child (or children) in 2002 who is under age 17 as of December 31, 2003, are satisfied (Code Sec. 6429(b), as added by the 2003 Act).

Example (4). On their 2002 tax return, Joe and Betsy Smart were allowed an $1,800 child tax credit for their children Michael (age 10), Mary (age 8), and David (age 4). Since all three children will be under age 17 on December 31, 2003, the Smarts are entitled to a CTC advance payment check in the amount of $1,200.

Comment. The advance payment of the CTC increase acknowledges that families with children have additional financial responsibilities. The goal is to improve their economic situation and jump start the economy by immediately providing them with this additional money. According to the Treasury Department, it is expected that approximately 27 million families will receive about $14 billion in advance payments.

The CTC refund amount will be paid or credited as quickly as possible. However, no refund or credit will be made after December 31, 2003 and no interest will be paid at any time on this CTC refund amount (Code Sec. 6429(c) and (e), as added by the 2003 Act).

Comment. It is anticipated that checks will be issued beginning in July of 2003 to put the tax savings into the hands of taxpayers more quickly. For taxpayers whose 2002 tax returns have already been filed and processed, it is expected that the advance payment checks will be mailed within the first three weeks of July. Prior to the mailing of the checks, notices are to be mailed to taxpayers stating the amount of their advance payment, the number of children used in computing the amount, and if any reduction in the amount was required due to the income phase-out provision or the tax liability and earned income limitations. For taxpayers whose returns are filed and processed later in the year, the advance payment checks will be mailed weekly through the end of December 2003 (Tax Complexity Analysis, Comments of the IRS and Treasury Department, Conference Committee Report).

Advance payment offset on 2003 tax return. The CTC claimed on the taxpayer's 2003 tax return must be reduced (but not below zero) by the amount of any advance CTC payment received by the taxpayer in 2003 (Code Sec. 6429(d)(1), as added by the 2003 Act). A failure to reduce the 2003 CTC by the advance payment amount will be treated as a mathematical or clerical error allowing the IRS to summarily assess the additional tax without issuing a notice of deficiency (Code Sec. 6429(d)(1), as added by the 2003 Act; Code Sec. 6213(b)(1)). If the CTC advance payment amount is paid based on a 2002 joint return, half of the payment will be treated as having been made to each joint filer (Code Sec. 6429(d)(2), as added by the 2003 Act).

¶ 225

Explanation

Comment. Similar to the rate reduction credit worksheet provided in the 2001 tax return instructions, a worksheet will be provided in the 2003 tax return instructions to calculate the allowable CTC for 2003 after deducting the advance CTC payment (Tax Complexity Analysis, Comments of the IRS and Treasury Department, Conference Committee Report).

Comment. For taxpayers subject to the CTC income phase-out provision in 2003, depending on how many qualifying children a taxpayer had in 2002 and the taxpayer's 2003 income level, it is possible that the CTC advance payment could be greater than the actual CTC allowable on the 2003 return. However, since the CTC calculated for 2003 must be reduced (*but not below zero*) by the CTC advance payment amount, potentially the "but not below zero" language provides a windfall of sorts for those taxpayers subject to the phase-out provisions.

Example (5). John and Mary Johansson claimed dependency exemptions for their children, Jack (age 3) and Sarah (age 1), on their 2002 tax return. Mary only worked part-time in 2002, but returned to work full-time in 2003. Because of Mary's reduced earnings in 2002, John and Mary's modified adjusted gross income for 2002 was less than $110,000, allowing them to claim the full amount of the CTC. They will receive a CTC advance payment check for $800. However, with Mary now a full-time attorney, John and Mary's 2003 modified adjusted gross income is expected to exceed the maximum phase-out amount of $130,000, therefore, their CTC may be zero for 2003. Since the CTC advance payment cannot reduce the CTC below zero, the $800 advance CTC payment may be a windfall for John and Mary.

Planning Note. The CTC remains a consideration in divorce and multiple support agreement situations because only the taxpayer entitled to the dependent exemption is entitled to the CTC. Furthermore, care must be exercised so that the relationship test applicable to the CTC is met between the child and the party claiming the dependent exemption. With the $400 increase in the CTC and its refundable component, the economic significance of the CTC is greater than ever in divorce and multiple support agreement situations.

PRACTICAL ANALYSIS. Sidney Kess, New York, CCH consulting editor, author and lecturer, points out that parents going through a divorce must be more sensitive than ever to planning for dependent children in view of the increased child tax credit to $1,000 per child and the refund checks to be paid in 2003 reflecting that increase. The parent entitled to the dependency exemption for a child is the parent who can claim the child tax credit. Divorced couples who alternate the year in which they take the dependency exemption may have a problem with the rebate checks since the parent who took the dependency exemption in 2002 will receive the refund check related to the 2003 return in 2003. The other parent, who would claim the dependency exemption in 2003, may attempt to claim the full $1,000 credit, without reduction for the check paid, since it was not paid to them. It may be difficult for divorced parents to resolve this problem.

PRACTICAL ANALYSIS. Vincent O'Brien, President of Vincent J. O'Brien, CPA, PC, Lynnbrook, New York, observes that the advance payment of the increase in the child credit creates some

¶ 225

interesting logistical questions that the IRS will need to address now and when the filing season for 2003 tax returns begins.

The IRS will calculate advance payments using information from 2002 income tax returns; however, these returns did not provide information about the ages of children for whom the credit was taken. If the child reaches age 17 during 2003, an individual who claimed a child credit for that child in 2002 will no longer be eligible for the credit in 2003.

Also, an individual's income for 2003 may exceed the phaseout threshold, causing the individual to be ineligible for some or all of the credit. As a result, it is possible that an individual may receive an advance payment and ultimately not be eligible for the child credit to which the advance payment relates.

Practitioners that have clients with children that turn 17 during 2003 or that have clients that expect significant increases in their income in 2003 should advise such clients that the advance payments received may be due back to the IRS when they file their 2003 returns.

Interestingly, when the Treasury Department issued advance payments in 2001 as part of the creation of the 10-percent tax bracket for that year, individuals who received amounts for which they were ultimately ineligible (due to lower income in 2001 versus 2000) did not have to repay those amounts when they filed their 2001 returns. While the Treasury Department may follow the same approach for the 2003 advance payments, practitioners and their clients should wait until the IRS issues guidance in this area before making any conclusions.

On a separate note, the increase in the child credit amount will be beneficial for any individual who is entitled to one or more full child credits. It will also benefit some individuals who have been subject to the phaseout of the child credit in prior years.

While the threshold for the phaseout of the credit and the formula under which that phaseout is calculated have not changed, the increased amount allowed per child credit may have the effect of making some higher-income individuals eligible for a portion of the credit for the first time.

The phaseout of the credit begins at modified adjusted gross income over $110,000 for married individuals filing joint returns ($75,000 for single individuals or heads of households). The phaseout reduces the allowable credit by $50 for each $1,000 (or fraction thereof) that modified adjusted gross income exceeds the applicable threshold.

Example. Joe and Mary have two children. In 2002 and 2003, they have modified adjusted gross income of $134,000. In 2002, their total child credit, before considering the phaseout, is $1,200 (2 × $600). Their allowable credit after the phaseout is zero. (This is calculated as $134,000 minus $110,000, which is $24,000. $24,000 divided by $1,000 is 24, and 24 multiplied by $50 results in a

Explanation

phaseout of $1,200, which equals the total credit for which they would otherwise be eligible.)

In 2003, their total child credit, before considering the phaseout, is $2,000 (2 × $1,000). Their allowable credit after the phaseout is $800 ($2,000 − $1,200 phaseout). The phaseout for 2003 is calculated in the same way as in 2002; however, with the higher total credit, the couple can now benefit from a portion of the child credit.

For further information about the child tax credit, see 2003FED ¶ 3770.01, FTS § A:19.200, or 2003FTG ¶ 2222.

★ *Effective date.* The child tax credit increase applies to tax years beginning after December 31, 2002 (Act Sec. 101(c)(1) of the Jobs and Growth Tax Relief Reconciliation Act of 2003). The advance payment provision is effective on the date of enactment (Act Sec. 101(c)(2) of the 2003 Act).

EGTRRA sunset provision. Amendments made by Title I of the 2003 Act are subject to the sunset provision found in Title IX of the Economic Growth and Tax Relief Reconciliation Act of 2001 (P.L. 107-16). These 2003 amendments are subject to the EGTRRA sunset provision in the same manner as the provision of EGTRRA to which the amendment relates (Act Sec. 107). See ¶ 29,001 for CCH Explanation and ¶ 10,070 for related committee report.

Act Sec. 101(a) of the Jobs and Growth Tax Relief Reconciliation Act of 2003, amending Code Sec. 24(a)(2); Act Sec. 101(b), adding Code Sec. 6429; Act Sec. 101(c). Law at ¶ 5010 and ¶ 5120. Committee Report at ¶ 10,010.

ALTERNATIVE MINIMUM TAX

Minimum Tax Relief for Individuals

¶ 230

Background

An alternative minimum tax (AMT) is payable to the extent that a taxpayer's tentative minimum tax exceeds the regular tax. The AMT imposed on noncorporate taxpayers is equal to 26 percent of the first $175,000 ($87,500 for married taxpayers filing separately) of alternative minimum taxable income (AMTI) in excess of an exemption amount and 28 percent of the remaining AMTI (Code Sec. 55(a) and (b)).

The AMT exemption amount for joint return filers and surviving spouses is $49,000 in tax years beginning in 2001, 2002, 2003 and 2004, and it is scheduled to revert to $45,000 for tax years beginning after 2004 (Code Sec. 55(d)(1)(A), prior to amendment by the Jobs and Growth Tax Relief Reconciliation Act of 2003). The AMT exemption amount for an unmarried individual who is not a surviving spouse is $35,750 in tax years beginning in 2001, 2002, 2003 and 2004, and it is scheduled to revert to $33,750 for tax years beginning after 2004 (Code Sec. 55(d)(1)(B), prior to amendment by the 2003 Act). The AMT exemption amount of a married taxpayer who files a separate return is one-half the AMT exemption amount of a joint return filer (Code Sec. 55(d)(1)(C)). Thus, the AMT exemption amount of a married taxpayer who files separately is $24,500 in the case of tax years beginning

Background

in 2001, 2002, 2003 and 2004, and it is scheduled to revert to $22,500 for tax years beginning after 2004.

The AMT exemption amounts are phased out for taxpayers with high AMTI. The exemption amounts are reduced by an amount equal to 25 percent of the amount by which the individual's AMTI exceeds:

- $150,000 in the case of joint return filers, surviving spouses and corporations;

- $112,500 in the case of single taxpayers; and

- $75,000 in the case of married taxpayers filing separate returns and estates and trusts (Code Sec. 55(d)(3)).

For married taxpayers filing joint returns and surviving spouses, the AMT exemption amount of $49,000 is not completely phased out until AMTI reaches $346,000. For single taxpayers, the exemption amount of $35,750 is completely phased out when AMTI reaches $255,500. For married taxpayers filing a separate return, the exemption amount of $24,500 is completely phased out when AMTI reaches $173,000. In order to prevent an incentive for separate filing by married taxpayers, a separate filer whose AMTI exceeds that $173,000 phase-out ceiling must also add back to AMTI the lesser of: (1) 25 percent of the excess of AMTI (as determined before this add-back computation) over the $173,000 phase-out ceiling, or (2) an amount equal to the $24,500 married filing separate AMT exemption amount. Thus, such a taxpayer with $271,000 of AMTI is subject to the full $24,500 add-back, as well as a complete exemption phase-out. The exemption and phase-out amounts are not adjusted for inflation.

Jobs and Growth Act Impact

AMT exemption amounts increased.—The AMT exemption amount is increased to:

- $58,000 for joint return filers and surviving spouses in tax years beginning in 2003 and 2004 (Code Sec. 55(d)(1)(A), as amended by the Jobs and Growth Tax Relief Reconciliation Act of 2003);

- $40,250 for a single individual who is not a surviving spouse in tax years beginning in 2003 and 2004 (Code Sec. 55(d)(1)(B), as amended by the 2003 Act); and

- $29,000 for a married taxpayer who files a separate return in tax years beginning in 2003 and 2004 (Code Sec. 55(d)(1)(C)).

Example. In 2003, Marge and Mike Midelinc have regular taxable income of $100,000 and file a joint income tax return. The Midelincs also have tax preferences and adjustments that total $30,000. Assume that the Midelincs' regular tax is $20,000. Their AMTI is $130,000 ($100,000 regular taxable income + $30,000 tax preferences and adjustments). The Midelincs' AMTI is reduced by the applicable exemption amount.

Under prior law, the AMT exemption amount for this married couple for the 2003 tax year would have been $49,000, the AMTI subject to the tentative minimum tax would have been $81,000 ($130,000 − $49,000), and the tentative minimum tax would have been $21,060 ($81,000 × 26%). Thus,

¶ 230

Explanation

the Midelincs' AMT would have been $1,060 ($21,060 tentative minimum tax − $20,000 regular tax).

Under the new law, the AMT exemption amount for this married couple for the 2003 tax year will be $58,000, the AMTI subject to the tentative minimum tax will be $72,000 ($130,000 − $58,000), and the tentative minimum tax will be $18,720 ($72,000 × 26%). Thus, the Midelincs' AMT will be $0 ($18,720 tentative minimum tax is less than the $20,000 regular tax).

Comment. Individuals' AMT exemption amounts were increased so that the benefits from the accelerated reduction in individuals' regular income tax rates were not diminished by the AMT (Treasury Department, Office of Public Affairs Release (May 22, 2003), Tax Provisions of the Jobs and Growth Tax Relief Reconciliation Act of 2003).

PRACTICAL ANALYSIS. Michael J. Grace of Jackson & Campbell, PC, Washington, D.C., points out that the 2003 Act leaves unresolved the AMT "creep" problem. The 2003 Act offers some relief from the alternative minimum tax on individuals by increasing somewhat the amounts of income exempt from the tax. It does not appear, however, that these increases will slow significantly the trend of increasing numbers of individuals having to pay alternative minimum tax.

Caution. Absent Congressional action, the AMT exemption amount for joint return filers and surviving spouses will statutorily revert to $45,000 for tax years beginning after 2004. Similarly, the AMT exemption amount for a single taxpayer who is not a surviving spouse will statutorily revert to $33,750 for tax years beginning after 2004. Finally, the AMT exemption amount of a married taxpayer who files a separate return will statutorily revert to $22,500 (one-half of the $45,000 AMT exemption amount for joint return filers) for tax years beginning after 2004 (Code Sec. 55(d)).

Caution. The AMT exemption amount of an estate or trust remains at $22,500 (Code Sec. 55(d)(1)(D)), and a corporation's AMT exemption amount remains at $40,000 (Code Sec. 55(d)(2)). Similarly, the AMT phase-out threshold for an estate or trust remains at $75,000, and the phase-out threshold for a corporation remains at $150,000 (Code Sec. 55(d)(3)).

AMT exemption phase-outs. Although an individual's AMT exemption amount increases for tax years beginning in 2003 and 2004, the threshold at which the AMT exemption begins to phase out remains the same. Exemption amounts are still reduced by an amount equal to 25 percent of the amount by which the individual's AMTI exceeds:

- $150,000 in the case of joint return filers and surviving spouses;
- $112,500 in the case of single taxpayers; and
- $75,000 in the case of married taxpayers filing separate returns.

Since the AMT exemption amounts for individuals have increased and the phase-out triggers have remained the same, the maximum amount of AMTI that a taxpayer may have before the exemption amount is fully phased out has increased under the new law. For married taxpayers filing joint returns and surviving

¶ 230

spouses, the increased AMT exemption amount of $58,000 is not completely phased out until AMTI reaches $382,000, up from $346,000. For single taxpayers, the exemption amount of $40,250 is completely phased out when AMTI reaches $273,500, up from $255,500. Similarly, for married taxpayers filing a separate return, the exemption amount of $29,000 is completely phased out when AMTI reaches $191,000, up from $173,000. As under prior law, the married taxpayer who files separately must also increase AMTI by the lesser of: (1) 25 percent of the excess of AMTI (as determined before this add-back computation) over the $191,000 phase-out ceiling, or (2) the $29,000 married filing separate AMT exemption. Thus, the ceiling on the amount of AMTI that would subject a married filing separate taxpayer to the full $29,000 add-back is $307,000, up from $271,000.

Comment. Absent Congressional action, the ceilings on the AMT exemption phase-outs will drop in tandem with the reversion in the AMT exemption amounts for tax years beginning after 2004. The phase-out ceiling for a married taxpayer filing a joint return and a surviving spouse will revert to $330,000 for tax years beginning after 2004. The phase-out ceiling for a single taxpayer who is not a surviving spouse will revert to $247,500 for tax years beginning after 2004. The phase-out ceiling for a married taxpayer who files a separate return will revert to $165,000 for tax years beginning after 2004 (Code Sec. 55(d)). Finally, the ceiling on the amount of AMTI that would subject a married filing separate taxpayer to a full $22,500 add-back will revert to $255,000.

PRACTICAL ANALYSIS. Mark Luscombe, Principal Analyst for the Federal and State Tax Group at CCH INCORPORATED, points out that the 2003 Act continues the band-aid approach that has been taken to the alternative minimum tax problem in the last several pieces of tax legislation. The Joint Committee on Taxation has estimated that over 17 million taxpayers will be subject to AMT by 2010, as compared to a little over one million taxpayers who pay AMT currently. Some recent legislation has specifically provided that new tax breaks will be allowed for both regular tax and AMT purposes, e.g., capital gains and nonrefundable tax credits. The 2001 Tax Act (EGTRRA) made a small increase in the AMT exemption amount for a four-year period. One of the principal sources of the projected rapid growth of taxpayers subjected to AMT is that the AMT amount is not adjusted annually for inflation.

The 2003 Act follows the same short-term approaches to the AMT problem. The 2003 Act increases the exemption amount for a period of two years, stemming the rise in additional taxpayers subjected to the AMT as a result of the tax reductions enacted as part of the 2003 Act for that period, but doing nothing to address the long-term AMT problem. The 2003 Act also specifically allows the reduced rate of tax on capital gains and dividends for both regular tax and AMT purposes, and also significantly reduces the AMT preference item associated with Code Sec. 1202 stock. While these changes are helpful in that they have a chance to stay in the Code at least as long as the underlying provision, they do not alone stem the rise in AMT. For example, even if the new capital gain and dividend rates are allowed for AMT purposes, the increased income associated with capital gains and dividends can

Explanation

still increase a taxpayer's likelihood of being subjected to the AMT because of the increase in other return items, such as the itemized deduction for state income taxes, which is an AMT preference item. Unless some further action is taken, the reach of the AMT will start its rapid rise in 2005.

For further information about the AMT exemption amounts, see 2003FED ¶ 5101.036, FTS § A:22.180, or 2003FTG ¶ 1320.

★ *Effective date.* The increases in the alternative minimum tax exemption amounts apply to tax years beginning after December 31, 2002 (Act Sec. 106(b) of the Jobs and Growth Tax Relief Reconciliation Act of 2003).

EGTRRA sunset provision. Amendments made by Title I of the 2003 Act are subject to the sunset provision found in Title IX of the Economic Growth and Tax Relief Reconciliation Act of 2001 (EGTRRA) (P.L. 107-16). These 2003 amendments are subject to the EGTRRA sunset provision in the same manner as the provision of EGTRRA to which the amendment relates (Act Sec. 107). See ¶ 29,001 for CCH Explanation and ¶ 10,070 for related committee report.

Comment. Since the AMT exemption increases apply only in tax years beginning in 2003 and 2004, the sunset provision has no impact on this provision. The increase in the AMT exemption amount ceases to apply in tax years beginning in 2005 and thereafter.

Act Sec. 106(a) of the Jobs and Growth Tax Relief Reconciliation Act of 2003, amending Code Sec. 55(d)(1); Act Sec. 106(b). Law at ¶ 5015. Committee Report at ¶ 10,060.

STATE AID

Temporary State Fiscal Relief

¶ 240

Background

States are mired in their worst fiscal crisis since World War II as they face a third consecutive year of significant budget shortfalls, according to the National Governors Association. For fiscal year 2004, which begins on July 1, 2003, the National Conference of State Legislatures estimates that 41 states face a cumulative budget gap of $78.4 billion. This comes on top of $200 billion in budget shortfalls for the last two fiscal years. Since most states are prohibited from running budget deficits, they must deal with these shortfalls by cutting spending and raising revenues.

State budget woes have several sources. The national economic downturn led to a general decline in state tax revenues, with capital gain and corporate tax revenues particularly hard-hit. At the same time, states were faced with unexpected expenses for items as diverse as homeland security needs and natural disasters. One of the largest single components of the fiscal crisis is increased health care expenditures, which account for about 30 percent of the average state budget, according to the National Governors Association.

Medicaid alone accounts for about 20 percent of state spending. This jointly funded, federal-state health insurance program for qualified low-income individuals is now larger than Medicare, the federal health insurance program for qualified

Background

disabled individuals and people over the age of 65. Medicaid covers 44 million people at an aggregate cost of $230 billion, while Medicare covers 40 million people at an aggregate cost of $215 billion. Medicaid eligibility is also growing twice as fast as Medicare eligibility, especially as people who lose their jobs also lose their health insurance. Medicaid costs increased by 14 percent last year, and are growing another 10 percent this year.

The federal share of state Medicaid expenditures is called the federal medical assistance percentage (FMAP). A state's FMAP is determined annually by a formula that compares the state's average per capita income level with the national income average. States with a higher per capita income receive a smaller share of their Medicaid costs. A higher FMAP means the federal government pays a greater share of the state's Medicaid expenses. Under current law, the FMAP cannot be lower than 50 percent or higher than 83 percent of the state's Medicaid expenditures. Some states also require their political subdivisions to pay a percentage of the state's share of Medicaid costs.

Jobs and Growth Act Impact

Temporary fiscal relief for states.—States will receive $20 billion in aid for fiscal years 2003 and 2004, with one-half devoted to Medicaid assistance, and one-half available for other government services (Act Sec. 401 of the Jobs and Growth Tax Relief Reconciliation Act of 2003).

Medicaid assistance. The federal share of state Medicaid expenditures is increased by increasing FMAPs in fiscal years 2003 and 2004 (Act Sec. 401(a) of the 2003 Act). If a state's FMAP for fiscal year 2003 is less than its FMAP for 2002, it may use its 2002 FMAP for the third and fourth quarters of fiscal year 2003. If the state's FMAP for fiscal year 2004 is less than its original FMAP for 2003 (that is, its 2003 FMAP before replacement by its 2002 FMAP), it may use its 2003 FMAP for the first, second and third quarters of fiscal year 2004. Whichever FMAP the state uses is also increased by 2.95 percent for the last two calendar quarters of fiscal year 2003, and the first three calendar quarters of fiscal year 2004. In addition, there is a 5.9-percent increase in the cap on Medicaid payments to Puerto Rico, the U.S. Virgin Islands, Guam, the Northern Mariana Islands, and American Samoa.

The FMAP increases do not apply with respect to certain expenses, such as disproportionate share hospital payments, Temporary Assistance to Needy Families (TANF), state child health plans, and enhanced FMAPs used for certain child health programs. In order for the increased FMAP or Medicaid cap to apply, Medicaid eligibility in the state or territory must be no more restrictive than it was on September 2, 2003. The share of state Medicaid expenses that political subdivisions are required to pay cannot be increased above the percentage required by the state on April 1, 2003.

General assistance. A total of $10 billion ($5 billion dollars for fiscal year 2003 and $5 billion for fiscal year 2004) will be distributed to the states (Act Sec. 401(b) of the 2003 Act, adding Section 601 to the Social Security Act (42 U.S.C. 301 et seq.)). These funds may be used only to provide essential government services or to cover the costs of complying with federal intergovernmental mandates. They cannot be used for any expenditures that were not permitted under the state's most recently approved budget.

¶ 240

Explanation

The amount of each state's payment is based on the state's population. For each year, the $5 billion appropriation is multiplied by the state's relative state population proportion, which is the state's total population divided by the total population of all states as determined by the 2000 census. These amounts are then prorated to ensure that each state, including the District of Columbia, receives no less that one-half of one percent of the total appropriation for the year, or $25 million. For Puerto Rico, the U.S. Virgin Islands, Guam, the Northern Mariana Islands, and American Samoa, the minimum payment is one-tenth of one percent of the total appropriation, or $5 million.

For fiscal year 2003, the funds will be disbursed on the later of the date the state certifies its appropriate use of the funds, or 45 days after the 2003 Act is enacted. For 2004, the funds will be disbursed on the later of the date the state certifies its appropriate use of the funds, or October 1, 2003.

PRACTICAL ANALYSIS. Harley T. Duncan of the Federation of Tax Administrators, Washington, D.C., observes that Title IV of the 2003 Act provides $20 billion in temporary fiscal assistance to states to assist them in dealing with revenue shortfalls and expenditure needs. One-half of the funding will assist in meeting Medicaid (joint federal-state program to provide health care to low income households) responsibilities, and the other $10 billion is flexible assistance that states must use for essential government services.

The Medicaid assistance will be provided by increasing the proportion of total program costs in each state that is paid for by the federal government by 2.95 percentage points for the last two quarters of federal Fiscal Year 2003 (April 2003–September 2003) and the first three quarters of FY 2004 (October 2003–June 2004). Currently, the federal government pays a varying percentage of total costs in each state (ranging from 50 to 77 percent), depending largely on income levels in the state. To qualify for the supplemental funds, a state may not restrict eligibility from that in place on September 3, 2003; neither may a state increase the proportion of costs paid by local governments in those states in which localities help finance the Medicaid program.

As to the flexible assistance, $5 billion will be provided in each of federal FY 2003 and 2004. States must use the funds for essential government services or to comply with an unfunded federal mandate. Funds must also be used for expenditures currently authorized in state budgets, *i.e.*, they may not be used to establish programs not approved by the state legislature. A state must certify to the Secretary of the Treasury that the funds will be utilized in accord with the 2003 Act in order to qualify for funding. The Secretary of Treasury is directed to disburse the FY 2003 funds within 45 days of enactment, and the FY 2004 funds by October 1, 2003, provided that a state has made the appropriate certification.

¶ 240

Funds are to be divided among the states, District of Columbia and five U.S. territories on the basis of population as determined in the 2000 Census, except that no territory shall receive less than 1/10th of one percent of the total appropriation ($10 million over 2 years), and no state (or D.C.) shall receive less than 1/2 of one percent of the amount appropriated ($50 million over 2 years).

★ *Effective date.* No specific effective date is provided by the Act. The provision is, therefore, considered effective on the date of enactment.

Act Sec. 401 of the Jobs and Growth Tax Relief Reconciliation Act of 2003. Law at ¶ 7040. Committee Report at ¶ 10,120.

Chapter 3
Business and Investment

CAPITAL GAINS
Reduction in capital gains rates for individuals .... ¶ 305
Elimination of five-year holding period .... ¶ 310
Small business stock .... ¶ 315
Transitional rule .... ¶ 320

DIVIDENDS
Dividend income of individuals taxed at capital gain rates .... ¶ 325
Dividends passed through RICs and REITs .... ¶ 335

DEPRECIATION
Increase and extension of bonus depreciation .... ¶ 350

DEDUCTIONS
Increased expensing for small businesses .... ¶ 355

CORPORATIONS
Repeal of collapsible corporation rules .... ¶ 360
Reduced accumulated earnings tax rate .... ¶ 365
Reduced personal holding company tax rate .... ¶ 370
Corporate estimated tax payments for 2003 .... ¶ 375

CAPITAL GAINS

Reduction in Capital Gains Rates for Individuals

¶ 305

Background

As a general rule, the maximum long-term capital gains tax rate for individuals is 20 percent (Code Sec. 1(h)(1)(C)). A lower rate of 10 percent may be used by individuals in a 10-percent or 15-percent tax bracket (Code Sec. 1(h)(1)(B)). However, if the capital asset was owned for at least five years, a maximum capital gains rate of 18 percent (8 percent for individuals in the 10-percent or 15-percent tax bracket) may be applied in some situations (Code Sec. 1(h)(2)). The applicable maximum capital gains tax rate (e.g., 20 percent or 18 percent) also is used when computing an individual's alternative minimum tax liability (Code Sec. 55(b)(3)).

Jobs and Growth Act Impact

Lower tax rates for some long-term capital gains.—The new legislation lowers the maximum tax rates that are generally applied to long-term capital gains. The following rate reductions have been made:

• A 15-percent maximum tax rate replaces the 20-percent rate that existed under prior law (Code Sec. 1(h)(1)(C), as amended by the Jobs and Growth Tax Relief Reconciliation Act of 2003).

• A 5-percent rate replaces the 10-percent rate for individuals in a 10-percent or 15-percent tax bracket (Code Sec. 1(h)(1)(B), as amended by the 2003 Act).

- A zero-percent rate replaces the 5-percent rate for tax years beginning after December 31, 2007 (Code Sec. 1(h)(1)(B), as amended by the 2003 Act).

Comment. Under Congress's sunset provisions, all these rate reductions will expire in tax years beginning after December 31, 2008, and the previous capital gains rates (e.g., 10 percent and 20 percent) will again apply (Act Sec. 303 of the 2003 Act).

Example (1). Assume that for 2002, Frank Keller, a single individual, had taxable income of $300,000 and that placed him in the 35% tax bracket. Included in the total amount of his taxable income was a $20,000 net long-term capital gain. Based on these facts, Keller would have paid a maximum capital gains tax of $4,000 ($20,000 × 20%).

Example (2). Assume the same facts pertain to Keller for 2003. In this situation, he would generally pay a maximum capital gains tax of $3,000 ($20,000 × 15%). As a result, Keller saves $1,000 in taxes.

Caution. Because the reduction in capital gains rates is not generally retroactive to January 1, 2003, special computations must be used to compute an individual's long-term capital gains tax for a tax year that includes May 6, 2003. See ¶ 320 for an explanation of the "transitional rule" that must be used for 2003.

Additional rate reductions. In addition to the reduction in the capital gains rates that are generally applicable, the 2003 Act made the following rate reductions:

(1) *Alternative minimum tax.* The new long-term capital gains tax rates of 5 percent (zero percent after 2007) or 15 percent are also used when computing an individual's liability for the alternative minimum tax (AMT) (Code Sec. 55(b)(3)(B) and (C), as amended by the 2003 Act). A separate rate reduction must be considered when determining the AMT of an investor who sold small business stock (see ¶ 315 for more information concerning this rate change).

(2) *Dividend income.* The 5-percent or 15-percent long-term capital gains tax rates apply to most types of dividend income (Code Sec. 1(h)(11), as added by the 2003 Act). Unlike the reduction in the capital gains tax rates, the rate reduction for dividend income will be effective as of January 1, 2003. See ¶ 325 and ¶ 335 for complete explanations of this new tax treatment of dividend income.

(3) *Nonqualified withdrawals of construction funds established under the Merchant Marine Act.* The maximum tax rate imposed on individuals who make nonqualified withdrawals from the capital gain account of a capital construction fund established under the Merchant Marine Act is reduced to 15 percent (Code Sec. 7518(g)(6)(A) and Act Sec. 607(h)(6)(A) of the Merchant Marine Act of 1936, as amended by the 2003 Act). (Note: The purpose of allowing these construction fund accounts is to encourage investment in United States shipyards that are used to construct or repair merchant vessels.)

(4) *Withholding by domestic partnerships, estates and trusts.* The IRS, by regulation, may reduce the amount of income tax required to be withheld on a foreign person's gain from the disposition of an interest in U.S. real property from 20 percent to 15 percent (Code Sec. 1445(e)(1), as amended by the 2003 Act). If the IRS does not include such a provision in its regulations, the domestic partnership, estate, or trust must withhold income tax at a rate of 35 percent (Code Sec. 1445(e)(1), as amended by the 2003 Act).

Explanation

Planning Note. The provision concerning withholding by partnerships, estates and trusts (see item (4), above), only comes into play when distributions from the sale of U.S. real property are made to a foreign person who is a partner or beneficiary. If the partner or beneficiary is not a foreign person, no income tax is required to be withheld from the distribution.

Comment. In addition to the capital gains tax rate reductions mentioned above, the new law has taken an important step in simplifying the taxation of long-term capital gains by eliminating the special five-year holding period rules. This topic is discussed at ¶ 310.

Caution. The 2003 Act did *not* bring about an overall reduction in maximum long-term capital gains rates. Left unchanged is the 28-percent rate imposed on long-term gain from collectibles and net gain from small business stock (Code Sec. 1(h)(4), as renumbered by the 2003 Act). The maximum rate of unrecaptured Section 1250 gain remains at 25 percent (Code Sec. 1(h)(1)(D)). Property must still be held for more than 12 months in order to be classified as "long-term" (Code Sec. 1222). Net capital losses are still subject to a limit of $3,000 per year (Code Sec. 1211(b)).

PRACTICAL ANALYSIS. Michael J. Grace of Jackson & Campbell, PC, Washington, D.C., notes that the 2003 Act leaves unchanged the 25-percent tax rate on unrecaptured Code Sec. 1250 gain. Under prior law, that rate generally exceeded the rate on capital gains by five percent (assuming the generally applicable 20-percent rate on capital gains). Under the 2003 Act, this excess has increased to 10 percent (20 percent in the case of taxpayers eligible for the five-percent rate on capital gains). Assume, for example, that a taxpayer sells commercial real property on which depreciation has been taken. The taxpayer will have to pay tax equaling 25 percent of the portion of the gain representing prior depreciation deductions and 15 percent (or five percent) of the remaining gain. Congress should consider reducing the 25-percent rate so as to preserve the differential that existed before the 2003 Act.

Reducing the five-percent rate on dividends and capital gains to zero percent for 2008 arguably will not stimulate investments because taxpayers subject to marginal rates below 25 percent tend not to invest significant amounts of money in capital assets.

PRACTICAL ANALYSIS. Martin Nissenbaum of Ernst & Young, New York, New York, makes the following comments:

The five-percent rate on gains otherwise taxed in the 10-percent and 15-percent brackets. The low five-percent potential rate on capital gains provides a substantial opportunity for income and transfer tax planning. Under prior law, the lowest rate on capital gains was eight percent for assets held over five years. High-bracket taxpayers could reduce the rate of tax on five-year appreciated assets (from 20 percent to eight percent), or one-year assets (from 20 percent to 10 percent), by gifting them to lower-income taxpayers, such as children 14 years or older, before sale. (The kiddie tax, which generally applies the parents' tax rate to the

¶ 305

unearned income of children who are under 14, continues to apply. The provision in the original Senate version of the bill which raised the kiddie tax age to under 18 did not pass.)

Under the 2003 Act, the five-percent rate applies to gains from assets held more than a year; the five-year holding period rule has been repealed. Taxpayers may wish to consider using a transfer to children, or other low-income taxpayers, to cut the effective rate of tax on such gains by two-thirds. Of course, if assets are transferred to a child or other taxpayer, the transferee will have legal ownership.

In light of the five-percent rate, which will apply to both capital gains and dividends through 2007 (the lower rate will be zero percent in 2008), parents may wish to reconsider the use of other tax-favored savings vehicles such as Code Sec. 529 plans and Coverdell Education Savings Accounts. The potential tax-free benefit of such vehicles, but with their various restrictions, may be outweighed by the extremely low rate of tax that a child might pay if the assets were held directly in his or her own name.

Alternative minimum tax effect. The new lower rates are effective for both regular and AMT purposes. Nevertheless, they may still result in greater exposure to the AMT.

(1) Inclusion of the gain in income may reduce the available AMT exemption.

(2) State and local taxes on capital gains, which are taxed at reduced federal rates, will reduce the spread between ordinary tax and AMT.

Qualified plans, IRAs, nonqualified plans and equity compensation. The benefit of the lower capital gains rates will not apply to gains generated within qualified plans, such as 401(k) plans, and IRAs. Distributions from these accounts will still be taxed as ordinary income regardless of the source of income. In light of this incongruity, taxpayers may wish to revisit their asset allocation between taxable accounts and these types of tax-favored accounts, taking into account the sunset of these rates at the end of 2008. If a taxpayer receives employer securities in a lump-sum distribution from an employer qualified plan which contain net unrealized appreciation (NUA), that NUA would be eligible for taxation at the new 15-percent/five-percent rates. Taxpayers may want to re-evaluate their participation in nonqualified deferred compensation plans. Distributions from such plans are taxed as ordinary wage income. If compensation is received and taxed up front but reinvested in capital gain/dividend generating securities, the net after-tax result may be greater than that of participating in a nonqualified plan.

The reduction in capital gains rates will also add luster to the Code Sec. 83(b) election for restricted stock. Because of the likely adoption of accounting proposals that will require book expensing on the grant of stock options, many companies will consider the grant of stock subject to performance restrictions instead. Under Code Sec. 83, the value of such stock is included in income of the

Explanation

recipient when the restrictions lapse, unless a Code Sec. 83(b) election is made. If the election is made, the value at grant is included in income and any subsequent appreciation is capital gain, recognized at the time of sale. The downside of the election is that no deduction is allowed to the recipient in the event of actual forfeiture.

Nevertheless, the Code Sec. 83(b) election may be valuable for two reasons: (1) the appreciation would potentially be taxed at maximum rate of 15 percent (and as low as five percent) instead of the 35-percent rate that could be imposed at vesting otherwise; and (2) dividends paid on restricted stock, which would be otherwise characterized as ordinary compensation income, would be eligible for the 15-percent capital gains rate.

The use of other types of compensation structures such as incentive stock options and partnership profits interests may also become more prevalent since these may generate long-term capital gains on the disposition of the underlying property.

Capital losses. The 2003 Act does not change the $3,000 annual capital loss limitation of Code Sec. 1211. Capital losses will also not be available for offset against qualifying dividends even though such dividends are subject to the same rates as capital gains. Thus, $3,000 of net capital losses will be applied against ordinary income; dividends will be taxed separately at capital gains rates.

Charitable giving. The lower capital gains rates may have a dampening effect on the use of appreciated property for charitable purposes, both directly and through split interest vehicles, such as charitable remainder trusts. Taxpayers will have less of an incentive to use such property if their tax rate on sale would be 15 percent or less.

Tax returns. The new capital gains rates generally apply to capital assets sold (and installment payments received) after May 5, 2003. As a result, the 2003 Schedule D will have to provide for at least three types of "long term" capital asset sales—sales of assets held for more than five years prior to May 6, 2003, sales of assets held for more than a year prior to May 6, 2003, and sales of assets held for more than a year after May 5, 2003. (Gains from collectibles will continue to be taxed at 28 percent.) Mutual fund companies and other passthrough entities will have to segregate these sales as well. Substantially more taxpayers would have to complete Schedule D, which will be much more complicated. Similar complexity will reach Form 6251 (AMT) and Form 8801 (AMT Credit).

For further information about capital gain rates for individuals, see 2003FED ¶ 3285.01, FTS § A:1.42[3], FTS § E:5.100, or 2003FTG ¶ 5581.

★ *Effective date.* These provisions generally apply to tax years ending on or after May 6, 2003 (Act Sec. 301(d)(1) of the Jobs and Growth Tax Relief Reconciliation Act of 2003). However, the new provision concerning the 15-percent withholding rate on certain payments made by domestic partnerships, estates and trusts to foreign persons applies to amounts paid after the date of enactment of the 2003 Act (Act Sec. 301(d)(2) of the 2003 Act).

Sunset provision. The provisions and amendments of Title III of the 2003 Act will not apply to tax years beginning after December 31, 2008. The Internal Revenue Code of 1986 will be applied and administered to these years as if the provisions and amendments had not been enacted (Act Sec. 303). See ¶ 29,001 for CCH Explanation.

Act Sec. 301(a)(1) of the Jobs and Growth Tax Relief Reconciliation Act of 2003, amending Code Sec. 1(h)(1)(B) and Code Sec. 55(b)(3)(B); Act Sec. 301(a)(2), amending Code Sec. 1(h)(1)(C), Code Sec. 55(b)(3)(C), Code Sec. 1445(e)(1) and Code Sec. 7518(g)(6)(A); Act Secs. 301(b)(1) and (2), amending Code Sec. 1(h) and Code Sec. 55(b)(3); Act Sec. 301(d)(1) and (2). Law at ¶ 5005 and ¶ 5015. Committee Report at ¶ 10,100.

Elimination of Five-Year Holding Period

¶ 310

Background

For tax years beginning after December 31, 2000, individuals can avail themselves of special low capital gains tax rates if they hold property for more than five years. Under this rule, the maximum rate is 18 percent (8 percent for those in the 10-percent or 15-percent brackets) (Code Sec. 1(h)(2)).

This "five-year-property rule" can be complicated to apply because the date that the five-year holding period begins is different for individuals in the 10-percent or 15-percent tax brackets than for individuals in higher brackets (Code Sec. 1(h)(2)(B)). Briefly, the following rules are used to determine when the five-year holding period starts:

(1) If an individual is in a tax bracket higher than 15 percent, the five-year holding period only applies to assets acquired after December 31, 2000. (However, a special "deemed sale election" could have been made on 2001 tax returns. See "Deemed Sale Election," below.)

(2) If an individual is in a 10-percent or 15-percent tax bracket, the assets do not have to be acquired after December 31, 2000, in order to have the five-year holding period begin.

Deemed sale election. Individuals in higher tax brackets who wanted to be able to use the lower tax rates for five-year assets that were acquired before January 1, 2001, could have elected on their 2001 tax returns to report a deemed sale. Under this election, the applicable capital gains tax was paid as though the asset had been sold on January 1, 2001, and the taxpayer's holding period began anew on that date (Act Sec. 311(e) of the Taxpayer Relief Act of 1997 (P.L. 105-34)). If the election was made on the original 2001 return, the individual filed a separate statement and indicated an election under "Section 311 of the Taxpayer Relief Act of 1997." The election, once made, was irrevocable (Act Sec. 311(e)(3) of P.L. 105-34).

Comment. Due to changes made by the 2003 legislation, the irrevocable nature of the deemed sale election may well raise problems for individuals who utilized this election. See "Planning Note," below, for more information.

Explanation

Jobs and Growth Act Impact

Five-year holding period and its lower rates eliminated.—The 2003 legislation has eliminated the special holding period rule that pertained to capital assets held for more than five years (Code Sec. 1(h)(9), repealed by the Jobs and Growth Tax Relief Reconciliation Act of 2003). Also eliminated are the lower capital gains tax rates (i.e., 8 percent for taxpayers in a 10-percent or 15-percent tax bracket and 18 percent for individuals in higher brackets) that could apply when computing an individual's capital gains tax (Code Sec. 1(h)(2), repealed by the 2003 Act) and alternative minimum tax liabilities (Code Sec. 55(b)(3), amended by the 2003 Act) (see ¶ 305).

Comment. Now that Congress has generally lowered the maximum capital gains tax rates to 5 percent and 15 percent, the cumbersome rules that applied to the taxation of gain from capital assets held more than five years are no longer needed. Naturally, those lower-income individuals who were able to use the five-year rule on their 2001 and 2002 tax returns can take some satisfaction from having utilized this tax savings device during its brief life. However, higher-income individuals who made a "deemed sale election" on their 2001 tax returns should consider filing amended returns (see "Planning Note," below).

Planning Note. High-income individuals who made a "deemed sale election" on their 2001 tax returns in order to have the five-year property rule apply to assets that they had acquired before January 1, 2001, should consider filing amended returns in order to reverse the election. Under the original 1997 legislation, the election, once made, was irrevocable (Act Sec. 311(e)(3) of the Taxpayer Relief Act of 1997 (P.L. 105-34)). The new legislation does not address the issue of allowing individuals to reverse their earlier election. However, given the speed in which Congress passed the 2003 Act, it is probable that this issue was overlooked. It is very likely that Congress will permit the revocation of the election in subsequent legislation. Amended returns should be filed at that time.

Computing capital gains tax for 2003. A special "transitional rule" has to be applied when computing an individual's maximum capital gains tax rate for a tax year that includes May 6, 2003. This rule is explained and illustrated at ¶ 320.

PRACTICAL ANALYSIS. Martin Nissenbaum of Ernst & Young, New York, New York, notes that the cut in the capital gains rate to 15 percent will cause consternation to those who made the mark-to-market election under Section 311(e) of the Taxpayer Relief Act of 1997. Under TRA 1997, gain on property, the holding period of which began after 2000 and which was held for more than five years, would be subject to a maximum tax rate of 18 percent. Pursuant to the election, a taxpayer could treat an asset as having been sold on January 1, 2001, for its fair market value. Any deemed gain was recognized and any loss was disallowed. The purpose of the Section 311(e) election was to allow the five-year period to begin for the 18 percent rate. Under the 2003 Act, the five-year holding period requirement has been repealed (at least until the end of 2008); gains on assets held for more than one year are eligible for the new capital gains rate.

In light of the blanket reduction of the maximum rate to 15 percent, the 311(e) election generally was of no value and may actually have had a detrimental effect. Unfortunately, as was clear in TRA 1997, the election is irrevocable.

¶ 310

For further information about the five-year holding period, see 2003FED ¶ 3285.03, FTS § E:5.180, or 2003FTG ¶ 5581.

★ *Effective date.* These provisions apply to tax years ending on or after May 6, 2003 (Act Sec. 301(d)(1) of the Jobs and Growth Tax Relief Reconciliation Act of 2003).

Sunset provision. The provisions and amendments of Title III of the 2003 Act will not apply to tax years beginning after December 31, 2008. The Internal Revenue Code of 1986 will be applied and administered to these years as if the provisions and amendments had not been enacted (Act Sec. 303). See ¶ 29,001 for CCH Explanation.

Act Sec. 301(b)(1)(A) of the Jobs and Growth Tax Relief Reconciliation Act of 2003, repealing Code Sec. 1(h)(2) and (9); Act Sec. 301(b)(1)(B) and (C), renumbering Code Sec. 1(h)(3) through (12); Act Sec. 301(b)(2), amending Code Sec. 55(b)(3); Act Sec. 301(d)(1). Law at ¶ 5005 and ¶ 5015. Committee Report at ¶ 10,100.

Small Business Stock

¶ 315

Background

If certain conditions are met, noncorporate investors may exclude up to 50 percent of the gain they realize on the sale or exchange of small business stock (Code Sec. 1202(a)(1)). Among the principal conditions that have to be satisfied are that the stock has to have been issued after August 10, 1993, and that the investor must have held the stock for more than five years (Code Sec. 1202(b)). "Small business stock" must be issued by a C corporation, at least 80 percent of the corporation's assets must be invested in assets used in the active conduct of a business, and the corporation's aggregate assets at the time the stock is issued must not exceed $50 million (Code Sec. 1202(c), (d) and (e)).

Exclusion and AMT liability. Generally, 42 percent of the excluded gain from small business stock is classified as a tax preference item when computing an investor's alternative minimum taxable income (AMTI) to determine liability for the alternative minimum tax (AMT) (Code Sec. 57(a)(7)). This means that 21 percent (50% × 42%) of the investor's total realized gain is used in the computation of AMTI. If the stock qualifies under the five-year holding period for capital assets (see ¶ 310), 28 percent of the excluded gain is classified as a tax preference item (Code Sec. 57(a)(7)). The result under the five-year rule is that 14 percent (50% × 28%) of the excluded gain is used in the computation of AMTI.

Jobs and Growth Act Impact

Tax preference percentage decreased.—Under the new legislation, and effective for dispositions of small business stock on or after May 6, 2003, only 7 percent of the 50-percent exclusion is treated as a tax preference item when computing AMTI (Code Sec. 57(a)(7), as amended by the Jobs and Growth Tax Relief Reconciliation Act of 2003). As a result of this change, 3.5 percent (50% ×

Explanation

7%) of the investor's total realized gain from the sale or exchange of small business stock will be used in the computation of AMTI. Due to the fact that the new law has eliminated the special capital gains tax rates that pertained to five-year property (see ¶ 310), the AMTI rules that applied to five-year property have also been eliminated (Code Sec. 57(a)(7), as amended by the 2003 Act).

Caution. Unlike many of the changes generated by the new legislation, this change is *not* effective as of January 1, 2003. The change is only effective for sales or exchanges of small business stock on or after May 6, 2003. Thus, when preparing their 2003 tax returns, investors who sold small business stock before *and* after the effective date will have to take two rates (i.e., 42 percent and 7 percent) into account when computing their AMTI. The IRS will have to include both rates when it designs the 2003 Form 6251 (Alternative Minimum Tax—Individuals).

Comment. This precipitous reduction in the percentage (i.e., from 42 percent to 7 percent) of the excluded gain from small business stock that is classified as a tax preference can be viewed as a demonstration of Congressional support for this type of investment. The reduction also highlights the attempt by Congress to reduce the number of taxpayers subject to the AMT. (See ¶ 230 for additional changes in the computation of AMT.)

For further information about small business stock, see 2003FED ¶ 5307.045, FTS § A:22.41, or 2003FTG ¶ 5586.

★ *Effective date.* The provision applies to sales or exchanges of small business stock on or after May 6, 2003 (Act Sec. 301(d)(3) of the Jobs and Growth Tax Relief Reconciliation Act of 2003).

Sunset provision. The provisions and amendments of Title III of the 2003 Act will not apply to tax years beginning after December 31, 2008. The Internal Revenue Code of 1986 will be applied and administered to these years as if the provisions and amendments had not been enacted (Act Sec. 303). See ¶ 29,001 for CCH Explanation.

Act Sec. 301(b)(3) of the Jobs and Growth Tax Relief Reconciliation Act of 2003, amending Code Sec. 57(a)(7); Act Sec. 301(d)(3). Law at ¶ 5020. Committee Report at ¶ 10,100.

Transitional Rule

¶ 320

Background

Starting with the Taxpayer Relief Act of 1997 (P.L. 105-34), Congress has made almost yearly changes concerning the taxation of net long-term capital gains. Basically, the process of computing an individual's correct capital gains tax has now evolved into a matter of putting each net capital gain into its proper group and applying the correct long-term capital gains tax rate to each group. The applicable groups are:

(1) a 28-percent group (e.g., assets as collectibles and recognized taxable gain from small business stock) (Code Sec. 1(h)(5));

(2) a 25-percent group for unrecaptured Section 1250 gain (Code Sec. 1(h)(1)(D));

(3) a 20-percent group (i.e., assets that do not fall within the 28-percent or 25-percent groups) (Code Sec. 1(h)(1)(C));

Background

(4) a 10-percent group (i.e., the same assets as the 20-percent group, but the 10-percent rate is used by lower-income individuals) (Code Sec. 1(h)(1)(B)); and

(5) an 8-percent group (i.e., the same assets as the 20-percent group, but the 8-percent rate is used by lower-income individuals who have held the assets for more than five years) (Code Sec. 1(h)(2)).

Jobs and Growth Act Impact

Capital gains tax for 2003 computed under a transitional rule.—Because the reduction in long-term capital gains rates was not retroactive to January 1, 2003 (see ¶ 305), most individuals will find that their capital gains tax for 2003 must be computed under a transitional rule. This rule applies in situations involving a tax year that includes May 6, 2003 (Act Sec. 301(c) of the Jobs and Growth Tax Relief Reconciliation Act of 2003).

Comment. The transitional rule is necessary in order to ensure that the lower rates (i.e., 5 percent or 15 percent) apply to capital assets sold or exchanged on or after May 6, 2003. The higher rates that were in effect before May 6, 2003 (i.e., 8 percent, 10 percent or 20 percent) will still apply to capital gains that were recognized before May 6, 2003. The following three rules are worth special note when determining an individual's capital gains tax rate for 2003:

(1) *Dividend income.* Qualified dividend income received in tax years beginning after December 31, 2002, qualifies for a maximum capital gains rate of 15 percent. Under the transitional computation rule in effect for 2003, qualified dividend income is treated as though it were taken into account by the individual on or after May 6, 2003 (Act Sec. 301(c)(5) of the 2003 Act). This stipulation ensures that the maximum 15-percent rate will apply to all qualified dividend income when computing an individual's maximum capital gains tax under the transitional rule. The maximum capital gains rate of 5 percent will apply to dividend income received by those individuals in the 10-percent or 15-percent tax brackets. For complete information concerning qualified dividend income, see ¶ 325 and ¶ 335.

(2) *Installment sale gain.* According to the Conference Committee Report, the lower rates will apply to *installment payments* received on or after May 6, 2003. In other words, the date the installment payment is received determines the capital gains rate that should be applied, not the date the asset was sold under an installment contract.

(3) *Gain or loss from mutual funds.* The 2003 legislation states that mutual funds and other types of pass-through entities have the responsibility to determine when capital gain or loss is properly taken into account (Act Sec. 301(c)(4) of the 2003 Act). It seems logical to assume that the entity will then notify its shareholders, or other type of distributees, whether distributions are determined under the lower rates that went into effect after May 5, 2003, or the higher rates that were in effect before the 2003 tax legislation.

Applying the transitional rule.—There are two main steps and a number of supplemental steps that have to be followed when computing an individual's capital gains tax under the 2003 transitional rule. The two main steps in applying the transitional rule are (1) computing the individual's capital gains tax by

¶ 320

Explanation

applying the lowest capital gains tax rates (i.e., 5 percent, 8 percent or 10 percent) (Act Sec. 301(c)(1) of the 2003 Act), and (2) computing the individual's capital gains tax by applying the highest capital gains rates that are generally applied (i.e., 15 percent or 20 percent) (Act Sec. 301(c)(2) of the 2003 Act). The two main steps are discussed and illustrated in the following material.

Planning Note. As a practical matter, step (1) of the transitional rule can be ignored if no portion of the individual's net long-term capital gain will be taxed at the lowest rate (e.g., 5 percent). The computations under step (2) of the transitional rule will have much broader application given the fact that the 15-percent rate applies to dividend income no matter how high the individual's marginal tax rate (e.g., 35 percent under the 2003 legislation). Also, keep in mind that the higher capital gains rates of 28 percent (e.g., for collectibles) (Code Sec. 1(h)(4), as renumbered by the 2003 Act), and 25 percent (e.g., for unrecaptured Section 1250 gain) (Code Sec. 1(h)(1)(D)) still have relevancy for individuals in the higher marginal tax rates of 33 percent and 35 percent.

Step 1. Applying the 5-percent, 8-percent and/or 10-percent rates. For lower-income individuals (i.e., those whose top marginal tax bracket does not exceed 15 percent), the maximum capital gains tax for 2003 is equal to the total tax determined under the following formula (Act Sec. 301(c)(1) of the 2003 Act):

(A) 5 percent of the *lesser* of (I) the net capital gain that is determined by taking into account gain or loss realized on or after May 6, 2003 (gain from collectibles and/or small business stock is ignored for purposes of this computation), *or* (II) the net capital gain computed under Code Sec. 1(h)(1)(B) without regard to this transitional rule (Act Sec. 301(c)(1)(A) of the 2003 Act), *plus*

(B) 8 percent of the *lesser* of (I) the gain from qualified five-year property that was correctly taken into account before May 6, 2003, *or* (II) the *excess* (if any) of the net capital gain computed under Code Sec. 1(h)(1)(B) without regard to the transitional rule, *over* the amount on which the 5-percent tax rate (see (A) above) was computed (Act Sec. 301(c)(1)(B) of the 2003 Act), *plus*

(C) 10 percent of the *excess* of the net capital gain computed under Code Sec. 1(h)(1)(B) without regard to the transitional rule, *over* the total of the amounts on which the 5-percent and/or 8-percent tax rates were computed (see (A) and (B), above) (Act Sec. 301(c)(1)(C) of the 2003 Act).

Example (1). For 2003, Helen Barkin, a single individual, has taxable income of $21,000. Included in her taxable income are the following income items: (1) $1,000 of qualified dividend income that was received on February 3, 2003, (2) $3,000 in long-term capital gain from the sale of stock she had purchased in 1990 (i.e., five-year property), and (3) $2,000 in long-term capital gain from the sale of stock on June 2, 2003. As a result of the new legislation, Barkin's total capital gains tax for 2003 will be $390 (the sum of $50 ($1,000 in dividends × 5%), $240 ($3,000 in five-year property gain × 8%) and $100 ($2,000 gain from sale of stock × 5%)). Her total regular income tax of $1,900 would be computed as follows: (1) 10% on the first $7,000 of taxable income ($7,000 × 10% = $700), plus (2) 15% on the amount over $7,000 that is not taxed under the capital gains rates ($21,000 taxable income − $7,000 = $14,000 excess − $6,000 in capital gains = $8,000 × 15% = $1,200). Including her capital gains tax, Barkin's total tax liability for 2003 would be $2,290 ($1,900 in regular income tax and $390 in capital gains tax).

¶ 320

(Note: Even though Barkin's dividend income was received before May 6, 2003, it is still subject to the new 5-percent capital gains tax rate (see ¶ 325 and ¶ 335).)

Step 2. Applying the 10-percent and/or 15-percent rates. For higher income individuals (i.e., those whose top marginal tax bracket exceeds 15 percent), maximum capital gains tax for 2003 is equal to the total tax determined under the following formula (Act Sec. 301(c)(2) of the 2003 Act):

(A) 15 percent of the *lesser* of (I) the *excess* of the amount of net capital gain determined under the transitional rule (see Step 1, (A), above) (i.e., the amount to which the 5-percent rate applies), *over* the total amount on which net capital gain is determined under all three computations set forth under Step 1, above (i.e., the total amount subject to the 5-percent, 8-percent and 10-percent rates), *or* (II) the net capital gain computed under Code Sec. 1(h)(1)(C) without regard to the transitional rule (Act Sec. 301(c)(2)(A) of the 2003 Act), *plus*

(B) 20 percent of the *excess* of (I) the net capital gain computed under Code Sec. 1(h)(1)(C) without regard to the transitional rule, *over* (II) the net capital gain on which the 15-percent tax rate is used under (A) of Step 2 (see above) (Act Sec. 301(c)(2)(B) of the 2003 Act).

Example (2). For 2003, Harold Bosch, a single individual, has taxable income of $350,000. As a result of the new legislation, Bosch's highest marginal tax rate for the year is 35%. Included in his taxable income are the following income items: (1) $5,000 in qualified dividends received throughout 2003, (2) $2,000 in long-term capital gain from the sale of stock on January 16, 2003, and (3) $3,000 in long-term capital gain from the sale of stock on May 6, 2003. Bosch's capital gains tax for 2003 would be $1,600 ($5,000 in dividends × 15% = $750; $2,000 in recognized long-term capital gain on January 16, 2003 × 20% = $400; and $3,000 in recognized long-term capital gain on May 6, 2003 × 15% = $450).

Comment. Due to the May 6, 2003, effective date for the reduction in capital gains tax rates, tax practitioners will experience new levels of complexity when preparing 2003 tax returns for their clients. According to the IRS, it will have to add eight new lines to Schedule D of Form 1040, the Schedule D worksheet, Form 6251 (Alternative Minimum Tax) and Form 8801 (Credit for Prior Year Tax). In addition, the IRS estimates that up to six million individuals who could file Form 1040A when reporting their capital gains distributions will now be required to file Form 1040 and attach Schedule D. Practitioners will not be the only group affected by the capital gains changes. Those who must file Form 1099-DIV will have to account separately for transactions that took place after May 5, 2003 (Tax Complexity Analysis, Comments of the IRS and Treasury Department, Conference Committee Report).

For further information about capital gains, see 2003FED ¶ 3285.01, FTS § A:1.42[3], or 2003FTG ¶ 5581.

★ *Effective date.* The transitional rule is in effect for a tax year that includes May 6, 2003 (Act Sec. 301(c) of the Jobs and Growth Tax Relief Reconciliation Act of 2003).

Act Sec. 301(c) of the Jobs and Growth Tax Relief Reconciliation Act of 2003; Act Sec. 301(d)(1). Law at ¶ 7030. Committee Report at ¶ 10,100.

¶ 320

DIVIDENDS

Dividend Income of Individuals Taxed at Capital Gain Rates

¶ 325

Background

The taxation of dividends has been a focal point for President Bush in 2003. Eliminate dividend taxes, the reasoning seemed to go, and the stock market will rise up to save the economy.

Dividend taxes can be high. Corporate dividends paid to individuals have long been taxed at ordinary income tax rates. Before the Jobs and Growth Tax Relief Reconciliation Act of 2003, the top rate for dividends was 38.6 percent for high-income couples (over $311,950) and 27 percent for middle-income joint filers (from $47,450–$114,650). There have been no special rate reductions, credits or exclusions for dividend income since 1986.

Amounts paid as dividends are also taxed as corporate income. Rates up to 38 percent apply at the corporate level. Assuming shareholders are the ultimate bearers of total taxes on corporate earnings, the double layers of tax can be viewed as a 60-percent tax on shareholder income. A profit of $100 can shrink to $38 in the shareholder's hands under the worst case scenario, reduced by $38 of corporate income tax (38 percent) and $24 of shareholder income tax (38.6 percent).

Double tax reality. In practice, the full effects of double tax shrinkage may rarely occur. Corporate income taxes can be minimized or eliminated through the use of tax subsidies such as accelerated depreciation, export subsidies, research subsidies, exemptions for state bond interest, and low-income housing credits, as well as less mainstream tax minimization techniques. Not all profits are distributed as dividends, meaning at least some corporate income dollars escape shareholder-level taxes. At the shareholder level, almost two-thirds of dividends are paid to institutional owners or those holding shares in tax-deferred vehicles such as pension plans, IRAs, 401(k)s or college savings plans. Foreign shareholders also escape U.S. shareholder-level taxes.

Double tax policy questions. The double tax scheme has been criticized as unjust for the high rates it produces and the inappropriate business incentives it supports. Even if tax levels are reflected in stock prices and affect mostly high-income shareholders, making them progressive and therefore accepted as fair, on paper it looks bad to tax stock income higher than other investments (bonds, pass-throughs and interest-bearing accounts).

The system favors debt financing over equity, since interest payments are deductible whereas dividends and retained earnings are not. Economists have connected this bias to a tendency for U.S. corporations to become highly leveraged, risking bankruptcy, instead of spreading financial risks among shareholders. Double taxes discourage companies from making cash distributions. With no need to show cash as concrete evidence of earnings, officers may have increased opportunities to manipulate the books or pursue questionable investments. The mere existence of corporate taxes also causes inefficiency, encouraging companies to engage in transactions for the sole purpose of saving taxes (moving businesses offshore and initiating transactions with no inherent economic value).

Corporate and individual tax integration. An ideal tax policy would eliminate the bad effects of double taxation. An ideal system for integrating corporate and

Background

individual taxes is difficult to achieve. Each solution holds potential to reduce the progressivity of the income tax (more benefits going to higher income individuals), to provide windfalls to shareholders (avoiding tax on profit altogether) or to add complexity to the tax system.

Simple dividend exclusion creates a zero-tax opportunity for clever entities taking full advantage of corporate tax subsidies. Dividend paid deductions for corporations would eliminate an incentive for retaining earnings, discouraging internal financing of corporate projects. Dividend deductions also raise tricky issues of how to treat tax preferences and what happens to companies with no income to offset. Shareholder credits for imputed corporate-level taxes require complicated gross-ups, while dividend received credits are regressive, removing a greater proportion of the additional tax burden for higher-income individuals.

As another possible solution, corporate items could be passed through to shareholders wholesale, eliminating corporate taxes once and for all—but this step would throw out $200 billion in corporate tax revenue and require millions of helpless shareholders (barely managing with Schedule D) to report complicated pass-through items on their individual returns.

Past U.S. attempts at integration. Early on, the United States only taxed dividend income paid to high-income individuals. Since 1936, dividends have been taxable to all at prevailing graduated rates. Dividend paid deductions were allowed for all U.S. corporations in 1936–1937 but were protested as discouraging investment. A limited dividend exclusion of $50 per individual was added in 1954, gradually increasing to $400 before being repealed in 1986. A tax credit equal to 4 percent of dividends received in excess of the exclusion also applied from 1954 to 1963. The credit was reduced to 2 percent in 1964 and repealed in 1965. Since 1986, dividends have been taxed at ordinary income tax rates with no exclusions, credits or other reductions.

The President Bush proposal—what happened to EDA, CREBA and REBA? In January 2003, President Bush revived the double taxation issue as part of his economic stimulus package. The President's original proposal called for a complete elimination of individual taxes on dividends. The tax exclusion would apply only to the extent the dividend was paid out of already-taxed corporate earnings. In this way the proposal sought to avoid replacing double taxation of corporate earnings with zero taxation of corporate earnings.

The proposal required corporations to keep track of taxed earnings in a special account (excludable dividend amount (EDA)). Adding to the complexity, earnings eligible for tax-free dividends could not be carried over to future years, but in lieu of distribution could be used to give shareholders an equivalent basis increase (retained earnings basis adjustment (REBA)). Basis increases for multiple years would be tracked in yet another corporate account (cumulative retained earnings basis adjustment account (CREBA)).

The overall scheme bore a respectable pedigree, having evolved out of carefully crafted Treasury Department recommendations taking into account all possible ill effects of integration. The combined complexity of these accounts plus the cost of the proposal (estimated by the JCT at $396 billion) ultimately killed the total dividend exclusion. Due to the tenacity of the underlying issues, however, taxpayers may not have seen the last of EDA, CREBA and REBA.

¶ 325

Explanation

Jobs and Growth Act Impact

Tax rates on dividend income reduced to 15 and 5 percent.—The top federal tax rate for dividends received by an individual is reduced by the new law to 15 percent (5 percent for those whose incomes fall in the 10- or 15-percent rate brackets) (Code Sec. 1(h)(11), as added by the Jobs and Growth Tax Relief Reconciliation Act of 2003). These are the same rates applicable to capital gains (see ¶ 305). The reduced rates apply to eligible dividends received from January 1, 2003, through December 31, 2008. A zero-percent rate applies to taxpayers in the 10- or 15-percent brackets for 2008 only. The reduced rates for dividends will expire in 2009.

Comment. Interest earned on savings accounts, certificates of deposits, and government bonds is still subject to federal income tax at ordinary tax rates. The new low tax rates apply only to stock dividends.

Comment. Investments in tax-deferred retirement vehicles such as regular IRAs, 401(k)s and deferred annuities receive no benefit from the rate reduction. Distributions from these accounts will be taxed at ordinary income tax rates even if the funds represent dividends paid on stocks held in the account.

Zero-percent rate for 2008. Qualified dividends will be tax free for taxpayers in the 10- and 15-percent bracket for one year only, in 2008 (Code Sec. 1(h)(1)(B) and Code Sec. 1(h)(11), as amended by the 2003 Act). The 10- and 15-percent rate brackets, as amended in 2003, include single taxpayers with taxable incomes up to $28,400 and married joint filers with incomes up to $56,800. These income limits are likely to increase for inflation by 2008. Since the reduced rate provision expires altogether at the end of 2008, the zero-percent rate also expires at that time.

Eligible dividends. The reduced tax rates apply to dividends received during the tax year from:

- a domestic corporation or
- a qualified foreign corporation.

Corporate stock dividends passed through to investors by a mutual fund or other regulated investment company, partnership, real estate investment trust, or held by a common trust fund are also eligible for the reduced rate assuming the distribution would otherwise be classified as qualified dividend income. See below and ¶ 335. Amounts received upon disposition of stock received as a nontaxable stock dividend that would otherwise be subject to ordinary income rules may also qualify for the reduced rate (Code Sec. 306(a)(1)(D), as added by the 2003 Act).

Comment. The President's original dividend proposal contained restrictions on the type of corporate earnings that would be eligible for dividend tax breaks. Eligible dividends needed to derive from taxed corporate earnings. The 2003 Act contains no restrictions on dividend tax cuts based on the earnings source of the payment. The reduced tax rates will apply even if the corporation had no current earnings, borrowed money to pay dividends, or paid no corporate-level tax on its earnings due to extensive tax credits.

Comment. The 2003 Act does not elaborate on the meaning of the phrase "dividends received from a corporation." Under accepted law, a dividend is defined as a corporate distribution with respect to its stock to the extent it is paid out of current or accumulated earnings and profits (Code Sec. 316). Salaries, payments to creditors, or other amounts unconnected to stock holdings are not dividends. A

¶ 325

payment in excess of historic earnings and profits is treated as a return of capital and applied against the shareholder's stock basis.

Planning Note. Excessive salaries paid to shareholders may be recharacterized by the IRS as constructive dividends. Under the reduced rates for dividends, employee-shareholders may actually prefer dividend treatment over salaries taxed at ordinary income rates. Dividends have the advantage of being free of employment taxes. Dividends would be preferable in situations in which the business did not need the salary deduction because its tax was fully offset by other deductions.

Dividends ineligible for the reduced tax rate. The reduced dividend rate does not apply to dividends paid by:

- credit unions
- mutual insurance companies
- farmers' cooperatives
- tax-exempt cemetery companies
- nonprofit voluntary employee benefit associations (VEBAs)
- employer securities owned by an employee stock ownership plan (ESOP), to the extent the dividends are deductible under Code Sec. 404(k) (Code Sec. 1(h)(11)(B)(ii), as added by the 2003 Act)
- any corporation exempt from federal tax under Code Sec. 501 or 521 in the tax year or preceding tax year of the dividend payment (Code Sec. 1(h)(11)(B)(ii), as added by the 2003 Act)
- any mutual savings bank, savings and loan, domestic building and loan, cooperative bank, or other type of bank eligible for the dividends paid deduction under Code Sec. 591 (Code Sec. 1(h)(11)(B)(ii), as added by the 2003 Act)
- stock owned for less than 60 days in the 120-day period surrounding the ex-dividend date
- stock purchased with borrowed funds if the dividend was included in investment income in claiming an interest deduction
- stock with respect to which related payments must be made with respect to substantially similar or related property
- substitute payments in lieu of a dividend made with respect to stock on loan in a short sale.

Comment. Credit union "dividends" paid on savings accounts, certificates of deposits, and other savings vehicles are taxed as interest and are not eligible for the reduced dividend tax rate.

Caution. A large number of investors currently receiving "preferred dividends" on "preferred stock" may be ineligible for the reduced dividend tax rate. The most popular preferred equity, hybrid preferred stock, is actually reported as debt by the corporate issuer and pays interest that is deducted by the corporation. Payments on these preferred instruments (hybrid preferred shares) are technically not dividends and are thus ineligible for the reduced dividend rate.

Dispositions of Code Sec. 306 stock otherwise taxed as ordinary income. Proceeds from a disposition of stock received as a nontaxable stock dividend, other than a redemption transaction, may be eligible for the reduced dividend tax rate

(Code Sec. 306(a)(1)(D), as added by the 2003 Act). The rule applies to "section 306 stock" that is disposed of in a disposition other than a redemption. In a typical transaction, a shareholder receives preferred stock as a nontaxable stock dividend and disposes of it following a brief holding period. Under Code Sec. 306, this transaction would result in ordinary income to the extent the distributed stock would have been treated as a dividend if the equivalent amount of cash had been distributed instead. The revised rule allows the "substitute dividend" to be taxed at preferential dividend rates.

Section 306 stock includes:

(1) stock other than common stock received as a tax-free stock dividend;

(2) stock other than common stock received in certain tax-free divisions or reorganizations; and

(3) stock (including common) with a substituted or carryover basis determined by reference to other section 306 stock.

The reduced dividend rate will apply to the extent that proceeds from a preferred stock bailout would be viewed as a dividend substitute and characterized as ordinary income under Code Sec. 306.

PRACTICAL ANALYSIS. Robert Keebler of Virchow, Krause & Company, LLP, Green Bay, Wisconsin, observes that the dividend provisions will affect all investors. The initial temptation will be to sell bonds and purchase preferred stocks. It is important however to focus on both the tax and investment aspects of investment selection.

Take the case of a client with a 50-percent bond—50-percent stock portfolio. The temptation is to sell the bonds and buy preferred stocks. But, will this result in a better overall return? One would be naive to think that preferred stocks carry the same risk as bonds. First, in a corporate bankruptcy, the preferred stock holder will have a lower priority. Second, the risk of price declines when interest rates rise may be greater with preferred stocks than with bonds. Why? Because bonds have a limited term (e.g., 20 years) where preferred stocks have an unlimited term.

In the next 120 days we will see a new wave of financial engineering designed to provide baskets of stocks with high dividends and high stability of principal. Advanced strategies of marrying put buying and writing covered calls to reduce risk will likely be the subject of articles and tax columns during this exciting time.

In the meantime, you should work collaboratively with your clients' investment advisors to balance the risk and rewards of this new investment paradigm.

Dividends paid by foreign corporations. Dividends received from qualified foreign corporations are eligible for the reduced tax rate (Code Sec. 1(h)(11)(B)(i)(II), as added by the 2003 Act). Any foreign corporation stock that is traded on an established U.S. securities market is considered qualified (Code Sec. 1(h)(11)(C)(ii), as added by the 2003 Act). Any corporation incorporated in a U.S. possession is also considered qualified. Non-U.S. traded stocks may be qualified if

¶ 325

certain treaty requirements are met (Code Sec. 1(h)(11)(C)(i), as added by the 2003 Act). Foreign dividends do *not* qualify for the reduced tax rate if the distributing corporation is one of the following types of companies in the year of the dividend or the preceding year (Code Sec. 1(h)(11)(C)(iii), as added by the 2003 Act):

- a foreign investment company (within the meaning of Code Sec. 1246(b))

- a passive foreign investment company (PFIC) (under Code Sec. 1297)

- a foreign personal holding company (FPHC) (under Code Sec. 552)

Treaty requirements. In order to be considered qualified, a foreign corporation that is not either incorporated in a U.S. possession or traded on a U.S. exchange must be eligible for benefits under a comprehensive income tax treaty which includes an exchange of information program (Code Sec. 1(h)(C)(i)(II), as added by the 2003 Act). The provision is worded in such a way that the requirement is met only when the IRS has determined that the treaty is satisfactory for purposes of Code Sec. 1(h)(11). The foreign corporation must qualify for the benefits of the treaty with respect to substantially all of its income in the tax year in which the dividend is paid, according to the Conference Report (H.R. Conf. Rept. No. 108-126).

Comment. The Conference Report specifically mentions Barbados as a country that does *not* qualify as having a satisfactory treaty with the United States. According to the conferees, that treaty may operate to eliminate double taxation for corporations that are not at risk for double taxation. Barbados has been named on the Organization for Economic Cooperation and Development (OECD) list of tax havens with "harmful tax practices."

The United States has entered into Tax Information Exchange Agreements (TIEA) with numerous countries, including Barbados. Countries that sign a TIEA agree to several layers of information exchange; however, the agreement is not equivalent to a comprehensive treaty designed to avoid double taxation and prevent tax evasion. Countries that have signed TIEAs but without comprehensive treaties include the Cayman Islands, Barbados, Bermuda, Costa Rica, Dominica, Dominican Republic, Grenada, Guyana, Honduras, Jamaica, Marshall Islands, Peru, Saint Lucia, Trinidad and Tobago. These countries would not satisfy the treaty requirement set forth in the Code. It is notable that it some cases the absence of a treaty is not an indicator of questionable practices in that jurisdiction, since the Treasury may have simply determined that the economic level of activity in the country was not sufficient to warrant a full-blown treaty.

Foreign tax credit adjustments. The foreign tax credit is subject to limitations designed to prevent taxpayers from using the credit to reduce taxes on income from sources within the United States. The maximum credit is roughly equal to the percentage of U.S. tax that equals the taxpayer's foreign source taxable income as a percentage of worldwide taxable income (Code Sec. 904(a)). In computing the foreign income part of the equation, capital gain is subject to special rules. The overall effect is to reduce capital gain by taxes saved due to special rates and to require domestic source net capital loss to be taken into account in determining foreign source capital gain (Code Sec. 904(b)(2)(B)). The capital gain reduction rule is invoked in any year there is a capital rate gain differential.

With the addition of the dividend rate differential, the capital gain adjustments in computing the foreign tax credit now apply to dividend income as well

Explanation

(Code Sec. 1(h)(11)(C)(iv), as added by the 2003 Act). According to the formula prescribed under Code Sec. 904(b)(2)(B), foreign source taxable income and worldwide taxable income are both reduced by the rate differential portion of any dividend income before calculating the proportions that make up the credit limitation. The rate differential proportion is defined as the excess of the highest applicable tax rate minus the maximum dividend rate under Code Sec. 1(h)(11) (Code Sec. 904(b)(3)(E) and Code Sec. 1(h)(11)(C)(iv), as added by the 2003 Act). At 2003 rates, as amended, the rate differential would be 20 percent (35 percent maximum individual rate minus the 15 percent maximum dividend rate). Thus, for example, a person with $10,000 in foreign dividend income would reduce this income to $8,000 ($10,000 − ($10,000 × 20%)) before using the dividend in the credit limitation equation.

Minimum holding period of 60 days. The law contains restrictions on reduced tax rates for investors who purchase stock very close to the ex-dividend date (the date following the record date on which the corporation finalizes the list of shareholders who will receive the dividend). An investor is required to hold a stock for at least 60 days in the 120-day period beginning 60 days before the ex-dividend date for the reduced rates to apply (Code Sec. 1(h)(11)(B)(iii), as added by the 2003 Act).

Comment. Although the House and Senate versions of the bill doubled the holding period for preferred dividends, the enacted version does not require a longer holding period.

Example (1). The ex-dividend date for General Electric is February 28, 2003. On January 20, 2003, Joe Rowley purchases 10,000 shares of GE for $260,000. On March 6, 2003, having held the shares long enough to avoid the wash sale rules, Rowley sells the 10,000 shares of GE for $258,000. Rowley receives the dividend of $.19 per share ($1,900). Rowley's economic loss is $100. Assuming this is his only transaction, he can use the capital loss from the stock sale to offset $2,000 of other income, for a potential tax savings of $700 (35% × $2,000). If the special dividend tax rate applied, Rowley's liability on the $1,900 dividend would be $285 (at 15%), meaning that his economic loss of $100 produced a tax savings of $415 ($700 − $285). However, since he did not hold the shares for at least 60 days during the December 28 to April 28 period (60 days before and after the 2/28/2003 ex-dividend date), Rowley's regular tax rate will apply (35%). His $665 ($1,900 × 35%) liability on the dividend, combined with the $700 saved by the capital loss, means that in this situation his $100 economic loss produces a net tax savings of only $35. The holding period rule prevents the taxpayer from using price drops due to dividends to generate capital loss to offset ordinary income while paying tax on the dividend at a lower rate.

Comment. The 60-day holding period requirement means that short-term traders or day traders will not be eligible for the reduced dividend tax rate. In all likelihood, however, short-term traders will not expect to derive a significant portion of their incomes from dividends.

Comment. The ex-dividend date is typically a few days before the official date of record on which shareholders receiving dividends are officially registered. Stock trades may take more than one day to settle.

Stocks with respect to which substantially similar positions are held. A dividend will not qualify for the reduced tax rates to the extent that the taxpayer is obligated to make related payments with respect to positions in substantially

¶ 325

similar or related property (Code Sec. 1(h)(11)(B)(iii)(II), as added by the 2003 Act). The related payments can be pursuant to a short sale or other arrangement.

This restriction is identical in wording to the restriction on corporations claiming the dividends received deduction (Code Sec. 246(c)(1)(B)). It anticipates situations in which taxpayers do not retain, or do not genuinely own, the dividends they receive. Under IRS regulations, the restriction applies regardless of how long the corporation has owned the dividend-paying stock, and this restriction would be expected to apply to the dividend rate as well (Reg. § 1.246-3(c)(3)).

Example (2). Joe Black purchases 100 shares of Microco on January 10, 1980. On February 10, 2003, Black short sells 25 shares of Microco and remains in the position on February 28, 2003, when the stock goes ex-dividend. Assuming Black receives a $100 dividend and is obligated to pay $25 to the lender for the sales that were sold short, only $75 of the dividend is eligible for the reduced dividend tax rate.

Comment. The IRS regulations illustrate the rule with an example in which identical company shares are held in offsetting positions. It is not clear to what extent positions in different company stocks will be considered substantially similar or related. Positions in different issuers in unrelated industries have been held not to be substantially similar (*Duke Energy Corp.*, 2000-1 USTC ¶ 50,143); however, the IRS has also ruled that groups of preferred shares in unrelated industry stocks were substantially similar property (IRS Letter Ruling 9128050 (April 4, 1991)).

Leveraged stock investments. Stock purchased with borrowed money may generate dividends eligible for the reduced dividend tax rates unless the taxpayer elects to count the dividend in calculating investment interest. Any taxpayer who elects to include a dividend in investment income for purposes of calculating the limit on the investment interest deduction under Code Sec. 163 is ineligible to use the reduced tax rate with respect to that dividend (Code Sec. 1(h)(D)(i), as added by the 2003 Act).

Election. A taxpayer must specifically elect to include a dividend in investment income (Code Sec. 163(d)(4)(B), as amended by the 2003 Act). If no election is made, the IRS will assume that the reduced dividend rate is to apply and the dividend is excluded in calculating the maximum permissible investment interest deduction. No further details regarding the election are provided by the new law.

An interest deduction is generally allowed for investment indebtedness. The deduction is limited to net investment income. Interest in excess of investment income can be carried over to succeeding years. Investment interest is interest properly allocated to property producing interest, dividends, annuities, royalties, or gain not derived in the ordinary course of business. Passive activities do not qualify. Investment indebtedness is reported on IRS Form 4952.

Capital gain income, like dividend income, is not included in investment income unless the taxpayer elects to tax it at regular tax rates.

Comment. Taxpayers can only benefit from the double-dip benefit of reduced tax rates on stock purchased with borrowed money plus an interest deduction for the investment loan if they have investment income from other sources. The amount of the investment interest deduction is limited to net investment income. Any unused deduction may be carried over to future tax years.

Caution. Securities on loan in connection with a short sale may generate substitute payments in lieu of a dividend. These payments are reported to inves-

¶ 325

Explanation

tors on Form 1099-MISC and are reported as other income. They are not considered dividends by the IRS and will not qualify for the reduced dividend rate. The Conference Committee Report states that individuals who have payments in lieu of dividends reported to them as dividends on Form 1099-DIV for calendar year 2003 should be allowed to treat the payments as dividends unless they know or have reason to know that the payments are in fact payments in lieu of dividends instead of actual dividends. Brokers and securities dealers will be given leeway in developing mechanisms for reporting qualified dividends eligible for the retroactive rate reductions.

PRACTICAL ANALYSIS. Michael J. Grace of Jackson & Campbell, PC, Washington, D.C., suggests that short-term traders should pay heed that in order to qualify for the 2003 Act's reduced rates on dividends, they must hold a stock for at least a minimum number of days. That minimum holding period is 60 days during the 120-day period beginning on the date which is 60 days before the date on which the stock goes "ex-dividend."

Under Code Sec. 163(d)(4)(B), taxpayers may elect to include in "investment income" net capital gains from property held for investment. Such gains do not qualify to be taxed as capital gains. However, they increase the amount of deductible investment interest expense. Piggybacking off that provision, the 2003 Act allows taxpayers to treat qualified dividend income (as defined in new Code Sec. 1(h)(11)(B)) as investment income. Dividends electively treated as investment income are not eligible to be taxed at the Act's reduced rates on dividends.

These elections suggest opportunities for individuals to reduce tax by leveraging purchases of stock. Individiual taxpayer borrows money and uses the debt proceeds to purchase dividend-yielding stocks. Interest on the debt generally qualifies as investment interest expense. See Code Sec. 163(d) and Temporary Reg. § 1.163-8T. Taxpayer collects dividends on the stock. To the extent of the taxpayer's investment interest expense, the taxpayer elects to include the dividends in investment income. Net investment income is offset by investment interest expense. Any excess investment interest expense carries forward to future years in which it may become deductible. On any dividends that the taxpayer did not elect to treat as investment income, the taxpayer pays tax at only 15 percent (or five percent, as the case may be).

Taxpayer then sells stock, realizing a capital gain. To the extent of the taxpayer's investment interest expense, the taxpayer elects to include the capital gain in investment income. Net investment income is offset by investment interest expense as previously described. On any capital gain that the taxpayer did not elect to treat as investment income, the taxpayer pays tax at only 15 percent (or five percent, as the case may be).

Extraordinary dividends. Corporate tax rules are designed to prevent abuse by corporations attempting to combine large dividends and dividend received deductions along with capital losses when the underlying stock is subsequently sold. The extraordinary dividend rule requires a corporation that receives a dividend in

¶ 325

connection with stock it has not held for more than two years before the ex-dividend date to reduce its basis in the stock by the amount of the dividend received (Code Sec. 1059(a)). The rule is invoked when the amount of the dividend exceeds 10 percent of the shareholder's adjusted basis in the stock (5 percent for preferred stock) (Code Sec. 1059(c)).

Individuals are now also subject to a special extraordinary dividend rule. If an individual receives a dividend qualifying for the reduced rate, and the dividend exceeds 10 percent of the shareholder's basis in the stock, then any loss on the sale of the stock to the extent of the dividends will be treated as long-term capital loss (Code Sec. 1(h)(11)(D)(ii), as added by the 2003 Act, and Code Sec. 1059(c)). The holding period of the stock on which the extraordinary dividend is paid is not taken into account in determining whether an individual is subject to the extraordinary dividend rule or whether the loss on the stock (to the extent of the extraordinary dividends) is long-term capital loss.

Comment. The long-term capital loss characterization rule affects taxpayers with both short-term capital gain and long-term capital gain from other transactions in excess of the loss generated by the extraordinary dividend transaction. The characterization makes no difference to a taxpayer having no capital gains, capital gain not in excess of the dividend transaction loss, or only capital losses.

> **Example (3).** Joe Grano purchases and sells 100 shares of Smallco at a $10,000 loss during 2004 and also receives a $10,000 extraordinary dividend from the company during the year. He also incurs $10,000 in net long-term capital gain and $10,000 in short-term capital gain in other unrelated transactions. He must use his $10,000 Smallco loss to offset the net long-term capital gain, leaving $10,000 of short-term capital gain to be taxed at ordinary income tax rates. Without the extraordinary dividend rule, Grano could characterize the loss as short-term and use it to offset his short-term capital gain, allowing his net $10,000 gain to be taxed at preferable long-term capital gain rates.

Comment. The Senate version of the bill, which was not adopted, would have required a stock basis adjustment in the amount of the dividend exclusion in the event the taxpayer received an extraordinary dividend.

Mutual funds. Dividends passed through to investors from a stock mutual fund or RIC are eligible for the reduced rate in the same manner as dividends received directly from a corporation. Dividends from a mutual fund would not be qualified dividends if they represented other types of earnings, such as interest. A shareholder will need to rely on the fund to report the portion of dividends paid that qualify for the reduced tax rate. See ¶ 335 for details.

Comment. Mutual funds charge management fees, and these are largely collected out of interest and dividends collected by the fund. A fund with stocks paying 1 percent dividends and charging a 1 percent fee may not pass along much dividend income to shareholders. This means that the dividend rate cut will have more impact on direct stockholders than those with mutual funds.

Comment. The IRS expects to revise Form 1099-DIV for 2004 to create a new box for reporting qualified dividends. A revised 2003 form may also be issued (Tax Complexity Analysis, Comments of the IRS and Treasury Department, Conference Committee Report).

REITs. Dividends paid by a real estate investment trust (REIT) are not generally eligible for the reduced dividend rate. These sums largely represent rents

Explanation

and other income that are passed through to shareholders as dividends deductible to the REIT, rather than corporate earnings subject to the corporate income tax. However, REIT distributions will qualify for the reduced dividend rate to the extent they represent qualified corporate dividends. See ¶ 335.

Conforming amendments. In connection with the reduced dividend rate, Congress also reduced the tax rate on personal holding companies to 15 percent (see ¶ 370), reduced the accumulated earnings tax rate to 15 percent (see ¶ 365), and repealed the collapsible corporation provisions (see ¶ 360). Each of these changes is subject to sunset in tax years beginning after 2008 (Act Sec. 303 of the 2003 Act).

Mechanism for reporting qualified dividends. The reduced dividend rate will be administered by including qualified dividends with net capital gain on Schedule D. Accordingly, the amount of net capital gain will be increased by the amount of qualified dividend income eligible for the reduced rate under Code Sec. 1(h)(11) (Code Sec. 1(h)(3), as amended by the 2003 Act).

Alternative minimum tax. The reduced dividend rates of 15 and 5 percent (zero percent in 2008 for taxpayers in the 10- or 15-percent bracket) are also used when computing an individual's liability for the alternative minimum tax (AMT) (Code Sec. 55(b)(3)(C), as amended by the 2003 Act). Alternative minimum tax rules ensure that at least a minimum amount of income tax is paid by high-income taxpayers with large amounts of deductions. An individual's AMT for a tax year is the excess of his tentative minimum tax over his regular tax (Code Sec. 55(a)). Generally, the maximum rate of tax, including alternative minimum tax, on the net capital gain of an individual is 15 percent; 5 percent to the extent the taxpayer's taxable income is taxed at a rate below 25 percent (currently equivalent to the 10- and 15-percent brackets) (Code Sec. 55(b)(3), as amended by the 2003 Act). Since qualified dividends are included in net capital gain for purposes of computing the tax, the dividends also qualify for the reduced AMT rate.

Reduced dividend rates to apply from 2003–2008. The reduced dividend rates apply for tax years 2003 through 2008. In 2009, dividends will once again be taxed at ordinary income tax rates. The reduced rate "sunsets" in 2009 and disappears along with all related provisions (including the reduced tax rates for accumulated earnings and personal holding company income).

Caution. The reduced rates for dividends apply to eligible dividends received at any point during 2003, even to first-quarter dividends received before the date of enactment. To compare, the reduced rate for capital gain (see ¶ 305 and ¶ 320) applies only to shares sold on or after May 6, 2003.

Planning Note. Since the reduced rates apply to first quarter dividends paid in 2003, some taxpayers may have already overpaid estimated taxes due in the first 2003 installment (payable April 15, 2003). Subsequent installments should be adjusted on Form 1040-ES to reflect the revised liability estimate. Subsequent installments are due June 16, 2003, September 15, 2003, and January 15, 2004.

PRACTICAL ANALYSIS. Michael J. Grace of Jackson & Campbell, PC, Washington, D.C., remarking on the consequences of the dividend rate reduction, finds that the "winners" will include common stocks and shares in stock mutual funds that pay meaningful dividends, preferred stocks compared to bonds and other debt instruments yielding taxable interest, and equity financing compared to debt financing. Concerning this third category, some commentators have flagged the risk that some corporations may

¶ 325

artificially increase their dividends in the short term only to reduce them after 2008 (assuming that dividends then become subject once again to regular rates on ordinary income). This concern appears unrealistic. Unless its financial condition so requires, no corporation wants to suffer the adverse publicity or possible panic selling of its stock that may result from reducing dividends.

Affected but not necessarily impaired. The reduced rates on dividends will affect but not necessarily impair other investment classes compared to common and preferred stocks.

REITs. Real estate investment trusts that distribute the required amounts of their income to shareholders will remain subject to a single level of tax. However, amounts distributed to shareholders will be taxable at the 2003 Act's reduced rates on dividends only to the extent that the distributions represent income previously taxed to the REIT or capital gains. All other distributions will be taxable as ordinary income. As a result, REITs may face increasing competition for investment capital from regular corporations paying dividends taxable at 15 percent (or five percent, as the case may be). However, REITs traditionally pay higher dividend yields than regular corporations, a pattern that should continue because REITs must distribute most of their income in order not to pay tax at the entity level. Long-term capital gains from selling shares in REITs will qualify to be taxed at the Act's reduced rates applicable to such gains.

Municipal bonds. Interest on municipal bonds will remain exempt from Federal and, in many situations, state and local income tax. To some investors, especially those seeking "growth" investments, the exemption may not prove comparatively as attractive as it did when dividends on stock were taxable as ordinary income. Long-term capital gains from selling municipal bonds will qualify to be taxed at the 2003 Act's reduced rates applicable to such gains.

Tax credits. Nothing in the 2003 Act will discourage corporations from continuing to invest in projects offering tax credits including the low-income housing credit and the rehabilitation credit. It had been argued that the Bush Administration's original proposal would have discouraged corporations from investing in such credits. Under that proposal, corporations generally could have paid nontaxable dividends only from fully taxed income, which credits would have reduced. Nonetheless, the reduced rates of tax on dividends and capital gains will alter the dynamics of comparing after-tax rates of return on investments in credits compared to investments in stocks paying dividends.

Losers. The 2003 Act disfavors short-term trading (including "day" trading) compared to long-term investing. Dividends on stock will not qualify for the reduced rates unless the stock is held for at least 60 days during the 120-day period beginning 60 days before the ex-dividend date. Gains from selling stocks held 12 months or less will be subject to tax at the rates applicable to ordinary income. The 2003 Act does not increase allowable capital

¶ 325

losses; capital losses exceeding capital gains may be deducted only to the extent of $3,000 per year.

PRACTICAL ANALYSIS. Harley T. Duncan of the Federation of Tax Administrators, Washington, D.C., finds that the most notable aspect of the bill from a state tax standpoint is that the federal tax relief for dividend and capital gains income will not flow through to state income taxes. Taxpayers will be required to include all the income from these sources on the federal and state return; thus, there is no diminution of the tax base. States may, if they so choose, establish a preferential rate for such income as some have done for certain capital gains.

The 2003 Act stands in sharp contrast to the Senate-passed bill and the Administration's original proposal, both of which would have excluded dividend income from taxation. The income exclusion would have potentially affected the state tax systems of all states with a federal starting point if the states had ultimately chosen to maintain their conformity.

The 2003 Act could have an indirect effect on state and local finances by increasing their borrowing costs. The current comparative advantage enjoyed by tax exempt state and local bonds will be diminished as a result of the reduced rate of federal tax on dividends. To the extent that investors view dividend-paying stocks as an alternative to municipal bonds, states and localities will be required to increase the interest paid on their bonds in order to attract investors. The 2003 Act will reduce the rate of tax on qualifying dividends by over 40 percent for many taxpayers.

For further information about the taxation of dividends and capital gains, see 2003FED ¶ 3285.01, 2003FED ¶ 5707B.01, FTS § E:5.100, FTS § I:5.40, or 2003FTG ¶ 3205.

★ *Effective date.* The provision applies to tax years beginning after December 31, 2002 (Act Sec. 302(f)(1) of the Jobs and Growth Tax Relief Reconciliation Act of 2003).

Sunset provision. The provisions and amendments of Title III of the 2003 Act will not apply to tax years beginning after December 31, 2008. The Internal Revenue Code of 1986 will be applied and administered to these years as if the provisions and amendments had not been enacted (Act Sec. 303). See the CCH Explanation at ¶ 29,001.

Act Sec. 302(a) of the Jobs and Growth Tax Relief Reconciliation Act of 2003, adding Code Sec. 1(h)(11); Act Sec. 302(b), amending Code Sec. 163(d)(4)(B); Act Sec. 302(e)(1), amending Code Sec. 1(h)(3); Act Sec. 302(e)(2), adding Code Sec. 301(f)(4); Act Sec. 302(e)(3), adding Code Sec. 306(a)(1)(D); Act Sec. 302(f)(1). Law at ¶ 5005, ¶ 5030, ¶ 5045 and ¶ 5050. Committee Report at ¶ 10,110.

Jobs and Growth Tax Relief Reconciliation Act of 2003

Dividends Passed Through RICs and REITs

¶ 335

Background

A regulated investment company (RIC) is a widely held corporation or common trust fund that invests in stocks and securities and satisfies a number of complex tests relating to income, assets and other matters. RICs are taxed as corporations but can deduct their dividends.

The shareholders of a RIC are taxed on distributions from RICs under the general rules applying to dividends. However, if the distributing RIC designates a distribution as a capital gain dividend, the shareholder treats it as capital gain. A RIC can designate a distribution as a capital gain dividend if it was realized from the disposition of capital assets and it represents some or all of the company's net capital gain for the tax year. However, if the shareholder receiving the distribution is not entitled to a share of the company's capital gains, it is taxed as if it received an ordinary dividend. Under Code Sec. 854(a), the dividends received deduction for corporations does not apply to capital gain dividends from RICs.

A corporation is entitled to a special deduction for dividends received (under Code Sec. 243) from a domestic corporation that is subject to income tax. The deduction is 70 percent of dividends received if the corporation receiving the dividend owns less than 20 percent of the distributing corporation; 80 percent of dividends received if 20 percent or more of the stock is owned by the receiving corporation; and, generally, 100 percent of the dividends received for dividends received from a member of an affiliated group. In order for a corporation receiving a distribution from a RIC to obtain a dividends received deduction, the RIC must designate the payment as a dividend. The amount designated as dividends cannot exceed the aggregate dividends received by the RIC for the tax year.

A real estate investment trust (REIT) is similar to a RIC that invests in real estate. A REIT is taxed on its income as a separate taxpayer, but it can deduct its dividends paid. However, if the distributing REIT designates a distribution as a capital gain dividend, the shareholders treat it as capital gain. Under Code Sec. 857(c), the dividends received deduction is *not* available for dividends from a REIT.

Under Code Sec. 337(d), the IRS has the authority to issue regulations to ensure that REITs and RICs cannot be used to circumvent the purpose of any provision of law or regulation. For example, the IRS issued regulations under this authority on March 13, 2003 (T.D. 9047), subjecting REITs which engage in conversion transactions to built-in gain treatment under Code Sec. 1374 as if they were S corporations.

Jobs and Growth Act Impact

Rules regarding dividends passed through RICs and REITs coordinated with new rules regarding taxation of dividends.—A provision of the Jobs and Growth Tax Relief Reconciliation Act of 2003 taxes dividends at the same rates as net capital gains with certain modifications (Code Sec. 1(h)(11), as added by the 2003 Act (see ¶ 325)). The rules regarding dividends passed through RICs and REITs are coordinated with these new rules regarding taxation of dividends.

Explanation

Planning Note. To qualify for the new favorable tax rates, it is important that the RIC designate its distributions as dividends to the full extent of its aggregate dividends received.

If the aggregate dividends received by a RIC during any tax year are less than 95 percent of its gross income, then, in computing the maximum rate on dividend income (under Code Sec. 1(h)(11)), rules similar to the existing rules of Code Sec. 854(b)(1)(A) apply (Code Sec. 854(b)(1)(B)(i), as amended by the 2003 Act).

Amounts will be treated as dividends for purposes of the 95-percent test only if the amount is "qualified dividend income" as described in new Code Sec. 1(h)(11)(B) (Code Sec. 854(b)(5), as added by the 2003 Act). See ¶ 325 for the definition of qualified dividend income.

Comment. The rules under Code Sec. 854(b)(1)(A), referred to above, allow a corporate shareholder that receives a dividend from a RIC that has met the minimum distribution requirements of Code Sec. 852(a) to claim a dividends received deduction under Code Sec. 243 only with respect to the amount of the distribution designated by the RIC as a dividend. Code Sec. 854(b)(1)(B) provides that the aggregate amount that may be designated by a RIC as a dividend for purposes of the dividends received deduction may not exceed the aggregate amount of dividends received by the RIC during the tax year. The new law imposes the same restriction with respect to the amount that may be designated by the RIC as a dividend for purposes of claiming the lower rates on dividends (Code Sec. 854(b)(1)(B), as amended by the 2003 Act).

Comment. The amount of dividends paid by a RIC that qualify for the reduced rate may not exceed the amount of aggregate qualifying dividends received by the RIC if the amount of aggregate qualifying dividends received by the RIC is less than 95 percent of its gross income.

Comment. Dividends received by a RIC or REIT before the date specified in the effective date section below are not treated as qualified dividend income.

For purposes of determining whether the aggregate dividends received by a RIC are less than 95 percent of gross income, a special rule applies to sales or dispositions of stock or securities. Specifically, the term "gross income" includes only the excess of:

- the net short-term capital gain from sales or dispositions of stock or securities, over

- the net long-term capital loss from such sales or dispositions included in gross income (Code Sec. 854(b)(1)(B)(ii), as added by the 2003 Act).

Special rules apply to distributions received by a RIC from a REIT. In determining the amount of aggregate dividends received by a RIC for purposes of applying the 95-percent gross income test, distributions received by a RIC from a qualifying REIT may be considered dividends (Code Sec. 854 (b)(1)(B)(iii), as added by the 2003 Act). The amount of a distribution from a REIT which is treated as a dividend is subject to the limitations under Code Sec. 857(c), as amended by the 2003 Act and explained below (Code Sec. 854(b)(1)(B)(iii)(II), as added by the 2003 Act).

Dividends received from qualified foreign corporations are also taken into account in computing the aggregate dividends received by a RIC (Code Sec. 854(b)(1)(B)(iv), as added by the 2003 Act).

¶ 335

REITs. The new law also makes changes to the REIT dividend rules in order to coordinate the new rules regarding taxing dividends at capital gains rates with the taxation of REITs.

Comment. The rule stating that dividends received from a REIT are not considered dividends for purposes of the Code Sec. 243 dividends received deduction is not affected.

Under the new law, rules similar to those that apply to a RIC will apply to a REIT. Thus, the amount of dividends paid by a REIT that will qualify for the reduced rate may not exceed the amount of aggregate qualifying dividends received by the REIT if the amount of aggregate qualifying dividends received by the REIT is less than 95 percent of its gross income (Code Sec. 857(c)(2)(A), as amended by the 2003 Act).

In applying these rules, however, a REIT is treated as receiving qualified dividend income (i.e., amounts which may be treated as dividends for purposes of the 95-percent gross income test) in an amount equal to the sum of:

(1) the excess of REIT taxable income computed under Code Sec. 857(b)(2) for the preceding tax year over the tax payable by the REIT under Code Sec. 857(b)(1) for that preceding tax year, and

(2) the excess of the income subject to tax by reason of the application of the Code Sec. 337(d) regulations for the preceding tax year over the tax payable by the REIT on that income for the preceding tax year (Code Sec. 857(c)(2)(B), as amended by the 2003 Act).

Caution. The IRS has the authority under Code Sec. 367(d) to issue regulations to ensure that REITs and RICs cannot be used to circumvent the purpose of any provision or regulation, which would apply to these new rules affecting the taxation of dividends.

PRACTICAL ANALYSIS. Keith Nakamoto of PricewaterhouseCoopers, Chicago, Illinois, notes that "qualified dividend income," which is taxed at capital gain rates, generally does not include dividends from a real estate investment trust (REIT). However, a portion of the REIT's dividend is classified as "qualified dividend income" if it is attributable to income which was subject to corporate tax at the REIT level or if it is attributable to "qualified dividend income" which was received by the REIT. (The REIT is subject to a corporate level tax on taxable income in excess of its dividends paid deduction and on other items such as Code Sec. 337(d) built-in gains.)

For further information about RICs and REITs, see 2003FED ¶ 26,433.01, 2003FED ¶ 26,512.01, FTS § F:9.20, FTS § I:21.20, 2003FTG ¶ 16,600, or 2003FTG ¶ 16,670.

★ *Effective date.* These amendments generally apply to tax years ending after December 31, 2002; however, dividends received by a RIC or a REIT on or before that date will not be treated as qualified dividend income (as defined in Code Sec. 1(h)(11)(B), as added by the 2003 Act) (Act Sec. 302(f)(2) of the Jobs and Growth Tax Relief Reconciliation Act of 2003).

Explanation

Sunset provision. The provisions and amendments of Title III of the 2003 Act will not apply to tax years beginning after December 31, 2008. The Internal Revenue Code of 1986 will be applied and administered to these years as if the provisions and amendments had not been enacted (Act Sec. 303). See ¶ 29,001 for CCH Explanation.

Act Sec. 302(c)(1) of the Jobs and Growth Tax Relief Reconciliation Act of 2003, amending Code Sec. 854(a); Act Sec. 302(c)(2), redesignating Code Sec. 854(b)(1)(B) as Code Sec. 854(b)(1)(C) and adding a new Code Sec. 854(b)(1)(B); Act Sec. 302(c)(3), amending Code Sec. 854(b)(1)(C) as redesignated; Act Sec. 302(c)(4), amending Code Sec. 854(b)(2); Act Sec. 302(c)(5), adding Code Sec. 854(b)(5); Act Sec. 302(d), amending Code Sec. 857(c); Act Sec. 302(e)(7), amending Code Sec. 584(c); Act Sec. 302(e)(8), amending Code Sec. 702(a)(5); Act Sec. 302(f)(2). Law at ¶ 5090 and ¶ 5095. Committee Report at ¶ 10,110.

DEPRECIATION

Increase and Extension of Bonus Depreciation

¶ 350

Background

The Job Creation and Worker Assistance Act of 2002 (P.L. 107-147) created a 30-percent additional first-year depreciation allowance for qualifying MACRS property (Code Sec. 168(k), as added by P.L. 107-147). The property must be acquired after September 10, 2001, and before September 11, 2004, and placed in service before January 1, 2005 (January 1, 2006, for property which (a) is produced by a taxpayer and is subject to the Code Sec. 263A uniform capitalization rules, (b) has a production period greater than two years, or greater than one year and a cost exceeding $1 million, and (c) has an MACRS recovery period of at least 10 years or is used in the trade or business of transporting persons for hire) (Code Sec. 168(k)(2)).

Property purchased by a taxpayer in a sale-leaseback transaction within three months after the original purchaser placed the property in service may qualify for the allowance if the original purchaser placed the property in service after September 10, 2001 (Code Sec. 168(k)(2)(D)(ii)).

Property acquired after September 10, 2001, pursuant to a written binding contract entered into before September 11, 2001, does not qualify for bonus depreciation (Code Sec. 168(k)(2)(A)(iii)).

The allowance is only available for new property that is depreciable under MACRS and has a recovery period of 20 years or less, is MACRS water utility property, is computer software depreciable over three years under Code Sec. 167, or is qualified leasehold improvement property, as defined below (Code Sec. 168(k)(2)(A)(i)).

Property which must be depreciated using the MACRS alternative depreciation system (ADS) does not qualify (Code Sec. 168(k)(2)(C)(i)). If ADS is elected, however, the property may qualify. A listed property, such as a passenger automobile, which is used 50 percent or less for business, does not qualify because it must be depreciated using ADS.

Bonus depreciation is allowed in full for alternative minimum tax (AMT) purposes. If bonus depreciation is claimed, no AMT adjustment is required on the

¶ 350

Background

regular MACRS deductions (i.e., the deductions are allowed in full for AMT purposes) (Code Sec. 168(k)(2)(F)).

Bonus depreciation is treated as depreciation for recapture purposes upon the sale of the property. Unlike the Code Sec. 179 expense allowance, there is no taxable income limitation or investment limitation on the bonus allowance.

A taxpayer may elect out of bonus depreciation with respect to any class of property (Code Sec. 168(k)(2)(C)(iii)).

Qualified leasehold improvement property. An improvement to an interior portion of *nonresidential real property* (whether or not depreciated under MACRS) by a lessor or lessee under or pursuant to a lease may qualify for bonus depreciation (Code Sec. 168(k)(3)). The improvement must be placed in service more than three years after the building was first placed in service (i.e., the building must be more than three years old). The lessor and lessee may not be related persons. Expenditures for (1) the enlargement of a building, (2) any elevator or escalator, (3) any structural component that benefits a common area, or (4) the internal structural framework of the building do not qualify.

Computation. The bonus depreciation deduction is claimed on the cost of the property after reduction by any Code Sec. 179 allowance claimed. Regular MACRS deductions are claimed on the cost, as reduced by any Code Sec. 179 allowance and bonus depreciation.

Example (1). On May 1, 2003, Jake Jackson purchases qualifying 5-year MACRS property subject to the half-year convention for $1,500 and claims a $500 Code Sec. 179 allowance. Bonus depreciation is $300 (($1,500 − $500) × 30%). Regular MACRS depreciation deductions are computed on $700 ($1,500 − $500 − $300). The regular first-year MACRS allowance is $140 ($700 × 20% (first-year table percentage)).

Example (2). Joseph Long purchases $100,000 of new machinery on January 17, 2002. Assume that the machinery is MACRS 5-year property, that the half-year convention applies, and that no amount is expensed under Code Sec. 179. Long is entitled to deduct a $30,000 ($100,000 × 30%) special depreciation allowance. The depreciable basis of the property is reduced to $70,000 ($100,000 − $30,000). Regular MACRS depreciation (using the table percentages for 5-year property) is computed as follows:

Recovery Year		Deduction
2002	bonus depreciation	$ 30,000
2002	$70,000 × 20% =	$ 14,000
2003	$70,000 × 32% =	$ 22,400
2004	$70,000 × 19.20% =	$ 13,440
2005	$70,000 × 11.52% =	$ 8,064
2006	$70,000 × 11.52% =	$ 8,064
2007	$70,000 × 5.76% =	$ 4,032
		$ 100,000

¶ 350

Explanation

Jobs and Growth Act Impact

Bonus depreciation deduction increased to 50 percent for post-May 5, 2003 acquisitions.—The new law increases the additional first-year depreciation allowance percentage from 30 percent to 50 percent. To qualify for the higher percentage, the property must be acquired after May 5, 2003, and placed in service before January 1, 2005 (January 1, 2006, for property with a longer production period, as described in the "Background" section). The 50-percent rate does not apply if a binding written contract for acquisition of the property was in effect before May 6, 2003 (Code Sec. 168(k)(4), as added by the Jobs and Growth Reconciliation Tax Act of 2003).

Property of the type which meets the requirements for the 30-percent bonus depreciation deduction will qualify for the 50-percent rate if the preceding acquisition and placed-in-service dates are met.

Taxpayers may elect to continue to use the 30-percent rate.

Example (1). Joseph Long purchases $100,000 of new machinery that is MACRS 5-year property, where the half-year convention applies and no amount is expensed under Code Sec. 179 (same facts as in "Background" Example (2), above). The property is purchased on June 1, 2003, and, therefore, qualifies for the 50-percent bonus depreciation rate. The 2003 bonus depreciation deduction is $50,000 ($100,000 cost × 50%). The depreciation table percentages for five-year property (Table 1, below) are applied to a depreciable basis of $50,000 ($100,000 − $50,000).

Recovery Year		Deduction
2003	bonus depreciation	$ 50,000
2003	$50,000 × 20% =	$ 10,000
2004	$50,000 × 32% =	$ 16,000
2005	$50,000 × 19.20% =	$ 9,600
2006	$50,000 × 11.52% =	$ 5,760
2007	$50,000 × 11.52% =	$ 5,760
2008	$50,000 × 5.76% =	$ 2,880
		$ 100,000

The following three depreciation tables may be used to compare the effect of claiming bonus depreciation on the rate of recovery over the applicable recovery period, assuming that the half-year convention applies. Table 1 is the official IRS table, which contains table percentages that do not reflect the bonus depreciation deduction. These table percentages are applied to the cost of an asset after reduction by any section 179 expense allowance and bonus depreciation. Table 2 shows recovery percentages that apply when 30-percent bonus depreciation is claimed. Table 2 percentages are applied to the cost of the property less any amount deducted under section 179. Table 3 shows the percentages that apply when 50-percent bonus depreciation is claimed. These percentages are also applied to the cost of the property less any amount expensed under section 179. The first recovery year percentages in Tables 2 and 3 were increased (relative to the Table 1 percentages) to reflect the applicable bonus depreciation rate. The Table 2 and Table 3 percentages for subsequent recovery years were reduced (relative to the Table 1 percentages) to reflect the required reduction in basis by the bonus depreciation amount. The IRS will not be issuing revised tables similar to Table 2

¶ 350

Jobs and Growth Tax Relief Reconciliation Act of 2003

and Table 3. This is because the bonus depreciation allowance must be calculated and reported separately on Form 4562. Tables 2 and 3 should not be used to prepare tax returns. They simply show the effect of claiming bonus depreciation on the rate of depreciation over the recovery period.

The following is the official IRS table used for the computing MACRS deductions on 3-, 5-, 7-, 10-, 15-, and 20-year MACRS property when the half-year convention applies.

TABLE 1   General Depreciation System
Applicable Depreciation Method: 200- or 150-Percent Declining Balance Switching to Straight Line
Applicable Recovery Periods: 3, 5, 7, 10, 15, 20 years
Applicable Convention: Half-Year

If the Recovery Year is:	3-year	5-year	7-year	10-year	15-year	20-year
			the Depreciation Rate is:			
1	33.33	20.00	14.29	10.00	5.00	3.750
2	44.45	32.00	24.49	18.00	9.50	7.219
3	14.81	19.20	17.49	14.40	8.55	6.677
4	7.41	11.52	12.49	11.52	7.70	6.177
5		11.52	8.93	9.22	6.93	5.713
6		5.76	8.92	7.37	6.23	5.285
7			8.93	6.55	5.90	4.888
8			4.46	6.55	5.90	4.522
9				6.56	5.91	4.462
10				6.55	5.90	4.461
11				3.28	5.91	4.462
12					5.90	4.461
13					5.91	4.462
14					5.90	4.461
15					5.91	4.462
16					2.95	4.461
17						4.462
18						4.461
19						4.462
20						4.461
21						2.231

¶ 350

Explanation

Caution: The following is an unofficial CCH prepared depreciation table which has adjusted percentages that reflect the 30-percent bonus depreciation deduction.

UNOFFICIAL CCH TABLE INCORPORATING 30-PERCENT BONUS DEPRECIATION

TABLE 2   General Depreciation System
Applicable Depreciation Method: 200- or 150-Percent
Declining Balance Switching to Straight Line
Applicable Recovery Periods: 3, 5, 7, 10, 15, 20 years
Applicable Convention: Half-Year

If the Recovery Year is:	3-year	5-year	7-year	10-year	15-year	20-year
			the Depreciation Rate is:			
1	53.331	44.00	40.003	37.00	33.50	32.625
2	31.115	22.40	17.143	12.60	6.65	5.0533
3	10.367	13.44	12.243	10.08	5.985	4.6739
4	5.187	8.064	8.743	8.064	5.39	4.3239
5		8.064	6.251	6.454	4.851	3.9991
6		4.032	6.244	5.159	4.361	3.6995
7			6.251	4.585	4.13	3.4216
8			3.122	4.585	4.13	3.1654
9				4.592	4.137	3.1234
10				4.585	4.13	3.1227
11				2.296	4.137	3.1234
12					4.13	3.1227
13					4.137	3.1234
14					4.13	3.1227
15					4.137	3.1234
16					2.065	3.1227
17						3.1234
18						3.1227
19						3.1234
20						3.1227
21						1.5617

Caution: The following is an unofficial CCH prepared depreciation table which has adjusted percentages that reflect the 50-percent bonus depreciation deduction.

UNOFFICIAL CCH DEPRECIATION TABLE INCORPORATING 50-PERCENT BONUS DEPRECIATION

TABLE 3   General Depreciation System
Applicable Depreciation Method: 200- or 150-Percent
Declining Balance Switching to Straight Line
Applicable Recovery Periods: 3, 5, 7, 10, 15, 20 years
Applicable Convention: Half-Year

If the Recovery Year is:	3-year	5-year	7-year	10-year	15-year	20-year
			the Depreciation Rate is:			
1	66.665	60.00	57.145	55.00	52.50	51.875
2	22.225	15.00	12.245	9.00	4.750	3.6095
3	7.405	9.60	8.745	7.20	4.275	3.3385
4	3.705	5.76	6.245	5.76	3.850	3.0885
5		5.76	4.465	4.61	3.465	2.8565
6		2.88	4.460	3.685	3.115	2.6425

¶ 350

Jobs and Growth Tax Relief Reconciliation Act of 2003

If the Recovery Year is:	3-year	5-year	and the Recovery Period is: 7-year	10-year	15-year	20-year
			the Depreciation Rate is:			
7			4.465	3.275	2.950	2.444
8			.2.23	3.275	2.950	2.261
9				3.28	2.955	2.231
10				3.275	2.950	2.2305
11				1.640	2.955	2.231
12					2.950	2.2305
13					2.955	2.231
14					2.950	2.2305
15					2.955	2.231
16					1.475	2.2305
17						2.231
18						2.2305
19						2.231
20						2.2305
21						1.1155

Example (2): Three-year property costing $100,000 and subject to the half-year convention is purchased on May 1, 2003. The taxpayer claims 30-percent bonus depreciation. The combined first-year depreciation deduction and 30-percent bonus depreciation allowance is $53,331 ($100,000 × 53.331%). The second-year depreciation deduction is $31,115 ($100,000 × 31.115%). The third-year depreciation deduction is $10,367 ($100,000 × 10.367%). The fourth-year deduction is $5,187 ($100,000 × 5.187%). Table 2 is used.

Example (3). Three-year property costing $100,000 and subject to the half-year convention is purchased on May 7, 2003. The taxpayer claims the 50 percent bonus depreciation deduction. The combined first-year depreciation deduction and 50-percent bonus depreciation allowance is $66,665 ($100,000 × 66.665%). The second-year depreciation deduction is $22,225 ($100,000 × 22.225%). The third-year depreciation deduction is $7,405 ($100,000 × 7.405%). The fourth-year deduction is $3,705 ($100,000 × 3.705%). Table 3 is used.

Comment. As originally enacted, 30-percent bonus depreciation applied to qualified property (1) acquired by a taxpayer after September 10, 2001, and before September 11, 2004, and (2) placed in service by the taxpayer before January 1, 2005 (January 1, 2006, for certain property with a longer production period). No written binding contract for the acquisition of the property may be in effect before September 11, 2001. Under the new law, bonus depreciation may be claimed on qualified property (1) acquired after September 10, 2001, and before January 1, 2005, and (2) placed in service before January 1, 2005 (January 1, 2006, for property with a longer production period). The bonus depreciation rate is increased from 30 percent to 50 percent if the property was acquired after May 5, 2003. The 50-percent rate does not apply if a written binding contract for the acquisition of the property was in effect prior to May 6, 2003. No bonus depreciation may be claimed if a written binding contract was in effect before September 11, 2001 (Code Sec. 168(k)(2)(A)(iii), as amended by the 2003 Act).

Comment. Although the rule that the bonus depreciation property must be placed in service before January 1, 2005, has not changed, there is no longer any requirement that the property must be acquired before September 11, 2004 (or, alternatively, that a binding contract for its acquisition be entered into before that date).

¶ 350

Explanation

50-percent bonus depreciation property. Property entitled to the 50-percent bonus depreciation rate is referred to as "50-percent bonus depreciation property."

50-percent bonus depreciation property is property that is described in Code Sec. 168(k)(2)(A)(i):

(1) the original use of which commences with the taxpayer after May 5, 2003,

(2) which is acquired by the taxpayer after May 5, 2003, and before January 1, 2005, but only if no written binding contract for the acquisition was in effect before May 6, 2003, and

(3) which is placed in service by the taxpayer before January 1, 2005 (January 1, 2006, for certain property with a long production period) (Code Sec. 168(k)(4)(B), as added by the 2003 Act).

Comment. The original use requirement means that the property must be new. Used property does not qualify for bonus depreciation at either the 30-percent or 50-percent rate.

Property described in Code Sec. 168(k)(2)(A)(i) is property which is:

(1) depreciable under MACRS and has a recovery period of 20 years or less;

(2) MACRS water utility property as defined in Code Sec. 168(e)(5);

(3) computer software which is depreciable under Code Sec. 167(f) using the straight-line method over 36 months; or

(4) qualified leasehold improvement property (as defined in the "Background" section).

Comment. Except for the post-May 5, 2003 acquisition date requirement, 50-percent bonus depreciation property is the same type of property which qualified for 30-percent bonus depreciation.

Binding contract to acquire a component of the property in effect before May 6, 2003. The controlling House Committee Report says that property will not fail to qualify for 50-percent bonus depreciation simply because a binding contract to acquire a component of the property is in effect prior to May 6, 2003 (footnote 22 at ¶ 10,080). The report says bonus depreciation may not be claimed on the component.

Comment. If a binding contract to acquire the component was in effect after September 10, 2001, and before May 6, 2003, it seems that the component should be eligible for bonus depreciation at the 30-percent rate.

The footnote goes on to say that no inference is intended as to the proper treatment of "components placed in service under the 30-percent additional first-year depreciation" provided by the 2001 Jobs Act. The Joint Committee on Taxation's General Explanation of Tax Legislation Enacted in the 107th Congress (footnote 211 of the "Blue Book" explanation relating to the 30-percent bonus depreciation deduction) (JCS-1-103)), however, states that Congress did not intend to preclude property from qualifying for the additional 30-percent first-year depreciation merely because a binding written contract to acquire a component of the property was in effect prior to September 11, 2001.

¶ 350

Comment. In this case, it seems that no bonus depreciation should be claimed on the component that was subject to the pre-September 11, 2001 contract.

PRACTICAL ANALYSIS. Keith Nakamoto of PricewaterhouseCoopers, Chicago, Illinois, observes that since bonus depreciation is not a deduction for "earnings and profits" purposes, a REIT can benefit from bonus depreciation only if its taxable income exceeds its dividends paid deduction. In this situation, a REIT can increase its distribution, reduce its taxable income, or pay a corporate level income tax. A REIT may be able to use bonus depreciation to reduce its taxable income so that its taxable income is equal to its dividends paid deduction.

A REIT with a distribution payout that already exceeds taxable income does not require additional deductions, nor can it reduce the taxable portion of its distribution by electing bonus depreciation.

Property with longer production periods. As explained in the "Background" section, certain property with a recovery period of 10 years or longer *or* which is transportation property only needs to be placed in service before January 1, 2006, rather than before January 1, 2005, in order to qualify for bonus depreciation (Code Sec. 168(k)(2)(B)). The 30-percent rate will continue to apply to this property if it was acquired after September 10, 2001, and before May 6, 2003, or if a binding contract for its acquisition was entered into after September 10, 2001, and before May 6, 2003. The 50-percent rate will apply if such property is acquired after May 5, 2003, or if a binding contract for its acquisition was entered into after May 5, 2003.

Under the prior rules, bonus depreciation on property with a longer production period only applied to the extent of the adjusted basis of the property that was attributable to manufacture, construction, or production before September 11, 2004. The new law allows the bonus depreciation deduction to be claimed on the adjusted basis of the property that is attributable to manufacture, construction, or production before January 1, 2005. This extension applies whether the taxpayer is claiming bonus depreciation at the 30-percent rate or the 50-percent rate (Code Sec. 168(k)(2)(B), as amended by the 2003 Act).

Comment. Progress expenditures incurred after September 10, 2004, through December 31, 2004, will now qualify for bonus depreciation provided that the property is placed in service by January 1, 2006.

Self-constructed property. Property which is manufactured, constructed, or produced for a taxpayer's own use will qualify for the 50-percent bonus depreciation rate if the taxpayer begins manufacture, construction, or production after May 5, 2003 (Code Sec. 168(k)(4)(C), as added by the 2003 Act). The 30-percent rate will continue to apply if the manufacture, etc., began after September 10, 2001 and before May 6, 2003. The former rule that the manufacture, construction, or production must begin before September 11, 2004, in order to claim bonus depreciation is changed to require that the manufacture, construction, or production must begin before January 1, 2005 (Code Sec. 168(k)(2)(D)(i), as amended by the 2003 Act; Code Sec. 168(k)(4)(C), as added by the 2003 Act).

Sale-leasebacks. A rule similar to the sale-leaseback provision of Code Sec. 168(k)(2)(D)(ii) applies except that the reference to September 10, 2001, is treated

¶ 350

Explanation

as a reference to May 5, 2003, so as to enable sale-leaseback property originally placed in service after this date to qualify for the 50-percent rate. Under the provision, as amended, if property is originally placed in service after May 5, 2003, by a person who sells it to the taxpayer and then leases it back from the taxpayer within three months after the date that the property was originally placed in service, then (1) the property is treated as originally placed in service by the taxpayer and (2) the placed-in-service date is deemed to occur no earlier than the date that the property is used under the leaseback (Code Sec. 168(k)(4)(C), as added by the 2003 Act).

Like-kind exchanges and involuntary conversions. The Controlling House Committee Report states that: "The Committee wishes to clarify that the adjusted basis of qualified property acquired by a taxpayer in a like kind exchange or an involuntary conversion is eligible for the additional first year depreciation deduction."

Comment. The House Report contains no other additional information on the subject. Although the reference to "qualified property" is made in the context of 50-percent bonus depreciation property, the statement should be equally applicable to 30-percent bonus depreciation property. Many taxpayers have assumed that the carryover basis of property acquired in a Code Sec. 1031 like-kind exchange or an involuntary conversion does not qualify for bonus depreciation. The issue arises due to IRS Notice 2000-4 (2001-1 CB 313). Under Notice 2000-4, a taxpayer must continue to depreciate the carryover basis of a depreciable asset acquired in a like-kind exchange or an involuntary conversion as if the exchange or conversion had not occurred. Only the non-carryover basis, if any, is treated as new property. Since bonus depreciation is a first-year depreciation allowance, the appropriateness of claiming the allowance on a carryover basis was in question. The IRS does not appear to have released any direct guidance on this issue.

Planning Note. Taxpayers who failed to claim bonus depreciation on the carryover basis portion of a depreciable asset acquired in a like-kind exchange or involuntary conversion (and who did not elect out of bonus depreciation) may want to file an amended return (if only one return has been filed) or file a request for a change in accounting method on Form 3115 if two or more returns have been filed. The automatic change of accounting method procedures in Rev. Proc. 2002-19 (2002-1 CB 696) should apply.

Caution. Taxpayers who failed to claim bonus depreciation on eligible property that should have been reported on a 2000 or 2001 return filed before June 1, 2002, may have made a deemed election out of bonus depreciation pursuant to the guidelines of Rev. Proc. 2002-33 (2002-1 CB 963). Since an election out of bonus depreciation cannot be revoked without IRS consent (Rev. Proc. 2002-33), these taxpayers will presumably need to obtain IRS permission to claim bonus depreciation on the carryover basis of property acquired in a like-kind exchange or an involuntary conversion. Taxpayers who did not make an affirmative election or deemed election out of bonus depreciation should be aware that the basis of property eligible for the allowance needs to be reduced even if the bonus allowance was not claimed on a return. This is the rule that applies to allowable depreciation that goes unclaimed.

PRACTICAL ANALYSIS. Michael J. Grace of Jackson & Campbell, PC, Washington, D.C., observes that under Code Sec. 168(k), as amended by the 2003 Act, taxpayers may take first-year "bonus" depreciation equaling 50 percent, 30 percent, or zero percent

¶ 350

of the adjusted basis of qualified property. The property must be acquired after May 5, 2003, and before January 1, 2005, and placed in service before January 1, 2005 (in some cases, January 1, 2006). Taxpayers desiring the 30-percent rather than the 50-percent bonus must elect the 30-percent bonus. Similarly, taxpayers desiring no bonus must elect out of Code Sec. 168(k). These elections must be made separately with respect to each class of qualified property. For purposes of computing otherwise allowable depreciation deductions, the property's basis must be reduced by any bonus depreciation taken. In evaluating their choices under Code Sec. 168(k), taxpayers should compare the benefit of taking bonus depreciation "upfront" to the cost of reducing other allowable depreciation on the property. Each taxpayer's unique circumstances must be considered.

The Conference Committee Report helpfully clarifies that taxpayers may take bonus depreciation on property received in a like-kind exchange or an involuntary conversion.

Luxury car depreciation cap adjustment. The first-year depreciation cap on a new vehicle subject to the Code Sec. 280F depreciation caps is increased by $4,600 if 30-percent bonus depreciation is claimed on the vehicle (i.e., an election out is not made) (Code Sec. 168(k)(2)(E)). The 2003 Act provides that the first-year cap is increased by $7,650 if 50-percent bonus depreciation is claimed on a new vehicle (Code Sec. 168(k)(4)(D), as added by the 2003 Act). In the case of a new electric vehicle, the $7,650 figure is tripled to $22,950. The $4,600 and $7,650 amounts are not adjusted for inflation.

Comment. If a taxpayer elects 30-percent bonus depreciation in place of 50-percent bonus depreciation under Code Sec. 168(k)(4)(E) (see above), then the first-year cap should, according to the controlling House Report, be increased by $4,600 rather than $7,650.

Comment. The IRS has not yet released the 2003 depreciation caps as of press time. CCH, however, projects that the caps on nonelectric vehicles will be unchanged for 2003. Thus, the first-year cap for a vehicle acquired after May 5, 2003, on which 50-percent bonus depreciation is claimed is $10,710 ($3,060 + $7,650). If bonus depreciation is claimed at the 30 percent rate, the first-year cap is $7,660 ($3,060 + $4,600).

Election to claim 30-percent bonus depreciation in place of 50-percent bonus depreciation. A taxpayer may elect to claim bonus depreciation at the 30-percent rate on one or more classes of property placed in service during a tax year even though the property otherwise qualifies for the 50-percent rate (Code Sec. 168(k)(4)(E)). The election is made on a property-class by property-class basis.

Election out of 30-percent bonus depreciation and 50-percent bonus depreciation. The election out of bonus depreciation is made separately for each class of property that qualifies for the 30-percent rate and for each class of property that qualifies for the 50-percent rate. Thus, for example, a taxpayer may elect out of bonus depreciation with respect to one class of property that qualifies for 30-percent bonus depreciation but decide not to elect out of bonus depreciation for property in the same class that qualifies for bonus depreciation at the 50-percent rate (Code Sec. 168(k)(2)(C)(iii), as amended by the 2003 Act).

¶ 350

Example. A calendar-year taxpayer places 10 machines in service in 2003 before May 6, 2003, and 5 cars in service in 2003 after May 5, 2003. The machines and cars are five-year property (same MACRS property class). The taxpayer may (1) claim bonus depreciation on the machines (30-percent rate applies) and bonus depreciation on the cars (a 50-percent rate applies unless a 30-percent rate is elected); (2) elect not to claim bonus depreciation on the machines and elect not to claim bonus depreciation on the cars; (3) claim bonus depreciation on the cars (at the 50-percent rate unless a 30-percent rate is elected) and elect not to claim bonus depreciation on the machines; or (4) elect not to claim bonus depreciation on the cars and claim bonus depreciation on the machines (30-percent rate applies).

Planning Note. Taxpayers who anticipate being in a higher tax bracket in future years may want to consider making the election out of bonus depreciation or making the election to use the 30-percent rate rather than the 50-percent rate. This situation may occur, for example, if the taxpayer is using NOL carryforwards to reduce taxable income in the year that bonus depreciation could be claimed.

Bonus depreciation on New York Liberty Zone property. The increased 50-percent rate does not apply to bonus depreciation that is claimed on "qualified New York Liberty Zone property" under Code Sec. 1400L(b). The 30-percent rate continues to apply to New York Liberty Zone property even if it is acquired after May 5, 2003.

Comment. Qualified New York Liberty Zone property is defined to exclude property which qualifies for bonus depreciation under Code Sec. 168(k) (Code Sec. 1400L(b)(2)(C)(i)). With the exception of used property, most property placed in service in the New York Liberty Zone will qualify for bonus depreciation under Code Sec. 168(k) during the period that the Code Sec. 168(k) allowance remains in effect. Thus, the failure to increase the allowance for New York Liberty Zone property from 30 percent to 50 percent is not particularly significant for taxpayers placing property in service in that area.

PRACTICAL ANALYSIS. Harley T. Duncan of the Federation of Tax Administrators, Washington, D.C., notes that prior to passage of the original bonus depreciation provisions in March 2002, each of 45 states with a personal or corporate income tax except California conformed to federal depreciation schedules and rules. Most states, however, chose not to conform to the bonus depreciation system, largely because of revenue concerns. Only fifteen states currently follow the bonus depreciation rules and will be affected by the revisions contained in the new Act, presuming they maintain their conformity. Those states are Alabama, Alaska, Colorado, Delaware, Florida, Kansas, Louisiana, Michigan, Montana, New Mexico, North Dakota, Oregon, Utah, Vermont and West Virginia.

In addition, five of the nonconforming states—Maine, Ohio, Nebraska, Minnesota and Oklahoma—provided a special schedule for recapturing the disallowed bonus depreciation, rather than simply disallowing the bonus and requiring the use of prior law depreciation schedules for the asset. The increased bonus may require that these states revisit their recapture schedule.

For further information about bonus depreciation, see 2003FED ¶ 11,279.058, FTS § G:16.260, or 2003FTG ¶ 9131.

★ *Effective date.* The provision applies to tax years ending after May 5, 2003 (Act Sec. 201(d), as added by the Jobs and Growth Tax Relief Reconciliation Act of 2003).

Act Sec. 201(a) of the Jobs and Growth Tax Relief Reconciliation Act of 2003, adding Code Sec. 168(k)(4); Act Secs. 201(b) and (c)(1), amending Code Sec. 168(k)(2); Act Sec. 201(c)(2), amending Code Sec. 1400L(b)(2)(C); Act Sec. 201(d). Law at ¶ 5035 and ¶ 5110. Committee Report at ¶ 10,080.

DEDUCTIONS

Increased Expensing for Small Businesses

¶ 355

Background

Taxpayers (other than estates, trusts and certain noncorporate lessors) that purchase qualifying tangible depreciable property may elect to deduct the cost of the property (new or used) in the year that it is placed in service (Code Sec. 179). This deduction is in lieu of depreciating the property and recovering the cost over a number of years through the modified accelerated cost recovery system (MACRS). The maximum allowable deduction for qualifying property placed in service in 2003 is $25,000. The $25,000 amount is reduced dollar-for-dollar (but not below zero) by the amount by which the cost of qualifying property placed in service during the tax year exceeds $200,000, the phase-out threshold. An election to expense these items is generally made on the taxpayer's original return for the tax year to which the election relates. In order to revoke the election, the taxpayer must obtain the consent of the IRS.

The amount eligible to be expensed may not exceed the taxable income derived by the taxpayer from the active conduct of any trade or business. The deduction disallowed under this limitation may be carried forward.

For property placed in service after 1990, Code Sec. 179 qualifying property is tangible Code Sec. 1245 property, depreciable under Code Sec. 168, and acquired by purchase for use in the active conduct of a trade or business. Generally, this includes (1) personal property; (2) other tangible property used as an integral part of manufacturing, production or extraction, or of furnishing electricity, gas, water or sewage disposal services or used in a research facility for these activities; (3) part of any real property that has an adjusted basis reflecting amortization deductions set forth in Code Sec. 1245(a)(3)(C); single-purpose agricultural or horticultural structures; storage facilities (other than buildings and their structural components) that are used in connection with the distribution of petroleum or primary products of petroleum; and any railroad grating or tunnel bore. Because property must be tangible to be eligible for expensing, generally, taxpayers may not elect to expense off-the-shelf computer software.

Jobs and Growth Act Impact

Dollar limitation increased to $100,000.—The maximum dollar amount that may be deducted under Code Sec. 179 is increased from $25,000 to $100,000

Explanation

for qualifying property placed in service in tax years beginning after 2002 and before 2006 and will be adjusted for inflation (Code Sec. 179(b)(1) and (5), as amended by the Jobs and Growth Tax Relief Reconciliation Act of 2003).

Comment. The National Federation of Independent Business (NFIB), the nation's largest small business lobbyist group, asked its 600,000 members to name their biggest tax problems. Among the top 10 tax problems cited by its members was the low Code Sec. 179 expensing limits. The NFIB found that the old business expensing limit was exceeded by the average company in only three months.

Planning Note. The deduction amount is limited to the aggregate taxable income of the taxpayer actively involved in a trade or business. An amount disallowed because of the taxable income limitation can be carried forward. Fully expensing qualifying property under Code Sec. 179, instead of depreciating the property, could provide additional benefits to the taxpayer. By lowering adjusted gross income (AGI), the taxpayer may qualify for itemized deductions that are limited by the taxpayer's AGI. Additionally, the Code Sec. 179 deduction is allowed in full for property placed in service even on the last day of the tax year. Taxpayers have the option of waiting until the end of the year before deciding if purchasing qualified property for their business will provide them with desired tax benefits.

Planning Note. Before deciding to elect the Code Sec. 179 deduction, consideration should be given to some long-range tax issues. For example, if the taxpayer is in a tax bracket of 15 percent or less, it may be better for the taxpayer not to take the deduction if the taxpayer expects to be in a higher income bracket in later years. Depreciation may provide a more valuable tax benefit to reduce taxable income in the following years.

Planning Note. If assets purchased in a tax year have different useful lives for depreciation purposes, and the taxpayer elects to take the Code Sec. 179 deduction, it is usually better to take the deduction on the longest-lived assets first.

Increase in qualifying investment at which phase-out begins. The $200,000 amount used to compute the phase-out of the deduction is increased to $400,000 for qualifying property placed in service in tax years beginning after 2002 and before 2006 (Code Sec. 179(b)(2), as amended by the 2003 Act). Thus, for tax years beginning in 2003, 2004 and 2005, the $100,000 maximum Code Sec. 179 deduction is reduced (but not below zero) by the amount by which the cost of qualifying property placed in service during the year exceeds $400,000. The $400,000 phase-out threshold will be adjusted for inflation.

Example. In 2003, Acme Co., a manufacturing company, purchases a machine to be used in its business. The cost of the machine is $410,000. Because the cost of the qualified property exceeds $400,000, the $100,000 deduction limitation must be reduced dollar-for-dollar by the amount that the cost of the machine exceeds $400,000. Thus, Acme Co. would be entitled to deduct $90,000 ($100,000 − $10,000) of the cost of the machine.

Comment. Code Sec. 179(b), as amended in 1986 by the Tax Reform Act of 1986 (P.L. 99-514), set the dollar deduction limitation at $10,000 and gradually it was raised to $25,000 for 2003 (prior to this new law). However, the phase-out amount of $200,000 had not been raised since 1986. Small business groups argued that increasing the $200,000 threshold might mean the difference between a company purchasing one machine or two. They also pointed out that purchasing additional machinery would lead to employing more people. The U.S. Small Business Administration's Office of Advocacy strongly supported the Code Sec. 179

¶355

changes made by the 2003 Act and pointed out that advocacy studies had shown that the small business community creates 67 percent of the new jobs in this country.

Planning Note. When a taxpayer is planning to make regular equipment purchases over several years, the acquisition of equipment should be structured, if possible, so that the purchases do not surpass the $400,000 phase-out threshold in any given year.

Caution. Taxpayers should also keep in mind that the $400,000 phase-out threshold will return to the previous $200,000 threshold in 2006 without the enactment of new legislation. In addition, the $100,000 maximum amount that can be deducted for qualifying property will revert to $25,000 in 2006 without the enactment of new legislation.

Off-the-shelf computer software. Off-the-shelf computer software to which Code Sec. 167 applies and that is placed in service in tax years beginning after 2002 and before 2006 is now included as qualifying property that may be expensed under Code Sec. 179 (Code Sec. 179(d)(1)(A), as amended by the 2003 Act). Computer software is defined as software that is readily available for purchase by the general public, is subject to a nonexclusive license, and has not been substantially modified. In addition, computer software does not include any database or similar item unless it is in the public domain and is incidental to the operation of otherwise qualifying computer software (Code Sec. 197(e)(3)(A)(i) and (B)).

Comment. Prior to the 2003 Act, small business off-the-shelf software purchases generally had to be amortized over 36 months. Software purchases were not allowed to be depreciated using the schedule allowed under MACRS. Instead, the cost of the software had to be depreciated and deducted on a straight-line basis over 36 months (Code Sec. 167(f)(1)(A)). In order to be depreciable, property has to have a useful life of more than one year. Software that had a useful life of less than one year (i.e., some tax-preparation software) could be expensed in the year it was placed in service.

PRACTICAL ANALYSIS. Michael Schlesinger of Schlesinger & Sussman of New York, New York, notes that under the 2003 Act's amendment to Code Sec. 179, the President and Congress want you to BUY! BUY! BUY! to stimulate the economy by prescribing that a taxpayer can expense up to $100,000 of qualified property in the year that the property is placed in service, more than quadruple the amount which could be expensed in 2002. While this is a boon to any taxpayer, particularly the small one, Congress still puts taxpayers through hoops to obtain this benefit, such as requiring taxpayers pursuant to Code Sec. 179(b)(3)'s trade or business income limitation to have taxable income equal to the Code Sec. 179(b)(1) amount expensed with a carryover provided by Code Sec. 179(b)(3)(B) for any amount in excess of the income limitation. Congress also under the 2003 Act did not simplify the analysis required to depreciate business assets; thus, taxpayers must read Code Secs. 179 and 168(k) very carefully to determine the best way to proceed. For instance, Congress under the 2003 Act, when it increased Code Sec. 168(k)'s bonus depreciation to 50 percent, left the requirement that taxpayers, to utilize this new provision, have to buy new property; in contrast, Code Sec. 179

Explanation

makes no such distinction allowing taxpayers to utilize this provision with new or used property.

While Congress has basically left Code Sec. 179's old qualification requirements in place, such as Code Sec. 179(b)(1)'s income requirement, it has added new dimensions to Code Sec. 179 which for the most part make it "taxpayer friendly." For instance, a new asset category has been created in Code Sec. 179(d)(1) "off-the-shelf computer software." Code Sec. 179(c)(2) has been amended to prescribe that any Code Sec. 179 elections made after 2002 and before 2006 can be revoked by taxpayers filing amended returns; previously, the election could only be revoked with the consent of the Secretary. Code Sec. 179(b)(2)'s investment dollar limitation has been raised from $200,000 to $400,000 with a new Code Sec. 179(b)(5) prescribing that Code Sec. 179(b)'s $100,000 expense limitation and $400,000 investment limitation is indexed for inflation commencing in 2004.

But Congress, instead of dovetailing effective dates for the changes to Code Secs. 168(k) and 179, prescribed that the changes to Code Sec. 179 commence after December 31, 2002, while Code Sec. 168(k)'s 50-percent depreciation bonus provisions do not apply until after May 5, 2003. Thus, for taxpayers who purchased property covered by both Code Secs. 179 and 168(k) between January 1 and May 5, 2003, they are bound by Code Sec. 168(k)'s old 30-percent bonus depreciation provisions but obtain the benefit of Code Sec. 179's new $100,000 expense limitations if they so elect; in contrast, taxpayers who purchase qualified property after May 5, 2003, can elect to acquire both Code Sec. 179's $100,000 expense provision and Code Sec. 168(k)'s 50-percent bonus provision.

Congress kept the elective provisions in Code Sec. 179 in tact; thus taxpayers can pick and choose what assets they want subject to Code Sec. 179 and the amount. Economically, taxpayers generally should choose assets for Code Sec. 179 treatment where they have long depreciation lives so that they can recover the cost of the assets quickly rather than over the lengthy period of depreciation.

The 2003 Act has a quirk in it not detailed in Code Sec. 179 in that taxpayers who purchase "large" SUVs in 2003 for business purposes can have Uncle Sam pay as much as $100,000 of the cost the first year the SUV is placed in service. The reason for this wrinkle is that Congress rejected the pleas of environmentalists. To qualify for this tax break, the SUV must be placed in service after December 31, 2002, and have a loaded gross vehicle weight rating of more than 6,000 pounds. Automobiles can also qualify providing that the curb weight exceeds 6,000 pounds. Otherwise, the maximum depreciation write-off for cars for the first year commencing under the revised Code Sec. 168(k) is a maximum of $7,650.

Besides creating this wrinkle with "large" SUVs, Congress left the wrinkles of the Job Creation and Worker Assistance Act of 2002

¶ 355

(JCWAA) in Code Secs. 179 and 168(k) rather than try to harmonize these provisions. For instance, Code Sec. 179 precludes estates, trusts and certain noncorporate lessors from utilizing this provision; Code Sec. 168(k) has no such limitation. Code Sec. 179 has an income limitation for use; Code Sec. 168(k) has no such requirement.

The changes made to Code Sec. 179 are of limited duration. The cost to the country for the amendment to Code Sec. 179 per the Joint Committee on Taxation is one billion dollars. It is unknown at this time if Congress will make the amendment to Code Sec. 179 permanent. If it does, the Joint Committee estimates the cost will be thirty-five billion dollars. Accordingly, since the status of Code Sec. 179 is unknown, taxpayers should if they are contemplating purchases of property for business, do it now while the law is certain rather than wait for the future.

Inflation adjustment for dollar limit and phase-out threshold. For tax years beginning after 2003 and before 2006, the $100,000 deduction limitation for qualifying property and the $400,000 phase-out threshold amount will be adjusted for inflation (Code Sec. 179(b)(5), as added by the 2003 Act). The inflation adjustment for the deduction limit and phase-out threshold amount is calculated by multiplying each respective dollar amount by the cost-of-living adjustment determined under Code Sec. 1(f)(3) for the calendar year in which the tax year begins and substituting calendar year 2002 for 1992 in the provision (Code Sec. 179(b)(5)).

If the amount of the dollar limitation ($100,000) as increased for inflation is not a multiple of $1,000, the amount will be rounded to the nearest multiple of $1,000 (Code Sec. 179(b)(5)(B)(i), as added by the 2003 Act). If the amount of the phase-out threshold as increased for inflation is not a multiple of $10,000, the amount will be rounded to the nearest multiple of $10,000 (Code Sec. 179(b)(5)(B)(ii), as added by the 2003 Act).

Comment. The cost-of-living adjustment under Code Sec. 1(f)(3) provides that a cost-of-living adjustment for any calendar year is the percentage by which the Consumer Price Index (CPI) for the preceding calendar year exceeds the CPI for calendar year 1992. The new law, as it applies the inflation adjustment to the deduction limit and the phase-out threshold amount, adopts this formula but substitutes calendar year 2002 for 1992 (Code Sec. 179(b)(5)(A)(ii), as added by the 2003 Act).

Revocation of election. Any election to expense property under Code Sec. 179 with respect to tax years beginning after 2002 and before 2006 may be revoked by the taxpayer with respect to any property. However, once the revocation is made, it is irrevocable (Code Sec. 179(c)(2), as amended by the 2003 Act).

Caution. The 2003 Act adds this language governing the revocation of a Code Sec. 179 election immediately under existing language stating that a Code Sec. 179 election may not be revoked except with the consent of the IRS. The Conference Committee Report states that the new provision permits taxpayers to make or

¶ 355

revoke expensing elections on amended returns without the consent of the IRS for tax years beginning after 2002 and before 2006.

PRACTICAL ANALYSIS. Michael J. Grace of Jackson & Campbell, PC, Washington, D.C., observes that the Act liberalizes the mechanics of elections under Code Sec. 179. Under prior law, an election to expense certain depreciable business assets generally could not be revoked without the IRS's permission. See Reg. § 1.179-5. Now, an election for tax years after 2002 and before 2006 may be revoked, although the revocation, once made, is irrevocable. See Code Sec. 179(c)(2) as amended by the 2003 Act. The Conference Committee Report permits taxpayers for such years to make or revoke expensing elections for those years on amended returns without the IRS's consent. Compare Reg. § 1.179-5, which allows taxpayers to make Code Sec. 179 elections on amended returns.

PRACTICAL ANALYSIS. Harley T. Duncan of the Federation of Tax Administrators, Washington, D.C., observes that provisions to increase the amount of business investment that small businesses may expense (as opposed to depreciate over time) are likely to affect most state income taxes. Of the 45 states with either an individual or business income tax, all but California generally follow federal rules for the computation of profit or loss and specifically conform to the small business expensing provisions of Code Sec. 179. Continuing their conformity to this provision will reduce state revenues by about $600 to $700 million per year for tax years 2003–2005, according to estimates from the Center on Budget and Policy Priorities (May 20, 2003). Not conforming to this change would likely prove problematic in that small business taxpayers would have to depreciate certain assets for state purposes that had been expensed at the federal level. This would make for a different basis in the asset and a different level of gain on any disposition. The resultant complexity and compliance issues would be substantial.

For further information about Code Sec. 179 expensing, see 2003FED ¶ 12,126.01, FTS § G:19.20, or 2003FTG ¶ 9130.

★ *Effective date.* These provisions apply to tax years beginning after December 31, 2002 (Act Sec. 202(f) of the Jobs and Growth Tax Relief Reconciliation Act of 2003). By their terms, the provisions apply to tax years beginning after 2002 and before 2006.

Act Sec. 202(a) of the Jobs and Growth Tax Relief Reconciliation Act of 2003, amending Code Sec. 179(b)(1); Act Sec. 202(b), amending Code Sec. 179(b)(2); Act Sec. 202(c), amending Code Sec. 179(d)(1); Act. Sec. 202(d), adding Code Sec. 179(b)(5); Act Sec. 202(e), amending Code Sec. 179(c)(2); Act Sec. 202(f). Law at ¶ 5040. Committee Report at ¶ 10,090.

¶ 355

CORPORATIONS

Repeal of Collapsible Corporation Rules

¶ 360

Background

Collapsible corporations are corporations used by shareholders to obtain favorable long-term capital gain treatment for income that would otherwise be taxable as ordinary income. Normally, gain on the sale or exchange of stock of a corporation and gain on complete or partial liquidating distributions constitute capital gain. However, if a corporation meets the definition of a collapsible corporation, the stockholder's gain on a sale or exchange of stock by the collapsible corporation's shareholders or distributions to shareholders that would otherwise be capital gain may be treated as ordinary income (Code Sec. 341).

A corporation is collapsible if it is formed or availed of principally for the manufacture, construction, or production of property, or for the purchase of inventory, unrealized receivables and specified trade or business assets (Section 341 assets), or the holding of stock in another collapsible corporation, with a view to the sale or exchange of stock by its shareholders or a distribution to its shareholders before it has realized two-thirds of the taxable income to be derived from the property and the realization of gain attributable to that property by the shareholders.

A corporation is presumed collapsible if, at the time of sale or distribution of the stock, the fair market value of its Section 341 assets is 50 percent or more of the fair market value of its total assets and 120 percent or more of the adjusted basis of its Section 341 assets. Both Section 341 assets and assets manufactured, constructed, or produced by the corporation are collectively treated as collapsible property.

Even if the corporation is collapsible, individual shareholders may be relieved from ordinary income characterization of gain if any one of the following applies:

(1) The shareholder owns 5 percent or less in value of the corporation's outstanding stock;

(2) At least 30 percent of the shareholder's gain on a distribution from the corporation or on a sale or exchange of stock is not attributable to collapsible property; or

(3) The shareholder's gain is realized more than three years after completion of the manufacture, construction, production, or purchase of a collapsible asset.

If a corporation is collapsible and none of the three exceptions above applies, collapsible treatment may be avoided if unrealized appreciation in the ordinary income assets is small in relation to the corporation's net worth. The collapsible provisions also do not apply to the sale of stock in a corporation that consents to the recognition of gain at the corporate level upon the disposition of noncapital assets.

Historically, collapsible corporations were utilized in the film and real estate industries. Actors, producers and others would receive stock in the corporation instead of salaries they might otherwise receive. After completion of the film, shares would be sold to the studio, the corporation would liquidate, and the shareholders would recognize capital gain from the sale of their shares. This result is no longer possible due to the repeal of the *General Utilities* doctrine.

Explanation

Background

The AICPA has long recommended repeal of the collapsible corporation rules in light of their ambiguity and because other laws already ensure corporate-level taxation upon the sale or liquidation of corporate assets. The provision was also criticized as at odds with the general preferential treatment of capital gain. The American Bar Association and, in turn, the Senate Finance Committee Report on the Simplification of the Income Taxation of Corporations (September 22, 1993) also recommended repeal of these outdated rules.

Jobs and Growth Act Impact

Collapsible corporation rules repealed.—The collapsible corporation rules under Code Sec. 341 are repealed (Act Sec. 302(e)(4) of the Jobs and Growth Tax Relief Reconciliation Act of 2003). Conforming amendments have also been made to strike references to the collapsible corporation rules under Code Secs. 338(h), 467(c)(5)(C), 1255(b)(2) and 1257(d).

Caution. The repeal of the collapsible corporation rules was made as a conforming amendment to the enactment of the temporary reduced dividend tax rate under Code Sec. 1(h)(11) (see ¶ 325). This means that the provision is scheduled to sunset for tax years beginning after December 31, 2008 (Act Sec. 303 of the 2003 Act). If nothing is done to permanently extend the provision, the collapsible corporation rules would revive in 2009.

Comment. There appears to be no direct connection between the repeal of the collapsible corporation rules and the reduced dividend tax rate. Rather, the repeal has been outstanding for some time as a recommended corporate tax reform due to the lack of necessity for the provision. Existing laws are viewed as sufficient to tax unrealized corporate gain at the corporate level.

For further information about collapsible corporations, see 2003FED ¶ 16,312.01, FTS § I:19.20, or 2003FTG ¶ 12,280.

★ *Effective date.* The provision applies to tax years beginning after December 31, 2002 (Act Sec. 302(f)(1) of the Jobs and Growth Tax Relief Reconciliation Act of 2003).

Sunset provision. The provisions and amendments of Title III of the 2003 Act will not apply to tax years beginning after December 31, 2008. The Internal Revenue Code of 1986 will be applied and administered to these years as if the provisions and amendments had not been enacted (Act Sec. 303). See ¶ 29,001 for CCH Explanation.

Act Sec. 302(e)(4)(A) of the Jobs and Growth Tax Relief Reconciliation Act of 2003, repealing Code Sec. 341; Act Sec. 302(e)(4)(B), amending Code Sec. 338(h), Code Sec. 467(c)(5)(C), Code Sec. 1255(b)(2) and Code Sec. 1257(d); Act Sec. 302(f)(1). Law at ¶ 5060. Committee Report at ¶ 10,110.

Reduced Accumulated Earnings Tax Rate

¶ 365

Background

The accumulated earnings tax is a penalty tax imposed on a corporation that is formed or availed of for the purpose of avoiding shareholder income tax by permitting its earnings and profits to accumulate (Code Sec. 531). It is imposed in addition to the regular corporate income tax. The accumulated earnings tax is imposed on accumulated taxable income at the highest rate of tax for single individuals. The highest rate of tax for individuals is 38.6 percent, decreasing to 35 percent in 2006 and thereafter.

All domestic corporations other than personal holding companies and tax-exempt corporations are potentially subject to the accumulated earnings tax. Foreign corporations other than foreign personal holding companies and passive foreign investment companies are also subject to the tax if they have income derived from U.S. sources and shareholders that are citizens or residents of the United States or subject to U.S. income tax.

Whether a corporation is formed or availed of for a tax avoidance purpose is decided based on the facts and circumstances in each case. The fact that a corporation is a mere holding or investment company is prima facie evidence of a tax avoidance purpose. Factors that are considered in deciding whether a corporation has a tax avoidance purpose include loans to shareholders, expenditures of corporate funds for personal benefits to shareholders, investments unrelated to its business, its dividend distribution history, and characteristics of the shareholders that make it likely they used the corporation to avoid tax.

A corporation is presumed to be availed of for a tax avoidance purpose if its earnings are accumulated beyond the reasonable needs of its business. A corporation's business can include any business that it has previously carried on and any business that it may undertake. The corporation can justify accumulating earnings and profits to pay any expenses that the corporation can demonstrate are for a business purpose.

Accumulated taxable income is taxable income, adjusted to make it a more accurate reflection of the corporation's ability to distribute its earnings, less the dividends paid deduction and the accumulated earnings credit. The accumulated earnings credit for corporations other than mere holding or investment companies is the greater of the amount of earnings and profits retained by the corporation for its reasonable business needs or the excess of $250,000 over the accumulated earnings and profits at the end of the previous tax year. The excess of $250,000 over the accumulated earnings and profits at the end of the previous tax year is the minimum credit amount. Corporations that are mere holding or investment companies are only entitled to the minimum credit amount; they cannot reduce their income by the amount they have accumulated for their reasonable needs in computing their accumulated taxable income.

Jobs and Growth Act Impact

Tax rate on accumulated earnings reduced to 15 percent.—The accumulated earnings tax rate is reduced to 15 percent (Code Sec. 531, as amended by the Jobs and Growth Tax Relief Reconciliation Act of 2003). The new rate equals the reduced rate on dividends that would apply to most shareholders if the accumulated earnings of the corporation were distributed to shareholders (see ¶ 325) (Code Sec. 1(h)(11), as amended by the 2003 Act). Prior to the law change, dividends and accumulated earnings were both taxed at ordinary income tax rates potentially as high as 38.6 percent.

Comment. The accumulated earnings tax rate still exceeds the rate that would apply on distributions for shareholders in the 10- or 15-percent rate brackets (under $56,800 for a married couple in 2003). These shareholders would be able to take advantage of the 5-percent rate on dividends (see ¶ 325).

Caution. As of 2009, the accumulated earnings tax rate is scheduled to return to highest ordinary income tax rate applicable to individuals. The rate following sunset is currently forecast to be 35 percent.

For further information about the accumulated earnings tax, see 2003FED ¶ 23,004.021, FTS § I:7.20, or 2003FTG ¶ 12,401.

★ *Effective date.* The provision applies to tax years beginning after December 31, 2002 (Act Sec. 302(f)(1) of the Jobs and Growth Tax Relief Reconciliation Act of 2003).

Sunset provision. The provisions and amendments of Title III of the 2003 Act will not apply to tax years beginning after December 31, 2008. The Internal Revenue Code of 1986 will be applied and administered to these years as if the provisions and amendments had not been enacted (Act Sec. 303). See ¶ 29,001 for CCH Explanation.

Act Sec. 302(e)(5) of the Jobs and Growth Tax Relief Reconciliation Act of 2003, amending Code Sec. 531; Act Sec. 302(f)(1). Law at ¶ 5070. Committee Report at ¶ 10,110.

Reduced Personal Holding Company Tax Rate

¶ 370

Background

The personal holding company rules penalize closely held corporations for earnings that remain undistributed to shareholders (Code Sec. 541). The rules are designed to prevent corporations from acting as incorporated pocketbooks of shareholders, collecting investment income or salaries on behalf of shareholders in order to avoid application of otherwise applicable individual income taxes.

Once classified as a personal holding company for the tax year, a corporation is subject to the personal holding company tax imposed on undistributed personal holding company income at the highest rate of tax for single individuals (38.6 percent before the law change). The personal holding company tax is in addition to other corporate income taxes that might apply, including regular and alternative minimum tax (AMT) liability.

A personal holding company is generally a corporation that meets the following tests:

(1) At any time during the last half of the tax year more than 50 percent in value of the corporation's outstanding stock is owned by not more than five individuals; and

(2) 60 percent or more of the corporation's adjusted ordinary income is personal holding company income.

Jobs and Growth Tax Relief Reconciliation Act of 2003

Background

Corporations that are exempt from the personal holding company tax include charitable and nonprofit corporations, banks, lending and finance companies, insurance and investment companies, S corporations and foreign personal holding companies.

Undistributed personal holding company income equals the corporation's taxable income less the dividends paid deduction. It is then increased to eliminate the dividends received deduction and to limit net operating loss carryovers and deductions on rented property and decreased to account for accrued taxes, a higher charitable deduction ceiling and excess of net long-term capital gains over short-term losses.

Jobs and Growth Act Impact

Personal holding company tax rate reduced to 15 percent.—The tax on undistributed personal holding company income is reduced to 15 percent (Code Sec. 541, as amended by the Jobs and Growth Tax Relief Reconciliation Act of 2003). The new rate equals the reduced rate on dividends that would apply to most shareholders if the income of the corporation were distributed to shareholders (see ¶ 325) (Code Sec. 1(h)(11), as amended by the 2003 Act). Prior to the law change, dividends and undistributed personal holding company income were both taxed at ordinary income tax rates potentially as high as 38.6 percent.

Comment. The personal holding company tax rate still exceeds the rate that would apply on distributions for shareholders in the 10- or 15-percent rate brackets (under $56,800 for a married couple in 2003). These individuals would be able to take advantage of the 5-percent rate for dividends.

Caution. As of 2009, the personal holding company tax rate is scheduled to return to ordinary income tax levels. The rate following sunset is currently forecast to be 35 percent.

For further information about the personal holding company tax, see 2003FED ¶ 23,154.021, FTS § I:20.20, or 2003FTG ¶ 12,450.

★ *Effective date.* The provision applies to tax years beginning after December 31, 2002 (Act Sec. 302(f)(1) of the Jobs and Growth Tax Relief Reconciliation Act of 2003).

Sunset provision. The provisions and amendments of Title III of the 2003 Act will not apply to tax years beginning after December 31, 2008. The Internal Revenue Code of 1986 will be applied and administered to these years as if the provisions and amendments had not been enacted (Act Sec. 303). See ¶ 29,001 for CCH Explanation.

Act Sec. 302(e)(6) of the Jobs and Growth Tax Relief Reconciliation Act of 2003, amending Code Sec. 541; Act Sec. 302(f)(1). Law at ¶ 5075. Committee Report at ¶ 10,110.

Explanation

Corporate Estimated Tax Payments for 2003

¶ 375

Background

Generally, most corporations are required to make quarterly estimated tax payments, due on the 15th day of the fourth, sixth, ninth and twelfth months of the corporation's tax year. A penalty may apply if a quarterly payment is underpaid (Code Sec. 6655).

Jobs and Growth Act Impact

Time for payment of 2003 corporate estimated taxes.—The new law provides that with respect to the corporate estimated tax payment that would have been due in September 2003, 25 percent of the amount of the required installment is not due until October 1, 2003 (Act Sec. 501 of the Jobs and Growth Reconciliation Act of 2003).

Comment. The provision provides a short deferral of corporate estimated tax payments. The legislative history of this act provides no insight on the purpose of the deferrals. However, the federal government's fiscal year begins on October 1st. It appears that Congress is pushing revenues from one fiscal year to another in order to meet budgetary requirements.

For further information about the payment of corporate estimated taxes, see 2003FED ¶ 39,575.021, FTS § P:6.62[1], or 2003FTG ¶ 22,519.

★ *Effective date.* No specific effective date is provided by the Act. The provision is, therefore, considered effective on the date of enactment.

Act Sec. 501 of the Jobs and Growth Tax Relief Reconciliation Act of 2003. Law at ¶ 7045. Committee Report at ¶ 10,130.

CODE SECTIONS ADDED, AMENDED OR REPEALED

[¶ 5001] INTRODUCTION.

The Internal Revenue Code provisions amended by the Jobs and Growth Tax Relief Reconciliation Act of 2003 (H.R. 2) are shown in the following paragraphs. Deleted Code material or the text of the Code Section prior to amendment appears in the amendment notes following each amended Code provision. *Any changed or added material is set out in italics.*

Many of the amendments made to the Internal Revenue Code by this Act are subject to a sunset provision. Thus, many of the law changes will cease to apply after a certain date unless Congress specifically acts to extend the amendments. Caution lines have been included and will alert the reader to the temporary status of these provisions. See ¶ 29,001 for more details on the sunset provisions.

[¶ 5005] CODE SEC. 1. TAX IMPOSED.

* * *

(f) PHASEOUT OF MARRIAGE PENALTY IN 15-PERCENT BRACKET; ADJUSTMENTS IN TAX TABLES SO THAT INFLATION WILL NOT RESULT IN TAX INCREASES.—

* * *

(8) PHASEOUT OF MARRIAGE PENALTY IN 15-PERCENT BRACKET.—

[Caution: Code Sec. 1(f)(8)(A), below, was amended by § 102(b)(1). For sunset provision, see H.R. 2, § 107, in the amendment notes.—CCH.]

(A) IN GENERAL.—With respect to taxable years beginning after December 31, *2002*, in prescribing the tables under paragraph (1)—

(i) the maximum taxable income in the 15-percent rate bracket in the table contained in subsection (a) (and the minimum taxable income in the next higher taxable income bracket in such table) shall be the applicable percentage of the maximum taxable income in the 15-percent rate bracket in the table contained in subsection (c) (after any other adjustment under this subsection), and

(ii) the comparable taxable income amounts in the table contained in subsection (d) shall be ½ of the amounts determined under clause (i).

[Caution: Code Sec. 1(f)(8)(B), below, was amended by § 102(a). For sunset provision, see H.R. 2, § 107, in the amendment notes.—CCH.]

(B) APPLICABLE PERCENTAGE.—For purposes of subparagraph (A), the applicable percentage shall be determined in accordance with the following table:

For taxable years beginning in calendar year—	The applicable percentage is—
2003 and 2004	200
2005	180
2006	187
2007	193
2008 and thereafter	200.

* * *

[CCH Explanation at ¶ 215. Committee Reports at ¶ 10,020.]

Amendment Notes

Act Sec. 102(a) amended the table contained in Code Sec. 1(f)(8)(B) by inserting before the item relating to 2005 a new item to read as above.

Act Sec. 102(b)(1) amended Code Sec. 1(f)(8)(A) by striking "2004" and inserting "2002".

The above amendments apply to tax years beginning after December 31, 2002.

Act Sec. 107 provides:

SEC. 107. APPLICATION OF EGTRRA SUNSET TO THIS TITLE.

Each amendment made by this title shall be subject to title IX of the Economic Growth and Tax Relief Reconciliation Act of 2001 to the same extent and in the same manner as the provision of such Act to which such amendment relates [applicable to years beginning after December 31, 2010.—CCH].

128 Jobs and Growth Tax Relief Reconciliation Act of 2003

(h) MAXIMUM CAPITAL GAINS RATE.—

(1) IN GENERAL.—If a taxpayer has a net capital gain for any taxable year, the tax imposed by this section for such taxable year shall not exceed the sum of—

(A) a tax computed at the rates and in the same manner as if this subsection had not been enacted on the greater of—

(i) taxable income reduced by the net capital gain, or

(ii) the lesser of—

(I) the amount of taxable income taxed at a rate below 25 percent; or

(II) taxable income reduced by the adjusted net capital gain;

[*Caution: Code Sec. 1(h)(1)(B), below, was amended by § 301(a)(1). For sunset provision, see H.R. 2, § 303, in the amendment notes.—CCH.*]

(B) *5 percent (0 percent in the case of taxable years beginning after 2007)* of so much of the adjusted net capital gain (or, if less, taxable income) as does not exceed the excess (if any) of—

(i) the amount of taxable income which would (without regard to this paragraph) be taxed at a rate below 25 percent, over

(ii) the taxable income reduced by the adjusted net capital gain;

[*Caution: Code Sec. 1(h)(1)(C), below, was amended by § 301(a)(2)(A). For sunset provision, see H.R. 2, § 303, in the amendment notes.—CCH.*]

(C) *15 percent* of the adjusted net capital gain (or, if less, taxable income) in excess of the amount on which a tax is determined under subparagraph (B);

(D) 25 percent of the excess (if any) of—

(i) the unrecaptured section 1250 gain (or, if less, the net capital gain), over

(ii) the excess (if any) of—

(I) the sum of the amount on which tax is determined under subparagraph (A) plus the net capital gain, over

(II) taxable income; and

(E) 28 percent of the amount of taxable income in excess of the sum of the amounts on which tax is determined under the preceding subparagraphs of this paragraph.

(2) NET CAPITAL GAIN TAKEN INTO ACCOUNT AS INVESTMENT INCOME.—For purposes of this subsection, the net capital gain for any taxable year shall be reduced (but not below zero) by the amount which the taxpayer takes into account as investment income under section 163(d)(4)(B)(iii).

[*Caution: Code Sec. 1(h)(3), below, was redesignated by § 301(b)(1)(B) and amended by § 302(e)(1). For sunset provision, see H.R. 2, § 303, in the amendment notes.—CCH.*]

(3) ADJUSTED NET CAPITAL GAIN.—*For purposes of this subsection, the term "adjusted net capital gain" means the sum of—*

(A) *net capital gain (determined without regard to paragraph (11)) reduced (but not below zero) by the sum of—*

(i) unrecaptured section 1250 gain, and

(ii) 28-percent rate gain, plus

(B) qualified dividend income (as defined in paragraph (11)).

(4) 28-PERCENT RATE GAIN.—For purposes of this subsection, the term "28-percent rate gain" means the excess (if any) of—

(A) the sum of—

(i) collectibles gain; and

(ii) section 1202 gain, over

(B) the sum of—

(i) collectibles loss;

(ii) the net short-term capital loss, and

¶ 5005 Code Sec. 1(h)

(iii) the amount of long-term capital loss carried under section 1212(b)(1)(B) to the taxable year.

(5) COLLECTIBLES GAIN AND LOSS.—For purposes of this subsection—

(A) IN GENERAL.—The terms "collectibles gain" and "collectibles loss" mean gain or loss (respectively) from the sale or exchange of a collectible (as defined in section 408(m) without regard to paragraph (3) thereof) which is a capital asset held for more than 1 year but only to the extent such gain is taken into account in computing gross income and such loss is taken into account in computing taxable income.

(B) PARTNERSHIPS, ETC.—For purposes of subparagraph (A), any gain from the sale of an interest in a partnership, S corporation, or trust which is attributable to unrealized appreciation in the value of collectibles shall be treated as gain from the sale or exchange of a collectible. Rules similar to the rules of section 751 shall apply for purposes of the preceding sentence.

(6) UNRECAPTURED SECTION 1250 GAIN.—For purposes of this subsection—

(A) IN GENERAL.—The term "unrecaptured section 1250 gain" means the excess (if any) of—

(i) the amount of long-term capital gain (not otherwise treated as ordinary income) which would be treated as ordinary income if section 1250(b)(1) included all depreciation and the applicable percentage under section 1250(a) were 100 percent, over

(ii) the excess (if any) of—

(I) the amount described in paragraph (5)(B); over

(II) the amount described in paragraph (5)(A).

(B) LIMITATION WITH RESPECT TO SECTION 1231 PROPERTY.—The amount described in subparagraph (A)(i) from sales, exchanges, and conversions described in section 1231(a)(3)(A) for any taxable year shall not exceed the net section 1231 gain (as defined in section 1231(c)(3)) for such year.

(7) SECTION 1202 GAIN.—For purposes of this subsection, the term "section 1202 gain" means the excess of—

(A) the gain which would be excluded from gross income under section 1202 but for the percentage limitation in section 1202(a), over

(B) the gain excluded from gross income under section 1202.

(8) COORDINATION WITH RECAPTURE OF NET ORDINARY LOSSES UNDER SECTION 1231.—If any amount is treated as ordinary income under section 1231(c), such amount shall be allocated among the separate categories of net section 1231 gain (as defined in section 1231(c)(3)) in such manner as the Secretary may by forms or regulations prescribe.

(9) REGULATIONS.—The Secretary may prescribe such regulations as are appropriate (including regulations requiring reporting) to apply this subsection in the case of sales and exchanges by pass-thru entities and of interests in such entities.

(10) PASS-THRU ENTITY DEFINED.—For purposes of this subsection, the term "pass-thru entity" means—

(A) a regulated investment company;

(B) a real estate investment trust;

(C) an S corporation;

(D) a partnership;

(E) an estate or trust;

(F) a common trust fund;

(G) a foreign investment company which is described in section 1246(b)(1) and for which an election is in effect under section 1247; and

(H) a qualified electing fund (as defined in section 1295).

Code Sec. 1(h)   ¶ 5005

[*Caution: Code Sec. 1(h)(11), below, was added by § 302(a). For sunset provision, see H.R. 2, § 303, in the amendment notes.—CCH.*]

(11) DIVIDENDS TAXED AS NET CAPITAL GAIN.—

(A) IN GENERAL.—For purposes of this subsection, the term "net capital gain" means net capital gain (determined without regard to this paragraph) increased by qualified dividend income.

(B) QUALIFIED DIVIDEND INCOME.—For purposes of this paragraph—

(i) IN GENERAL.—The term "qualified dividend income" means dividends received during the taxable year from—

(I) domestic corporations, and

(II) qualified foreign corporations.

(ii) CERTAIN DIVIDENDS EXCLUDED.—Such term shall not include—

(I) any dividend from a corporation which for the taxable year of the corporation in which the distribution is made, or the preceding taxable year, is a corporation exempt from tax under section 501 or 521,

(II) any amount allowed as a deduction under section 591 (relating to deduction for dividends paid by mutual savings banks, etc.), and

(III) any dividend described in section 404(k).

(iii) COORDINATION WITH SECTION 246(c).—Such term shall not include any dividend on any share of stock—

(I) with respect to which the holding period requirements of section 246(c) are not met (determined by substituting in section 246(c)(1) "60 days" for "45 days" each place it appears and by substituting "120-day period" for "90-day period"), or

(II) to the extent that the taxpayer is under an obligation (whether pursuant to a short sale or otherwise) to make related payments with respect to positions in substantially similar or related property.

(C) QUALIFIED FOREIGN CORPORATIONS.—

(i) IN GENERAL.—Except as otherwise provided in this paragraph, the term "qualified foreign corporation" means any foreign corporation if—

(I) such corporation is incorporated in a possession of the United States, or

(II) such corporation is eligible for benefits of a comprehensive income tax treaty with the United States which the Secretary determines is satisfactory for purposes of this paragraph and which includes an exchange of information program.

(ii) DIVIDENDS ON STOCK READILY TRADABLE ON UNITED STATES SECURITIES MARKET.—A foreign corporation not otherwise treated as a qualified foreign corporation under clause (i) shall be so treated with respect to any dividend paid by such corporation if the stock with respect to which such dividend is paid is readily tradable on an established securities market in the United States.

(iii) EXCLUSION OF DIVIDENDS OF CERTAIN FOREIGN CORPORATIONS.—Such term shall not include any foreign corporation which for the taxable year of the corporation in which the dividend was paid, or the preceding taxable year, is a foreign personal holding company (as defined in section 552), a foreign investment company (as defined in section 1246(b)), or a passive foreign investment company (as defined in section 1297).

(iv) COORDINATION WITH FOREIGN TAX CREDIT LIMITATION.—Rules similar to the rules of section 904(b)(2)(B) shall apply with respect to the dividend rate differential under this paragraph.

(D) SPECIAL RULES.—

(i) AMOUNTS TAKEN INTO ACCOUNT AS INVESTMENT INCOME.—Qualified dividend income shall not include any amount which the taxpayer takes into account as investment income under section 163(d)(4)(B).

(ii) EXTRAORDINARY DIVIDENDS.—If an individual receives, with respect to any share of stock, qualified dividend income from 1 or more dividends which are extraordinary dividends (within the meaning of section 1059(c)), any loss on the sale or exchange of such share shall, to the extent of such dividends, be treated as long-term capital loss.

(iii) TREATMENT OF DIVIDENDS FROM REGULATED INVESTMENT COMPANIES AND REAL ESTATE INVESTMENT TRUSTS.—A dividend received from a regulated investment company or a real estate investment trust shall be subject to the limitations prescribed in sections 854 and 857.

[CCH Explanation at ¶ 305, ¶ 310, ¶ 320, ¶ 325 and ¶ 335. Committee Reports at ¶ 10,100 and ¶ 10,110.]

Amendment Notes

Act Sec. 301(a)(1) amended Code Sec. 1(h)(1)(B) by striking "10 percent" and inserting "5 percent (0 percent in the case of taxable years beginning after 2007)".

Act Sec. 301(a)(2)(A) amended Code Sec. 1(h)(1)(C) by striking "20 percent" and inserting "15 percent".

Act Sec. 301(b)(1)(A)-(C) amended Code Sec. 1(h) by striking paragraphs (2) and (9), by redesignating paragraphs (3) through (8) as paragraphs (2) through (7), respectively, and by redesignating paragraphs (10), (11), and (12) as paragraphs (8), (9), and (10), respectively. Prior to being stricken, Code Sec. 1(h)(2) and (9) read as follows:

(2) REDUCED CAPITAL GAIN RATES FOR QUALIFIED 5-YEAR GAIN.—

(A) REDUCTION IN 10-PERCENT RATE.—In the case of any taxable year beginning after December 31, 2000, the rate under paragraph (1)(B) shall be 8 percent with respect to so much of the amount to which the 10-percent rate would otherwise apply as does not exceed qualified 5-year gain, and 10 percent with respect to the remainder of such amount.

(B) REDUCTION IN 20-PERCENT RATE.—The rate under paragraph (1)(C) shall be 18 percent with respect to so much of the amount to which the 20-percent rate would otherwise apply as does not exceed the lesser of—

(i) the excess of qualified 5-year gain over the amount of such gain taken into account under subparagraph (A) of this paragraph; or

(ii) the amount of qualified 5-year gain (determined by taking into account only property the holding period for which begins after December 31, 2000),

and 20 percent with respect to the remainder of such amount. For purposes of determining under the preceding sentence whether the holding period of property begins after December 31, 2000, the holding period of property acquired pursuant to the exercise of an option (or other right or obligation to acquire property) shall include the period such option (or other right or obligation) was held.

* * *

(9) QUALIFIED 5-YEAR GAIN.—For purposes of this subsection, the term "qualified 5-year gain" means the aggregate long-term capital gain from property held for more than 5 years. The determination under the preceding sentence shall be made without regard to collectibles gain, gain described in paragraph (7)(A)(i), and section 1202 gain.

The above amendments apply to tax years ending on or after May 6, 2003. For a transition rule, see Act Sec. 301(c), below.

Act Sec. 301(c) provides:

(c) TRANSITIONAL RULES FOR TAXABLE YEARS WHICH INCLUDE MAY 6, 2003.—For purposes of applying section 1(h) of the Internal Revenue Code of 1986 in the case of a taxable year which includes May 6, 2003—

(1) The amount of tax determined under subparagraph (B) of section 1(h)(1) of such Code shall be the sum of—

(A) 5 percent of the lesser of—

(i) the net capital gain determined by taking into account only gain or loss properly taken into account for the portion of the taxable year on or after May 6, 2003 (determined without regard to collectibles gain or loss, gain described in section 1(h)(6)(A)(i) of such Code, and section 1202 gain), or

(ii) the amount on which a tax is determined under such subparagraph (without regard to this subsection),

(B) 8 percent of the lesser of—

(i) the qualified 5-year gain (as defined in section 1(h)(9) of the Internal Revenue Code of 1986, as in effect on the day before the date of the enactment of this Act) properly taken into account for the portion of the taxable year before May 6, 2003, or

(ii) the excess (if any) of—

(I) the amount on which a tax is determined under such subparagraph (without regard to this subsection), over

(II) the amount on which a tax is determined under subparagraph (A), plus

(C) 10 percent of the excess (if any) of—

(i) the amount on which a tax is determined under such subparagraph (without regard to this subsection), over

(ii) the sum of the amounts on which a tax is determined under subparagraphs (A) and (B).

(2) The amount of tax determined under subparagraph (C) of section (1)(h)(1) of such Code shall be the sum of—

(A) 15 percent of the lesser of—

(i) the excess (if any) of the amount of net capital gain determined under subparagraph (A)(i) of paragraph (1) of this subsection over the amount on which a tax is determined under subparagraph (A) of paragraph (1) of this subsection, or

(ii) the amount on which a tax is determined under subparagraph (C) (without regard to this subsection), plus

(B) 20 percent of the excess (if any) of—

(i) the amount on which a tax is determined under subparagraph (C) (without regard to this subsection), over

(ii) the amount on which a tax is determined under subparagraph (A) of this paragraph.

(3) For purposes of applying section 55(b)(3) of such Code, rules similar to the rules of paragraphs (1) and (2) of this subsection shall apply.

(4) In applying this subsection with respect to any pass-thru entity, the determination of when gains and losses are properly taken into account shall be made at the entity level.

(5) For purposes of applying section 1(h)(11) of such Code, as added by section 302 of this Act, to this subsection, dividends which are qualified dividend income shall be treated as gain properly taken into account for the portion of the taxable year on or after May 6, 2003.

(6) Terms used in this subsection which are also used in section 1(h) of such Code shall have the respective meanings that such terms have in such section.

Act Sec. 302(a) amended Code Sec. 1(h), as amended by Act Sec. 301, by adding at the end a new paragraph (11) to read as above.

Act Sec. 302(e)(1) amended Code Sec. 1(h)(3), as redesignated by Act Sec. 301, to read as above. Prior to amendment, but as redesignated, Code Sec. 1(h)(3) read as follows:

(3) ADJUSTED NET CAPITAL GAIN.—For purposes of this subsection, the term "adjusted net capital gain" means net capital gain reduced (but not below zero) by the sum of—

(A) unrecaptured section 1250 gain; and

(B) 28-percent rate gain.

The above amendments generally apply to tax years beginning after December 31, 2002. For a special rule, see Act Sec. 302(f)(2), below.

Act Sec. 302(f)(2) provides:

(2) REGULATED INVESTMENT COMPANIES AND REAL ESTATE INVESTMENT TRUSTS.—In the case of a regulated investment company or a real estate investment trust, the amendments made by this section shall apply to taxable years ending after December 31, 2002; except that dividends received by such a company or trust on or before such date shall not be treated as qualified dividend income (as defined in section 1(h)(11)(B) of the Internal Revenue Code of 1986, as added by this Act).

Act Sec. 303 provides:

SEC. 303. SUNSET OF TITLE.

All provisions of, and amendments made by, this title shall not apply to taxable years beginning after December 31, 2008, and the Internal Revenue Code of 1986 shall be applied and administered to such years as if such provisions and amendments had never been enacted.

(i) RATE REDUCTIONS AFTER 2000.—

(1) 10-PERCENT RATE BRACKET.—

* * *

(B) INITIAL BRACKET AMOUNT.—For purposes of this paragraph, the initial bracket amount is—

[Caution: Code Sec. 1(i)(1)(B)(i), below, was amended by § 104(a). For sunset provision, see H.R. 2, § 107, in the amendment notes.—CCH.]

(i) $14,000 ($12,000 in the case of taxable years beginning after December 31, 2004, and before January 1, 2008) in the case of subsection (a),

(ii) $10,000 in the case of subsection (b), and

(iii) ½ the amount applicable under clause (i) (after adjustment, if any, under subparagraph (C)) in the case of subsections (c) and (d).

[Caution: Code Sec. 1(i)(1)(C), below, was amended by § 104(b). For sunset provision, see H.R. 2, § 107, in the amendment notes.—CCH.]

(C) INFLATION ADJUSTMENT.—In prescribing the tables under subsection (f) which apply with respect to taxable years beginning in calendar years after 2000—

(i) except as provided in clause (ii), the Secretary shall make no adjustment to the initial bracket amounts for any taxable year beginning before January 1, 2009,

(ii) there shall be an adjustment under subsection (f) of such amounts which shall apply only to taxable years beginning in 2004, and such adjustment shall be determined under subsection (f)(3) by substituting "2002" for "1992" in subparagraph (B) thereof,

(iii) the cost-of-living adjustment used in making adjustments to the initial bracket amounts for any taxable year beginning after December 31, 2008, shall be determined under subsection (f)(3) by substituting "2007" for "1992" in subparagraph (B) thereof, and

(iv) the adjustments under clauses (ii) and (iii) shall not apply to the amount referred to in subparagraph (B)(iii).

If any amount after adjustment under the preceding sentence is not a multiple of $50, such amount shall be rounded to the next lowest multiple of $50.

* * *

[Caution: The table contained in Code Sec. 1(i)(2), below, was amended by § 105(a). For sunset provision, see H.R. 2, § 107, in the amendment notes.—CCH.]

(2) REDUCTIONS IN RATES AFTER JUNE 30, 2001.—In the case of taxable years beginning in a calendar year after 2000, the corresponding percentage specified for such calendar year in the following table shall be substituted for the otherwise applicable tax rate in the tables under subsections (a), (b), (c), (d), and (e).

Law Added, Amended or Repealed

In the case of taxable years beginning during calendar year:	The corresponding percentages shall be substituted for the following percentages:			
	28%	31%	36%	39.6%
2001	27.5%	30.5%	35.5%	39.1%
2002	27.0%	30.0%	35.0%	38.6%
2003 and thereafter	25.0%	28.0%	33.0%	35.0%

* * *

[CCH Explanation at ¶ 205 and ¶ 210. Committee Reports at ¶ 10,040 and ¶ 10,050.]

Amendment Notes

Act Sec. 104(a) amended Code Sec. 1(i)(1)(B)(i) by striking "($12,000 in the case of taxable years beginning before January 1, 2008)" and inserting "($12,000 in the case of taxable years beginning after December 31, 2004, and before January 1, 2008)".

Act Sec. 104(b) amended Code Sec. 1(i)(1)(C) to read as above. Prior to amendment, Code Sec. 1(i)(1)(C) read as follows:

(C) INFLATION ADJUSTMENT.—In prescribing the tables under subsection (f) which apply with respect to taxable years beginning in calendar years after 2000—

(i) the Secretary shall make no adjustment to the initial bracket amount for any taxable year beginning before January 1, 2009,

(ii) the cost-of-living adjustment used in making adjustments to the initial bracket amount for any taxable year beginning after December 31, 2008, shall be determined under subsection (f)(3) by substituting "2007" for "1992" in subparagraph (B) thereof, and

(iii) such adjustment shall not apply to the amount referred to in subparagraph (B)(iii).

If any amount after adjustment under the preceding sentence is not a multiple of $50, such amount shall be rounded to the next lowest multiple of $50.

The above amendments apply to tax years beginning after December 31, 2002.

Act Sec. 104(c)(2) provides:

(2) TABLES FOR 2003.—The Secretary of the Treasury shall modify each table which has been prescribed under section 1(f) of the Internal Revenue Code of 1986 for taxable years beginning in 2003 and which relates to the amendment made by subsection (a) to reflect such amendment.

Act Sec. 105(a) amended the table contained in Code Sec. 1(i)(2) to read as above. Prior to amendment, the table contained in Code Sec. 1(i)(2) read as follows:

In the case of taxable years beginning during calendar year:	The corresponding percentages shall be substituted for the following percentages:			
	28%	31%	36%	39.6%
2001	27.5%	30.5%	35.5%	39.1%
2002 and 2003	27.0%	30.0%	35.0%	38.6%
2004 and 2005	26.0%	29.0%	34.0%	37.6%
2006 and thereafter	25.0%	28.0%	33.0%	35.0%

The above amendment applies to tax years beginning after December 31, 2002.

Act Sec. 107 provides:

SEC. 107. APPLICATION OF EGTRRA SUNSET TO THIS TITLE.

Each amendment made by this title shall be subject to title IX of the Economic Growth and Tax Relief Reconciliation Act of 2001 to the same extent and in the same manner as the provision of such Act to which such amendment relates [applicable to years beginning after December 31, 2010.—CCH].

[¶ 5010] CODE SEC. 24. CHILD TAX CREDIT.

(a) ALLOWANCE OF CREDIT.—

* * *

[Caution: Code Sec. 24(a)(2), below, was amended by § 101(a). For sunset provision, see H.R. 2, § 107, in the amendment notes.—CCH.]

(2) PER CHILD AMOUNT.—For purposes of paragraph (1), the per child amount shall be determined as follows:

In the case of any taxable year beginning in—	The per child amount is—
2003 or 2004	$1,000
2005, 2006, 2007, or 2008	700
2009	800
2010 or thereafter	1,000

* * *

[CCH Explanation at ¶ 225. Committee Reports at ¶ 10,010.]

Amendment Notes

Act Sec. 101(a) amended the item relating to calendar years 2001 through 2004 in the table contained in Code Sec. 24(a)(2) to read as above. Prior to amendment, the item relating to calendar years 2001 through 2004 read as follows:

2001, 2002, 2003, or 2004 .... $ 600

Code Sec. 24(a) ¶ 5010

The above amendment applies to tax years beginning after December 31, 2002.

Act Sec. 107 provides:

SEC. 107. APPLICATION OF EGTRRA SUNSET TO THIS TITLE.

Each amendment made by this title shall be subject to title IX of the Economic Growth and Tax Relief Reconciliation Act of 2001 to the same extent and in the same manner as the provision of such Act to which such amendment relates [applicable to years beginning after December 31, 2010.—CCH].

[¶ 5015] CODE SEC. 55. ALTERNATIVE MINIMUM TAX IMPOSED.

* * *

(b) TENTATIVE MINIMUM TAX.—For purposes of this part—

* * *

[*Caution: Code Sec. 55(b)(3), below, was amended by § 301(a)-(b). For sunset provision, see H.R. 2, § 303, in the amendment notes.—CCH.*]

(3) MAXIMUM RATE OF TAX ON NET CAPITAL GAIN OF NONCORPORATE TAXPAYERS.—The amount determined under the first sentence of paragraph (1)(A)(i) shall not exceed the sum of—

(A) the amount determined under such first sentence computed at the rates and in the same manner as if this paragraph had not been enacted on the taxable excess reduced by the lesser of—

(i) the net capital gain; or

(ii) the sum of—

(I) the adjusted net capital gain, plus

(II) the unrecaptured section 1250 gain, plus

(B) *5 percent (0 percent in the case of taxable years beginning after 2007)* of so much of the adjusted net capital gain (or, if less, taxable excess) as does not exceed the amount on which a tax is determined under section 1(h)(1)(B), plus

(C) *15 percent* of the adjusted net capital gain (or, if less, taxable excess) in excess of the amount on which tax is determined under subparagraph (B), plus

(D) 25 percent of the amount of taxable excess in excess of the sum of the amounts on which tax is determined under the preceding subparagraphs of this paragraph.

Terms used in this paragraph which are also used in section 1(h) shall have the respective meanings given such terms by section 1(h) but computed with the adjustments under this part.

* * *

[CCH Explanation at ¶ 305 and ¶ 310. Committee Reports at ¶ 10,100.]

Amendment Notes

Act Sec. 301(a)(1) amended Code Sec. 55(b)(3)(B) by striking "10 percent" and inserting "5 percent (0 percent in the case of taxable years beginning after 2007)".

Act Sec. 301(a)(2)(B) amended Code Sec. 55(b)(3)(C) by striking "20 percent" and inserting "15 percent".

Act Sec. 301(b)(2) amended Code Sec. 55(b)(3) by striking "In the case of taxable years beginning after December 31, 2000, rules similar to the rules of section 1(h)(2) shall apply for purposes of subparagraphs (B) and (C)." in the flush text before "Terms used in this paragraph".

The above amendments apply to tax years ending on or after May 6, 2003. For a transition rule, see Act Sec. 301(c) in the amendment notes following Code Sec. 1(h).

Act Sec. 303 provides:

SEC. 303. SUNSET OF TITLE.

All provisions of, and amendments made by, this title shall not apply to taxable years beginning after December 31, 2008, and the Internal Revenue Code of 1986 shall be applied and administered to such years as if such provisions and amendments had never been enacted.

(d) EXEMPTION AMOUNT.—For purposes of this section—

[*Caution: Code Sec. 55(d)(1), below, was amended by § 106(a)(1)-(2). For sunset provision, see H.R. 2, § 107, in the amendment notes.—CCH.*]

(1) EXEMPTION AMOUNT FOR TAXPAYERS OTHER THAN CORPORATIONS.—In the case of a taxpayer other than a corporation, the term "exemption amount" means—

(A) $45,000 (*$58,000 in the case of taxable years beginning in 2003 and 2004*) in the case of—

(i) a joint return, or

Law Added, Amended or Repealed 135

(ii) a surviving spouse,

(B) $33,750 (*$40,250 in the case of taxable years beginning in 2003 and 2004*) in the case of an individual who—

(i) is not a married individual, and

(ii) is not a surviving spouse,

(C) 50 percent of the dollar amount applicable under paragraph (1)(A) in the case of a married individual who files a separate return, and

(D) $22,500 in the case of an estate or trust.

For purposes of this paragraph, the term "surviving spouse" has the meaning given to such term by section 2(a), and marital status shall be determined under section 7703.

* * *

[CCH Explanation at ¶ 230. Committee Reports at ¶ 10,060.]

Amendment Notes

Act Sec. 106(a)(1) amended Code Sec. 55(d)(1)(A) by striking "$49,000 in the case of taxable years beginning in 2001, 2002, 2003, and 2004" and inserting "$58,000 in the case of taxable years beginning in 2003 and 2004".

Act Sec. 106(a)(2) amended Code Sec. 55(d)(1)(B) by striking "$35,750 in the case of taxable years beginning in 2001, 2002, 2003, and 2004" and inserting "$40,250 in the case of taxable years beginning in 2003 and 2004".

The above amendments apply to tax years beginning after December 31, 2002.

Act Sec. 107 provides:

SEC. 107. APPLICATION OF EGTRRA SUNSET TO THIS TITLE.

Each amendment made by this title shall be subject to title IX of the Economic Growth and Tax Relief Reconciliation Act of 2001 to the same extent and in the same manner as the provision of such Act to which such amendment relates [applicable to years beginning after December 31, 2010.—CCH].

[¶ 5020] CODE SEC. 57. ITEMS OF TAX PREFERENCE.

(a) GENERAL RULE.—For purposes of this part, the items of tax preference determined under this section are—

* * *

[Caution: Code Sec. 57(a)(7), below, was amended by § 301(b)(3)(A)-(B). For sunset provision, see H.R. 2, § 303, in the amendment notes.—CCH.]

(7) EXCLUSION FOR GAINS ON SALE OF CERTAIN SMALL BUSINESS STOCK.—An amount equal to *7 percent* of the amount excluded from gross income for the taxable year under section 1202.

* * *

[CCH Explanation at ¶ 315. Committee Reports at ¶ 10,100.]

Amendment Notes

Act Sec. 301(b)(3)(A)-(B) amended Code Sec. 57(a)(7) by striking "42 percent" the first place it appears and inserting "7 percent", and by striking the last sentence. Prior to being stricken, the last sentence of Code Sec. 57(a)(7) read as follows:

In the case of stock the holding period of which begins after December 31, 2000 (determined with the application of the last sentence of section 1(h)(2)(B)), the preceding sentence shall be applied by substituting "28 percent" for "42 percent".

The above amendment applies to dispositions on or after May 6, 2003.

Act Sec. 303 provides:

SEC. 303. SUNSET OF TITLE.

All provisions of, and amendments made by, this title shall not apply to taxable years beginning after December 31, 2008, and the Internal Revenue Code of 1986 shall be applied and administered to such years as if such provisions and amendments had never been enacted.

[¶ 5025] CODE SEC. 63. TAXABLE INCOME DEFINED.

* * *

(c) STANDARD DEDUCTION.—For purposes of this subtitle—

* * *

[Caution: Code Sec. 63(c)(7), below, was amended by § 103(a). For sunset provision, see H.R. 2, § 107, in the amendment notes.—CCH.]

(7) APPLICABLE PERCENTAGE.—For purposes of paragraph (2), the applicable percentage shall be determined in accordance with the following table:

For taxable years beginning in calendar year—	The applicable percentage is—
2003 and 2004	200
2005	174
2006	184
2007	187
2008	190
2009 and thereafter	200.

* * *

[CCH Explanation at ¶ 220. Committee Reports at ¶ 10,030.]

Amendment Notes

Act Sec. 103(a) amended the table contained in Code Sec. 63(c)(7) by inserting before the item relating to 2005 a new item to read as above.

The above amendment applies to tax years beginning after December 31, 2002.

Act Sec. 107 provides:

SEC. 107. APPLICATION OF EGTRRA SUNSET TO THIS TITLE.

Each amendment made by this title shall be subject to title IX of the Economic Growth and Tax Relief Reconciliation Act of 2001 to the same extent and in the same manner as the provision of such Act to which such amendment relates [applicable to years beginning after December 31, 2010.—CCH.].

[¶ 5030] CODE SEC. 163. INTEREST.

* * *

(d) LIMITATION ON INVESTMENT INTEREST.—

* * *

(4) NET INVESTMENT INCOME.—For purposes of this subsection—

* * *

[Caution: Code Sec. 163(d)(4)(B), below, was amended by § 302(b). For sunset provision, see H.R. 2, § 303, in the amendment notes.—CCH.]

(B) INVESTMENT INCOME.—The term "investment income" means the sum of—

(i) gross income from property held for investment (other than any gain taken into account under clause (ii)(I)),

(ii) the excess (if any) of—

(I) the net gain attributable to the disposition of property held for investment, over

(II) the net capital gain determined by only taking into account gains and losses from dispositions of property held for investment, plus

(iii) so much of the net capital gain referred to in clause (ii)(II) (or, if lesser, the net gain referred to in clause (ii)(I)) as the taxpayer elects to take into account under this clause.

Such term shall include qualified dividend income (as defined in section 1(h)(11)(B)) only to the extent the taxpayer elects to treat such income as investment income for purposes of this subsection.

* * *

[CCH Explanation at ¶ 325 and ¶ 335. Committee Reports at ¶ 10,110.]

Amendment Notes

Act Sec. 302(b) amended Code Sec. 163(d)(4)(B) by adding at the end a new flush sentence to read as above.

The above amendment generally applies to tax years beginning after December 31, 2002. For a special rule, see Act Sec. 302(f)(2), below.

Act Sec. 302(f)(2) provides:

(2) REGULATED INVESTMENT COMPANIES AND REAL ESTATE INVESTMENT TRUSTS.—In the case of a regulated investment company or a real estate investment trust, the amendments made by this section shall apply to taxable years ending after December 31, 2002; except that dividends received by such a company or trust on or before such date shall not be treated

¶ 5030 Code Sec. 163(d)

as qualified dividend income (as defined in section 1(h)(11)(B) of the Internal Revenue Code of 1986, as added by this Act).

Act Sec. 303 provides:
SEC. 303. SUNSET OF TITLE.

All provisions of, and amendments made by, this title shall not apply to taxable years beginning after December 31, 2008, and the Internal Revenue Code of 1986 shall be applied and administered to such years as if such provisions and amendments had never been enacted.

[¶ 5035] CODE SEC. 168. ACCELERATED COST RECOVERY SYSTEM.

* * *

(k) SPECIAL ALLOWANCE FOR CERTAIN PROPERTY ACQUIRED AFTER SEPTEMBER 10, 2001, AND BEFORE JANUARY 1, 2005.—

* * *

(2) QUALIFIED PROPERTY.—For purposes of this subsection—

(A) IN GENERAL.—The term "qualified property" means property—

(i)(I) to which this section applies which has a recovery period of 20 years or less,

(II) which is computer software (as defined in section 167(f)(1)(B)) for which a deduction is allowable under section 167(a) without regard to this subsection,

(III) which is water utility property, or

(IV) which is qualified leasehold improvement property,

(ii) the original use of which commences with the taxpayer after September 10, 2001,

(iii) which is—

(I) acquired by the taxpayer after September 10, 2001, and before *January 1, 2005,* but only if no written binding contract for the acquisition was in effect before September 11, 2001, or

(II) acquired by the taxpayer pursuant to a written binding contract which was entered into after September 10, 2001, and before *January 1, 2005,* and

(iv) which is placed in service by the taxpayer before January 1, 2005, or, in the case of property described in subparagraph (B), before January 1, 2006.

(B) CERTAIN PROPERTY HAVING LONGER PRODUCTION PERIODS TREATED AS QUALIFIED PROPERTY.—

* * *

(ii) ONLY *PRE-JANUARY 1, 2005,* BASIS ELIGIBLE FOR ADDITIONAL ALLOWANCE.—In the case of property which is qualified property solely by reason of clause (i), paragraph (1) shall apply only to the extent of the adjusted basis thereof attributable to manufacture, construction, or production before *January 1, 2005.*

* * *

(C) EXCEPTIONS.—

* * *

(iii) ELECTION OUT.—If a taxpayer makes an election under this clause with respect to any class of property for any taxable year, this subsection shall not apply to all property in such class placed in service during such taxable year. *The preceding sentence shall be applied separately with respect to property treated as qualified property by paragraph (4) and other qualified property.*

(D) SPECIAL RULES.—

(i) SELF-CONSTRUCTED PROPERTY.—In the case of a taxpayer manufacturing, constructing, or producing property for the taxpayer's own use, the requirements of clause (iii) of subparagraph (A) shall be treated as met if the taxpayer begins manufacturing, constructing, or producing the property after September 10, 2001, and before *January 1, 2005.*

* * *

(4) 50-PERCENT BONUS DEPRECIATION FOR CERTAIN PROPERTY.—

(A) IN GENERAL.—In the case of 50-percent bonus depreciation property—

(i) paragraph (1)(A) shall be applied by substituting "50 percent" for "30 percent", and

(ii) except as provided in paragraph (2)(C), such property shall be treated as qualified property for purposes of this subsection.

(B) 50-PERCENT BONUS DEPRECIATION PROPERTY.—For purposes of this subsection, the term "50-percent bonus depreciation property" means property described in paragraph (2)(A)(i)—

(i) the original use of which commences with the taxpayer after May 5, 2003,

(ii) which is acquired by the taxpayer after May 5, 2003, and before January 1, 2005, but only if no written binding contract for the acquisition was in effect before May 6, 2003, and

(iii) which is placed in service by the taxpayer before January 1, 2005, or, in the case of property described in paragraph (2)(B) (as modified by subparagraph (C) of this paragraph), before January 1, 2006.

(C) SPECIAL RULES.—Rules similar to the rules of subparagraphs (B) and (D) of paragraph (2) shall apply for purposes of this paragraph; except that references to September 10, 2001, shall be treated as references to May 5, 2003.

(D) AUTOMOBILES.—Paragraph (2)(E) shall be applied by substituting "$7,650" for "$4,600" in the case of 50-percent bonus depreciation property.

(E) ELECTION OF 30-PERCENT BONUS.—If a taxpayer makes an election under this subparagraph with respect to any class of property for any taxable year, subparagraph (A)(i) shall not apply to all property in such class placed in service during such taxable year.

[CCH Explanation at ¶ 350. Committee Reports at ¶ 10,080.]

Amendment Notes

Act Sec. 201(a) amended Code Sec. 168(k) by adding at the end a new paragraph (4) to read as above.

Act Sec. 201(b)(1)(A) amended Code Sec. 168(k)(2)(B)(ii) and (D)(i) by striking "September 11, 2004" each place it appears in the text and inserting "January 1, 2005".

Act Sec. 201(b)(1)(B) amended Code Sec. 168(k)(2)(B)(ii) by striking "PRE-SEPTEMBER 11, 2004" in the heading and inserting "PRE-JANUARY 1, 2005".

Act Sec. 201(b)(2) amended Code Sec. 168(k)(2)(A)(iii) by striking "September 11, 2004" each place it appears and inserting "January 1, 2005".

Act Sec. 201(b)(3) amended Code Sec. 168(k)(2)(C)(iii) by adding at the end a new sentence to read as above.

Act Sec. 201(c)(1) amended the subsection heading for Code Sec. 168(k) by striking "SEPTEMBER 11, 2004" and inserting "JANUARY 1, 2005".

The above amendments apply to tax years ending after May 5, 2003.

[¶ 5040] CODE SEC. 179. ELECTION TO EXPENSE CERTAIN DEPRECIABLE BUSINESS ASSETS.

* * *

(b) LIMITATIONS.—

(1) DOLLAR LIMITATION.—The aggregate cost which may be taken into account under subsection (a) for any taxable year shall not exceed $25,000 ($100,000 in the case of taxable years beginning after 2002 and before 2006).

(2) REDUCTION IN LIMITATION.—The limitation under paragraph (1) for any taxable year shall be reduced (but not below zero) by the amount by which the cost of section 179 property placed in service during such taxable year exceeds $200,000 ($400,000 in the case of taxable years beginning after 2002 and before 2006).

* * *

(5) INFLATION ADJUSTMENTS.—

(A) IN GENERAL.—In the case of any taxable year beginning in a calendar year after 2003 and before 2006, the $100,000 and $400,000 amounts in paragraphs (1) and (2) shall each be increased by an amount equal to—

i) such dollar amount, multiplied by

ii) the cost-of-living adjustment determined under section 1(f)(3) for the calendar year in which the taxable year begins, by substituting "calendar year 2002" for "calendar year 1992" in subparagraph (B) thereof.

(B) ROUNDING.—

Law Added, Amended or Repealed

(i) DOLLAR LIMITATION.—If the amount in paragraph (1) as increased under subparagraph (A) is not a multiple of $1,000, such amount shall be rounded to the nearest multiple of $1,000.

(ii) PHASEOUT AMOUNT.—If the amount in paragraph (2) as increased under subparagraph (A) is not a multiple of $10,000, such amount shall be rounded to the nearest multiple of $10,000.

[CCH Explanation at ¶ 355. Committee Reports at ¶ 10,090.]

Amendment Notes

Act Sec. 202(a) amended Code Sec. 179(b)(1) to read as above. Prior to amendment, Code Sec. 179(b)(1) read as follows:

(1) DOLLAR LIMITATION.—The aggregate cost which may be taken into account under subsection (a) for any taxable year shall not exceed the following applicable amount:

If the taxable year begins in:	The applicable amount is:
1997	18,000
1998	18,500
1999	19,000
2000	20,000
2001 or 2002	24,000
2003 or thereafter	25,000

Act Sec. 202(b) amended Code Sec. 179(b)(2) by inserting "($400,000 in the case of taxable years beginning after 2002 and before 2006)" after "$200,000".

Act Sec. 202(d) amended Code Sec. 179(b) by adding at the end a new paragraph (5) to read as above.

The above amendments apply to tax years beginning after December 31, 2002.

(c) ELECTION.—

* * *

(2) ELECTION IRREVOCABLE.—Any election made under this section, and any specification contained in any such election, may not be revoked except with the consent of the Secretary. *Any such election or specification with respect to any taxable year beginning after 2002 and before 2006 may be revoked by the taxpayer with respect to any property, and such revocation, once made, shall be irrevocable.*

[CCH Explanation at ¶ 355. Committee Reports at ¶ 10,090.]

Amendment Notes

Act Sec. 202(e) amended Code Sec. 179(c)(2) by adding at the end a new sentence to read as above.

The above amendment applies to tax years beginning after December 31, 2002.

(d) DEFINITIONS AND SPECIAL RULES.—

(1) SECTION 179 PROPERTY.—For purposes of this section, the term "section 179 property" means property—

(A) which is—

(i) tangible property (to which section 168 applies), or

(ii) computer software (as defined in section 197(e)(3)(B)) which is described in section 197(e)(3)(A)(i), to which section 167 applies, and which is placed in service in a taxable year beginning after 2002 and before 2006,

(B) which is section 1245 property (as defined in section 1245(a)(3)), and

(C) which is acquired by purchase for use in the active conduct of a trade or business.

Such term shall not include any property described in section 50(b) and shall not include air conditioning or heating units.

* * *

[CCH Explanation at ¶ 355. Committee Reports at ¶ 10,090.]

Amendment Notes

Act Sec. 202(c) amended Code Sec. 179(d)(1) to read as above. Prior to amendment, Code Sec. 179(d)(1) read as follows:

(1) SECTION 179 PROPERTY.—For purposes of this section, the term "section 179 property" means any tangible property (to which section 168 applies) which is section 1245 property (as defined in section 1245(a)(3) and which is acquired by purchase for use in the active conduct of a trade or business. Such term shall not include any property described in section 50(b) and shall not include air conditioning or heating units.

The above amendment applies to tax years beginning after December 31, 2002.

[¶ 5045] CODE SEC. 301. DISTRIBUTIONS OF PROPERTY.

* * *

(f) SPECIAL RULES.—

(1) For distributions in redemption of stock, see section 302.

(2) For distributions in complete liquidation, see part II (sec. 331 and following).

(3) For distributions in corporate organizations and reorganizations, see part III (sec. 351 and following).

[*Caution: Code Sec. 301(f)(4), below, was added by § 302(e)(2). For sunset provision, see H.R. 2, § 303, in the amendment notes.—CCH.*]

(4) *For taxation of dividends received by individuals at capital gain rates, see section 1(h)(11).*

[CCH Explanation at ¶ 325 and ¶ 335. Committee Reports at ¶ 10,110.]

Amendment Notes

Act Sec. 302(e)(2) amended Code Sec. 301(f) by adding at the end a new paragraph (4) to read as above.

The above amendment generally applies to tax years beginning after December 31, 2002. For a special rule, see Act Sec. 302(f)(2), below.

Act Sec. 302(f)(2) provides:

(2) REGULATED INVESTMENT COMPANIES AND REAL ESTATE INVESTMENT TRUSTS.—In the case of a regulated investment company or a real estate investment trust, the amendments made by this section shall apply to taxable years ending after December 31, 2002; except that dividends received by such a company or trust on or before such date shall not be treated as qualified dividend income (as defined in section 1(h)(11)(B) of the Internal Revenue Code of 1986, as added by this Act).

Act Sec. 303 provides:

SEC. 303. SUNSET OF TITLE.

All provisions of, and amendments made by this title shall not apply to taxable years beginning after December 31, 2008, and the Internal Revenue Code of 1986 shall be applied and administered to such years as if such provisions and amendments had never been enacted.

[¶ 5050] CODE SEC. 306. DISPOSITIONS OF CERTAIN STOCK.

(a) GENERAL RULE.—If a shareholder sells or otherwise disposes of section 306 stock (as defined in subsection (c))—

(1) DISPOSITIONS OTHER THAN REDEMPTIONS.—If such disposition is not a redemption (within the meaning of section 317(b))—

(A) The amount realized shall be treated as ordinary income. This subparagraph shall not apply to the extent that—

(i) the amount realized, exceeds

(ii) such stock's ratable share of the amount which would have been a dividend at the time of distribution if (in lieu of section 306 stock) the corporation had distributed money in an amount equal to the fair market value of the stock at the time of distribution.

(B) Any excess of the amount realized over the sum of—

(i) the amount treated under subparagraph (A) as ordinary income, plus

(ii) the adjusted basis of the stock,

shall be treated as gain from the sale of such stock.

(C) No loss shall be recognized.

[*Caution: Code Sec. 306(a)(1)(D), below, was added by § 302(e)(3). For sunset provision, see H.R. 2, § 303, in the amendment notes.—CCH.*]

(D) TREATMENT AS DIVIDEND.—For purposes of section 1(h)(11) and such other provisions as the Secretary may specify, any amount treated as ordinary income under this paragraph shall be treated as a dividend received from the corporation.

* * *

[CCH Explanation at ¶ 325 and ¶ 335. Committee Reports at ¶ 10,110.]

Amendment Notes

Act Sec. 302(e)(3) amended Code Sec. 306(a)(1) by adding at the end a new subparagraph (D) to read as above.

The above amendment generally applies to tax years beginning after December 31, 2002. For a special rule, see Act Sec. 302(f)(2), below.

Act Sec. 302(f)(2) provides:

(2) REGULATED INVESTMENT COMPANIES AND REAL ESTATE INVESTMENT TRUSTS.—In the case of a regulated investment company or a real estate investment trust, the amendments made by this section shall apply to taxable years ending after December 31, 2002; except that dividends received by such a company or trust on or before such date shall not be treated as qualified dividend income (as defined in section 1(h)(11)(B) of the Internal Revenue Code of 1986, as added by this Act).

Act Sec. 303 provides:

SEC. 303. SUNSET OF TITLE.

All provisions of, and amendments made by, this title shall not apply to taxable years beginning after December 31, 2008, and the Internal Revenue Code of 1986 shall be applied and administered to such years as if such provisions and amendments had never been enacted.

Law Added, Amended or Repealed

[¶ 5055] CODE SEC. 338. CERTAIN STOCK PURCHASES TREATED AS ASSET ACQUISITIONS.

* * *

(h) DEFINITIONS AND SPECIAL RULES.—For purposes of this section—

* * *

[Caution: Code Sec. 338(h)(14), below, was stricken by § 302(e)(4)(B)(i). For sunset provision, see H.R. 2, § 303, in the amendment notes.—CCH.]

(14) *[Stricken.]*

* * *

[CCH Explanation at ¶ 335 and ¶ 360. Committee Reports at ¶ 10,110.]

Amendment Notes

Act Sec. 302(e)(4)(B)(i) amended Code Sec. 338(h) by striking paragraph (14). Prior to being stricken, Code Sec. 338(h)(14) read as follows:

(14) COORDINATION WITH SECTION 341.—For purposes of determining whether section 341 applies to a disposition within 1 year after the acquisition date of stock by a shareholder (other than the acquiring corporation) who held stock in the target corporation on the acquisition date, section 341 shall be applied without regard to this section.

The above amendment generally applies to tax years beginning after December 31, 2002. For a special rule, see Act Sec. 302(f)(2), below.

Act Sec. 302(f)(2) provides:

(2) REGULATED INVESTMENT COMPANIES AND REAL ESTATE INVESTMENT TRUSTS.—In the case of a regulated investment company or a real estate investment trust, the amendments made by this section shall apply to taxable years ending after December 31, 2002; except that dividends received by such a company or trust on or before such date shall not be treated as qualified dividend income (as defined in section 1(h)(11)(B) of the Internal Revenue Code of 1986, as added by this Act).

Act Sec. 303 provides:

SEC. 303. SUNSET OF TITLE.

All provisions of, and amendments made by, this title shall not apply to taxable years beginning after December 31, 2008, and the Internal Revenue Code of 1986 shall be applied and administered to such years as if such provisions and amendments had never been enacted.

[Caution: Code Sec. 341, below, was repealed by § 302(e)(4)(A). For sunset provision, see H.R. 2, § 303, in the amendment notes.—CCH.]

[¶ 5060] CODE SEC. 341. COLLAPSIBLE CORPORATIONS. *[Repealed.]*

[CCH Explanation at ¶ 335 and ¶ 360. Committee Reports at ¶ 10,110.]

Amendment Notes

Act Sec. 302(e)(4)(A) repealed subpart C of part II of subchapter C of chapter 1 (Code Sec. 341). Prior to repeal, Code Sec. 341 read as follows:

SEC. 341. COLLAPSIBLE CORPORATIONS.

(a) TREATMENT OF GAIN TO SHAREHOLDERS.—Gain from—

(1) the sale or exchange of stock of a collapsible corporation,

(2) a distribution—

(A) in complete liquidation of a collapsible corporation if such distribution is treated under this part as in part or full payment in exchange for stock, or

(B) in partial liquidation (within the meaning of section 302(e)) of a collapsible corporation if such distribution is treated under section 302(b)(4) as in part or full payment in exchange for the stock, and

(3) a distribution made by a collapsible corporation which, under section 301(c)(3)(A), is treated, to the extent it exceeds the basis of the stock, in the same manner as a gain from the sale or exchange of property,

to the extent that it would be considered (but for the provisions of this section) as gain from the sale or exchange of a capital asset shall, except as otherwise provided in this section, be considered as ordinary income.

(b) DEFINITIONS.—

(1) COLLAPSIBLE CORPORATION.—For purposes of this section, the term "collapsible corporation" means a corporation formed or availed of principally for the manufacture, construction, or production of property, for the purchase of property which (in the hands of the corporation) is property described in paragraph (3), or for the holding of stock in a corporation so formed or availed of, with a view to—

(A) the sale or exchange of stock by its shareholders (whether in liquidation or otherwise), or a distribution to its shareholders, before the realization by the corporation manufacturing, constructing, producing, or purchasing the property of 2/3 of the taxable income to be derived from such property, and

(B) the realization by such shareholders of gain attributable to such property.

(2) PRODUCTION OR PURCHASE OF PROPERTY.—For purposes of paragraph (1), a corporation shall be deemed to have manufactured, constructed, produced, or purchased property, if—

(A) it engaged in the manufacture, construction, or production of such property to any extent,

(B) it holds property having a basis determined, in whole or in part, by reference to the cost of such property in the hands of a person who manufactured, constructed, produced, or purchased the property, or

(C) it holds property having a basis determined, in whole or in part, by reference to the cost of property manufactured, constructed, produced, or purchased by the corporation.

(3) SECTION 341 ASSETS.—For purposes of this section, the term "section 341 assets" means property held for a period of less than 3 years which is—

(A) stock in trade of the corporation, or other property of a kind which would properly be included in the inventory of the corporation if on hand at the close of the taxable year;

(B) property held by the corporation primarily for sale to customers in the ordinary course of its trade or business;

(C) unrealized receivables or fees, except receivables from sales of property other than property described in this paragraph; or

(D) property described in section 1231(b) (without regard to any holding period therein provided), except such property which is or has been used in connection with the manufacture, construction, production, or sale of property described in subparagraph (A) or (B).

In determining whether the 3-year holding period specified in this paragraph has been satisfied, section 1223 shall apply, but no such period shall be deemed to begin before the completion of the manufacture, construction, production, or purchase.

(4) UNREALIZED RECEIVABLES.—For purposes of paragraph (3) (C), the term "unrealized receivables or fees" means, to the extent not previously includible in income under the method of accounting used by the corporation, any rights (contractual or otherwise) to payment for—

(A) goods delivered, or to be delivered, to the extent the proceeds therefrom would be treated as amounts received from the sale or exchange of property other than a capital asset, or

(B) services rendered or to be rendered.

(c) PRESUMPTION IN CERTAIN CASES.—

(1) IN GENERAL.—For purposes of this section, a corporation shall, unless shown to the contrary, be deemed to be a collapsible corporation if (at the time of the sale or exchange, or the distribution, described in subsection (a)) the fair market value of its section 341 assets (as defined in subsection (b) (3)) is—

(A) 50 percent or more of the fair market value of its total assets, or

(B) 120 percent or more of the adjusted basis of such section 341 assets.

Absence of the conditions described in subparagraphs (A) and (B) shall not give rise to a presumption that the corporation was not a collapsible corporation.

(2) DETERMINATION OF TOTAL ASSETS.—In determining the fair market value of the total assets of a corporation for purposes of paragraph (1) (A), there shall not be taken into account—

(A) cash,

(B) obligations which are capital assets in the hands of the corporation, and

(C) stock in any other corporation.

(d) LIMITATIONS ON APPLICATION OF SECTION.—In the case of gain realized by a shareholder with respect to his stock in a collapsible corporation, this section shall not apply—

(1) unless, at any time after the commencement of the manufacture, construction, or production of the property, or at the time of the purchase of the property described in subsection (b) (3) or at any time thereafter, such shareholder (A) owned (or was considered as owning) more than 5 percent in value of the outstanding stock of the corporation, or (B) owned stock which was considered as owned at such time by another shareholder who then owned (or was considered as owning) more than 5 percent in value of the outstanding stock of the corporation;

(2) to the gain recognized during a taxable year, unless more than 70 percent of such gain is attributable to the property described in subsection (b)(1); and

(3) to gain realized after the expiration of 3 years following the completion of such manufacture, construction, production, or purchase.

For purposes of paragraph (1), the ownership of stock shall be determined in accordance with the rules prescribed in paragraphs (1), (2), (3), (5), and (6) of section 544(a) (relating to personal holding companies); except that, in addition to the persons prescribed by paragraph (2) of that section, the family of an individual shall include the spouses of that individual's brothers and sisters (whether by the whole or half blood) and the spouses of that individual's lineal descendants. In determining whether property is described in subsection (b)(1) for purposes of applying paragraph (2), all property described in section 1221(a)(1) shall, to the extent provided in regulations prescribed by the Secretary, be treated as one item of property.

(e) EXCEPTIONS TO APPLICATION OF SECTION.—

(1) SALES OR EXCHANGES OF STOCK.—For purposes of subsection (a)(1), a corporation shall not be considered to be a collapsible corporation with respect to any sale or exchange of stock of the corporation by a shareholder, if, at the time of such sale or exchange, the sum of—

(A) the net unrealized appreciation in subsection (e) assets of the corporation (as defined in paragraph (5)(A)), plus

(B) if the shareholder owns more than 5 percent in value of the outstanding stock of the corporation, the net unrealized appreciation in assets of the corporation (other than assets described in subparagraph (A)) which would be subsection (e) assets under clauses (i) and (iii) of paragraph (5)(A) if the shareholder owned more than 20 percent in value of such stock, plus

(C) if the shareholder owns more than 20 percent in value of the outstanding stock of the corporation and owns, or at any time during the preceding 3-year period owned, more than 20 percent in value of the outstanding stock of any other corporation more than 70 percent in value of the assets of which are, or were at any time during which such shareholder owned during such 3-year period more than 20 percent in value of the outstanding stock, assets similar or related in service or use to assets comprising more than 70 percent in value of the assets of the corporation, the net unrealized appreciation in assets of the corporation (other than assets described in subparagraph (A)) which would be subsection (e) assets under clauses (i) and (iii) of paragraph (5)(A) if the determination whether the property, in the hands of such shareholder, would be property gain from the sale or exchange of which would under any provision of this chapter be considered in whole or in part as ordinary income, were made—

(i) by treating any sale or exchange by such shareholder of stock in such other corporation within the preceding 3-year period (but only if at the time of such sale or exchange the shareholder owned more than 20 percent in value of the outstanding stock in such other corporation) as a sale or exchange by such shareholder of his proportionate share of the assets of such other corporation, and

(ii) by treating any liquidating sale or exchange of property by such other corporation within such 3-year period (but only if at the time of such sale or exchange the shareholder owned more than 20 percent in value of the outstanding stock in such other corporation), as a sale or exchange by such shareholder of his proportionate share of the property sold or exchanged,

does not exceed an amount equal to 15 percent of the net worth of the corporation. This paragraph shall not apply to any sale or exchange of stock to the issuing corporation or, in the case of a shareholder who owns more than 20 percent in value of the outstanding stock of the corporation, to any sale or exchange of stock by such shareholder to any person related to him (within the meaning of paragraph (8)).

(2) [Repealed.]

(3) [Repealed.]

(4) [Repealed.]

(5) SUBSECTION (e) ASSET DEFINED.—

(A) For purposes of paragraph (1), the term "subsection (e) asset" means, with respect to property held by any corporation—

¶ 5060   Code Sec. 341

Law Added, Amended or Repealed

(i) property (except property used in the trade or business, as defined in paragraph (9)) which in the hands of the corporation is, or, in the hands of a shareholder who owns more than 20 percent in value of the outstanding stock of the corporation, would be, property gain from the sale or exchange of which would under any provision of this chapter be considered in whole or in part as ordinary income;

(ii) property used in the trade or business (as defined in paragraph (9)), but only if the unrealized depreciation on all such property on which there is unrealized depreciation exceeds the unrealized appreciation on all such property on which there is unrealized appreciation;

(iii) if there is net unrealized appreciation on all property used in the trade or business (as defined in paragraph (9)), property used in the trade or business (as defined in paragraph (9)) which, in the hands of a shareholder who owns more than 20 percent in value of the outstanding stock of the corporation, would be property gain from the sale or exchange of which would under any provision of this chapter be considered in whole or in part as ordinary income; and

(iv) property (unless included under clause (i), (ii), or (iii)) which consists of a copyright, a literary, musical, or artistic composition, a letter or memorandum, or similar property, or any interest in any such property, if the property was created in whole or in part by the personal efforts of, or (in the case of a letter, memorandum, or similar property) was prepared, or produced in whole or in part for, any individual who owns more than 5 percent in value of the stock of the corporation.

The determination as to whether property of the corporation in the hands of the corporation is, or in the hands of a shareholder would be, property gain from the sale or exchange of which would under any provision in this chapter be considered in whole or in part as ordinary income shall be made as if all property of the corporation had been sold or exchanged to one person in one transaction.

(B) [Repealed.]

(6) NET UNREALIZED APPRECIATION DEFINED.—

(A) For purposes of this subsection, the term "net unrealized appreciation" means, with respect to the assets of a corporation, the amount by which—

(i) the unrealized appreciation in such assets on which there is unrealized appreciation, exceeds

(ii) the unrealized depreciation in such assets on which there is unrealized depreciation.

(B) For purposes of subparagraph (A) and paragraph (5)(A), the term "unrealized appreciation" means, with respect to any asset, the amount by which—

(i) the fair market value of such asset, exceeds

(ii) the adjusted basis for determining gain from the sale or other disposition of such asset.

(C) For purposes of subparagraph (A) and paragraph (5)(A), the term "unrealized depreciation" means, with respect to any asset, the amount by which—

(i) the adjusted basis for determining gain from the sale or other disposition of such asset, exceeds

(ii) the fair market value of such asset.

(D) For purposes of this paragraph (but not paragraph (5)(A)), in the case of any asset on the sale or exchange of which only a portion of the gain would under any provision of this chapter be considered as ordinary income, there shall be taken into account only an amount of the unrealized appreciation in such asset which is equal to such portion of the gain.

(7) NET WORTH DEFINED.—For purposes of this subsection, the net worth of a corporation, as of any day, is the amount by which—

(A) (i) the fair market value of all its assets at the close of such day, plus

(ii) the amount of any distribution in complete liquidation made by it on or before such day, exceeds

(B) all its liabilities at the close of such day.

For purposes of this paragraph, the net worth of a corporation as of any day shall not take into account any increase in net worth during the one-year period ending on such day to the extent attributable to any amount received by it for stock, or as a contribution to capital or as paid-in surplus, if it appears that there was not a bona fide business purpose for the transaction in respect of which such amount was received.

(8) RELATED PERSON DEFINED.—For purposes of paragraphs (1) and (4), the following persons shall be considered to be related to a shareholder:

(A) If the shareholder is an individual—

(i) his spouse, ancestors, and lineal descendants, and

(ii) a corporation which is controlled by such shareholder.

(B) If the shareholder is a corporation—

(i) a corporation which controls, or is controlled by, the shareholder, and

(ii) if more than 50 percent in value of the outstanding stock of the shareholder is owned by any person, a corporation more than 50 percent in value of the outstanding stock of which is owned by the same person.

For purposes of determining the ownership of stock in applying subparagraphs (A) and (B), the rules of section 267(c) shall apply, except that the family of an individual shall include only his spouse, ancestors, and lineal descendants. For purposes of this paragraph, control means the ownership of stock possessing at least 50 percent of the total combined voting power of all classes of stock entitled to vote or at least 50 percent of the total value of shares of all classes of stock of the corporation.

(9) PROPERTY USED IN THE TRADE OR BUSINESS.—For purposes of this subsection, the term "property used in the trade or business" means property described in section 1231(b), without regard to any holding period therein provided.

(10) OWNERSHIP OF STOCK.—For purposes of this subsection (other than paragraph (8)), the ownership of stock shall be determined in the manner prescribed by subsection (d).

(11) CORPORATIONS AND SHAREHOLDERS NOT MEETING REQUIREMENTS.—In determining whether or not any corporation is a collapsible corporation within the meaning of subsection (b), the fact that such corporation, or such corporation with respect to any of its shareholders, does not meet the requirements of paragraph (1), (2), (3), or (4) of this subsection shall not be taken into account, and such determination, in the case of a corporation which does not meet such requirements, shall be made as if this subsection had not been enacted.

(12) NONAPPLICATION OF SECTION 1245(a), ETC.—For purposes of this subsection, the determination of whether gain from the sale or exchange of property would under any provision of this chapter be considered as ordinary income shall be made without regard to the application of sections 617(d)(1), 1245(a), 1250(a), 1252(a),1254(a), and 1276(a).

(f) CERTAIN SALES OF STOCK OF CONSENTING CORPORATIONS.—

(1) IN GENERAL.—Subsection (a)(1) shall not apply to a sale of stock of a corporation (other than a sale to the issuing corporation) if such corporation (hereinafter in this subsection referred to as "consenting corporation") consents (at such time and in such manner as the Secretary may by regulations prescribe) to have the provisions of paragraph (2) apply. Such consent shall apply with respect to each sale of stock of such corporation made within the 6-month period beginning with the date on which such consent is filed.

(2) RECOGNITION OF GAIN.—Except as provided in paragraph (3), if a subsection (f) asset (as defined in paragraph (4)) is disposed of at any time by a consenting corporation (or, if paragraph (3) applies, by a transferee corporation), then the amount by which—

Code Sec. 341 ¶5060

(A) in the case of a sale, exchange, or involuntary conversion, the amount realized, or

(B) in the case of any other disposition, the fair market value of such asset,

exceeds the adjusted basis of such asset shall be treated as gain from the sale or exchange of such asset. Such gain shall be recognized notwithstanding any other provision of this subtitle, but only to the extent such gain is not recognized under any other provision of this subtitle.

(3) EXCEPTION FOR CERTAIN TAX-FREE TRANSACTIONS.—If the basis of a subsection (f) asset in the hands of a transferee is determined by reference to its basis in the hands of the transferor by reason of the application of section 332, 351, or 361, then the amount of gain taken into account by the transferor under paragraph (2) shall not exceed the amount of gain recognized to the transferor on the transfer of such asset (determined without regard to this subsection). This paragraph shall apply only if the transferee—

(A) is not an organization which is exempt from tax imposed by this chapter, and

(B) agrees (at such time and in such manner as the Secretary may by regulations prescribe) to have the provisions of paragraph (2) apply to any disposition by it of such subsection (f) asset.

(4) SUBSECTION (f) ASSET DEFINED.—For purposes of this subsection—

(A) IN GENERAL.—The term "subsection (f) asset" means any property which, as of the date of any sale of stock referred to in paragraph (1), is not a capital asset and is property owned by, or subject to an option to acquire held by, the consenting corporation. For purposes of this subparagraph, land or any interest in real property (other than a security interest), and unrealized receivables or fees (as defined in subsection (b)(4)), shall be treated as property which is not a capital asset.

(B) PROPERTY UNDER CONSTRUCTION.—If manufacture, construction, or production with respect to any property described in subparagraph (A) has commenced before any date of sale described therein, the term "subsection (f) asset" includes the property resulting from such manufacture, construction, or production.

(C) SPECIAL RULE FOR LAND.—In the case of land or any interest in real property (other than a security interest) described in subparagraph (A), the term "subsection (f) asset" includes any improvements resulting from construction with respect to such property if such construction is commenced (by the consenting corporation or by a transferee corporation which has agreed to the application of paragraph (2)) within 2 years after the date of any sale described in subparagraph (A).

(5) 5-YEAR LIMITATION AS TO SHAREHOLDER.—Paragraph (1) shall not apply to the sale of stock of a corporation by a shareholder if, during the 5-year period ending on the date of such sale, such shareholder (or any related person within the meaning of subsection (e)(8)(A)) sold any stock of another consenting corporation within any 6-month period beginning on a date on which a consent was filed under paragraph (1) by such other corporation.

(6) SPECIAL RULE FOR STOCK OWNERSHIP IN OTHER CORPORATIONS.—If a corporation (hereinafter in this paragraph referred to as "owning corporation") owns 5 percent or more in value of the outstanding stock of another corporation on the date of any sale of stock of the owning corporation during a 6-month period with respect to which a consent under paragraph (1) was filed by the owning corporation, such consent shall not be valid with respect to such sale unless such other corporation has (within the 6-month period ending on the date of such sale) filed a valid consent under paragraph (1) with respect to sales of its stock. For purposes of applying paragraph (4) to such other corporation, a sale of stock of the owning corporation to which paragraph (1) applies shall be treated as a sale of stock of such other corporation. In the case of a chain of corporations connected by the 5-percent ownership requirements of this paragraph, rules similar to the rules of the two preceding sentences shall be applied.

(7) ADJUSTMENTS TO BASIS.—The Secretary shall prescribe such regulations as he may deem necessary to provide for adjustments to the basis of property to reflect gain recognized under paragraph (2).

(8) SPECIAL RULE FOR FOREIGN CORPORATIONS.—Except to the extent provided in regulations prescribed by the Secretary—

(A) any consent given by a foreign corporation under paragraph (1) shall not be effective, and

(B) paragraph (3) shall not apply if the transferee is a foreign corporation.

The above amendment generally applies to tax years beginning after December 31, 2002. For a special rule, see Act Sec. 302(f)(2), below.

Act Sec. 302(f)(2) provides:

(2) REGULATED INVESTMENT COMPANIES AND REAL ESTATE INVESTMENT TRUSTS.—In the case of a regulated investment company or a real estate investment trust, the amendments made by this section shall apply to taxable years ending after December 31, 2002; except that dividends received by such a company or trust on or before such date shall not be treated as qualified dividend income (as defined in section 1(h)(11)(B) of the Internal Revenue Code of 1986, as added by this Act).

Act Sec. 303 provides:

SEC. 303. SUNSET OF TITLE.

All provisions of, and amendments made by, this title shall not apply to taxable years beginning after December 31, 2008, and the Internal Revenue Code of 1986 shall be applied and administered to such years as if such provisions and amendments had never been enacted.

[¶ 5065] CODE SEC. 467. CERTAIN PAYMENTS FOR THE USE OF PROPERTY OR SERVICES.

* * *

(c) RECAPTURE OF PRIOR UNDERSTATED INCLUSIONS UNDER LEASEBACK OR LONG-TERM AGREEMENTS.—

* * *

(5) SPECIAL RULES.—Under regulations prescribed by the Secretary—

(A) exceptions similar to the exceptions applicable under section 1245 or 1250 (whichever is appropriate) shall apply for purposes of this subsection,

(B) any transferee in a disposition excepted by reason of subparagraph (A) who has a transferred basis in the property shall be treated in the same manner as the transferor, and

[*Caution: Code Sec. 467(c)(5)(C), below, was amended by § 302(e)(4)(B)(ii). For sunset provision, see H.R. 2, § 303, in the amendment notes.—CCH.*]

(C) for purposes of sections 170(e) and 751(c), amounts treated as ordinary income under this section shall be treated in the same manner as amounts treated as ordinary income under section 1245 or 1250.

* * *

[CCH Explanation at ¶ 335 and ¶ 360. Committee Reports at ¶ 10,110.]

Amendment Notes

Act Sec. 302(e)(4)(B)(ii) amended Code Sec. 467(c)(5)(C) by striking ", 341(e)(12)," following "sections 170(e)".

The above amendment generally applies to tax years beginning after December 31, 2002. For a special rule, see Act Sec. 302(f)(2), below.

Act Sec. 302(f)(2) provides:

(2) REGULATED INVESTMENT COMPANIES AND REAL ESTATE INVESTMENT TRUSTS.—In the case of a regulated investment company or a real estate investment trust, the amendments made by this section shall apply to taxable years ending after December 31, 2002; except that dividends received by such a company or trust on or before such date shall not be treated as qualified dividend income (as defined in section 1(h)(11)(B) of the Internal Revenue Code of 1986, as added by this Act).

Act Sec. 303 provides:

SEC. 303. SUNSET OF TITLE.

All provisions of, and amendments made by, this title shall not apply to taxable years beginning after December 31, 2008, and the Internal Revenue Code of 1986 shall be applied and administered to such years as if such provisions and amendments had never been enacted.

[*Caution: Code Sec. 531, below, was amended by § 302(e)(5). For sunset provision, see H.R. 2, § 303, in the amendment notes.—CCH.*]

[¶ 5070] CODE SEC. 531. IMPOSITION OF ACCUMULATED EARNINGS TAX.

In addition to other taxes imposed by this chapter, there is hereby imposed for each taxable year on the accumulated taxable income (as defined in section 535) of each corporation described in section 532, an accumulated earnings tax *equal to 15 percent of the accumulated taxable income.*

[CCH Explanation at ¶ 335 and ¶ 365. Committee Reports at ¶ 10,110.]

Amendment Notes

Act Sec. 302(e)(5) amended Code Sec. 531 by striking "equal to" and all that follows and inserting "equal to 15 percent of the accumulated taxable income.". Prior to amendment, Code Sec. 531 read as follows:

SEC. 531. IMPOSITION OF ACCUMULATED EARNINGS TAX.

In addition to other taxes imposed by this chapter, there is hereby imposed for each taxable year on the accumulated taxable income (as defined in section 535) of each corporation described in section 532, an accumulated earnings tax equal to the product of the highest rate of tax under section 1(c) and the accumulated taxable income.

The above amendment generally applies to tax years beginning after December 31, 2002. For a special rule, see Act Sec. 302(f)(2), below.

Act Sec. 302(f)(2) provides:

(2) REGULATED INVESTMENT COMPANIES AND REAL ESTATE INVESTMENT TRUSTS.—In the case of a regulated investment company or a real estate investment trust, the amendments made by this section shall apply to taxable years ending after December 31, 2002; except that dividends received by such a company or trust on or before such date shall not be treated as qualified dividend income (as defined in section 1(h)(11)(B) of the Internal Revenue Code of 1986, as added by this Act).

Act Sec. 303 provides:

SEC. 303. SUNSET OF TITLE.

All provisions of, and amendments made by, this title shall not apply to taxable years beginning after December 31, 2008, and the Internal Revenue Code of 1986 shall be applied and administered to such years as if such provisions and amendments had never been enacted.

[*Caution: Code Sec. 541, below, was amended by § 302(e)(6). For sunset provision, see H.R. 2, § 303, in the amendment notes.—CCH.*]

[¶ 5075] CODE SEC. 541. IMPOSITION OF PERSONAL HOLDING COMPANY TAX.

In addition to other taxes imposed by this chapter, there is hereby imposed for each taxable year on the undistributed personal holding company income (as defined in section 545) of every personal holding company (as defined in section 542) a personal holding company tax *equal to 15 percent of the undistributed personal holding company income.*

[CCH Explanation at ¶ 335 and ¶ 370. Committee Reports at ¶ 10,110.]

Amendment Notes

Act Sec. 302(e)(6) amended Code Sec. 541 by striking "equal to" and all that follows and inserting "equal to 15 percent of the undistributed personal holding company income.". Prior to amendment, Code Sec. 541 read as follows:

SEC. 541. IMPOSITION OF PERSONAL HOLDING COMPANY TAX.

In addition to other taxes imposed by this chapter, there is hereby imposed for each taxable year on the undistributed personal holding company income (as defined in section 545) of every personal holding company (as defined in section 542) a personal holding company tax equal to the product of the highest rate of tax under section 1(c) and the undistributed personal holding company income.

The above amendment generally applies to tax years beginning after December 31, 2002. For a special rule, see Act Sec. 302(f)(2), below.

Act Sec. 302(f)(2) provides:

(2) REGULATED INVESTMENT COMPANIES AND REAL ESTATE INVESTMENT TRUSTS.—In the case of a regulated investment company or a real estate investment trust, the amendments made by this section shall apply to taxable years ending after December 31, 2002; except that dividends received by such a company or trust on or before such date shall not be treated as qualified dividend income (as defined in section 1(h)(11)(B) of the Internal Revenue Code of 1986, as added by this Act).

Act Sec. 303 provides:

SEC. 303. SUNSET OF TITLE.

All provisions of, and amendments made by, this title shall not apply to taxable years beginning after December 31, 2008, and the Internal Revenue Code of 1986 shall be applied and administered to such years as if such provisions and amendments had never been enacted.

[¶ 5080] CODE SEC. 584. COMMON TRUST FUNDS.

* * *

[*Caution: Code Sec. 584(c), below, was amended by § 302(e)(7). For sunset provision, see H.R. 2, § 303, in the amendment notes.—CCH.*]

(c) INCOME OF PARTICIPANTS IN FUND.—Each participant in the common trust fund in computing its taxable income shall include, whether or not distributed and whether or not distributable—

(1) as part of its gains and losses from sales or exchanges of capital assets held for not more than 1 year, its proportionate share of the gains and losses of the common trust fund from sales or exchanges of capital assets held for not more than 1 year,

(2) as part of its gains and losses from sales or exchanges of capital assets held for more than 1 year, its proportionate share of the gains and losses of the common trust fund from sales or exchanges of capital assets held for more than 1 year, and

(3) its proportionate share of the ordinary taxable income or the ordinary net loss of the common trust fund, computed as provided in subsection (d).

The proportionate share of each participant in the amount of dividends received by the common trust fund and to which section 1(h)(11) applies shall be considered for purposes of such paragraph as having been received by such participant.

* * *

[CCH Explanation at ¶ 335. Committee Reports at ¶ 10,110.]

Amendment Notes

Act Sec. 302(e)(7) amended Code Sec. 584(c) by adding at the end a new flush sentence to read as above.

The above amendment generally applies to tax years beginning after December 31, 2002. For a special rule, see Act Sec. 302(f)(2), below.

Act Sec. 302(f)(2) provides:

(2) REGULATED INVESTMENT COMPANIES AND REAL ESTATE INVESTMENT TRUSTS.—In the case of a regulated investment company or a real estate investment trust, the amendments made by this section shall apply to taxable years ending after December 31, 2002; except that dividends received by such a company or trust on or before such date shall not be treated as qualified dividend income (as defined in section 1(h)(11)(B) of the Internal Revenue Code of 1986, as added by this Act).

Act Sec. 303 provides:

SEC. 303. SUNSET OF TITLE.

All provisions of, and amendments made by, this title shall not apply to taxable years beginning after December 31, 2008, and the Internal Revenue Code of 1986 shall be applied and administered to such years as if such provisions and amendments had never been enacted.

[¶ 5085] CODE SEC. 702. INCOME AND CREDITS OF PARTNER.

(a) GENERAL RULE.—In determining his income tax, each partner shall take into account separately his distributive share of the partnership's—

(1) gains and losses from sales or exchanges of capital assets held for not more than 1 year,

(2) gains and losses from sales or exchanges of capital assets held for more than 1 year,

(3) gains and losses from sales or exchanges of property described in section 1231 (relating to certain property used in a trade or business and involuntary conversions),

(4) charitable contributions (as defined in section 170(c)),

¶ 5080 Code Sec. 584(c)

[*Caution: Code Sec. 702(a)(5), below, was amended by § 302(e)(8). For sunset provision, see H.R. 2, § 303, in the amendment notes.—CCH.*]

(5) dividends with respect to which section 1(h)(11) or part VIII of subchapter B applies,

(6) taxes, described in section 901, paid or accrued to foreign countries and to possessions of the United States,

(7) other items of income, gain, loss, deduction, or credit, to the extent provided by regulations prescribed by the Secretary, and

(8) taxable income or loss, exclusive of items requiring separate computation under other paragraphs of this subsection.

* * *

[CCH Explanation at ¶ 335. Committee Reports at ¶ 10,110.]

Amendment Notes

Act Sec. 302(e)(8) amended Code Sec. 702(a)(5) to read as above. Prior to amendment, Code Sec. 702(a)(5) read as follows:

(5) dividends with respect to which there is a deduction under part VIII of subchapter B,

The above amendment generally applies to tax years beginning after December 31, 2002. For a special rule, see Act Sec. 302(f)(2), below.

Act Sec. 302(f)(2) provides:

(2) REGULATED INVESTMENT COMPANIES AND REAL ESTATE INVESTMENT TRUSTS.—In the case of a regulated investment company or a real estate investment trust, the amendments made by this section shall apply to taxable years ending after December 31, 2002; except that dividends received by such a company or trust on or before such date shall not be treated as qualified dividend income (as defined in section 1(h)(11)(B) of the Internal Revenue Code of 1986, as added by this Act).

Act Sec. 303 provides:

SEC. 303. SUNSET OF TITLE.

All provisions of, and amendments made by, this title shall not apply to taxable years beginning after December 31, 2008, and the Internal Revenue Code of 1986 shall be applied and administered to such years as if such provisions and amendments had never been enacted.

[¶ 5090] CODE SEC. 854. LIMITATIONS APPLICABLE TO DIVIDENDS RECEIVED FROM REGULATED INVESTMENT COMPANY.

[*Caution: Code Sec. 854(a), below, was amended by § 302(c)(1). For sunset provision, see H.R. 2, § 303, in the amendment notes.—CCH.*]

(a) CAPITAL GAIN DIVIDEND.—For purposes of *section 1(h)(11) (relating to maximum rate of tax on dividends) and* section 243 (relating to deductions for dividends received by corporations), a capital gain dividend (as defined in section 852(b)(3)) received from a regulated investment company shall not be considered as a dividend.

[CCH Explanation at ¶ 335. Committee Reports at ¶ 10,110.]

Amendment Notes

Act Sec. 302(c)(1) amended Code Sec. 854(a) by inserting "section 1(h)(11) (relating to maximum rate of tax on dividends) and" after "For purposes of".

The above amendment generally applies to tax years beginning after December 31, 2002. For a special rule, see Act Sec. 302(f)(2), below.

Act Sec. 302(f)(2) provides:

(2) REGULATED INVESTMENT COMPANIES AND REAL ESTATE INVESTMENT TRUSTS.—In the case of a regulated investment company or a real estate investment trust, the amendments made by this section shall apply to taxable years ending after December 31, 2002; except that dividends received by such a company or trust on or before such date shall not be treated as qualified dividend income (as defined in section 1(h)(11)(B) of the Internal Revenue Code of 1986, as added by this Act).

Act Sec. 303 provides:

SEC. 303. SUNSET OF TITLE.

All provisions of, and amendments made by, this title shall not apply to taxable years beginning after December 31, 2008, and the Internal Revenue Code of 1986 shall be applied and administered to such years as if such provisions and amendments had never been enacted.

(b) OTHER DIVIDENDS.—

(1) AMOUNT TREATED AS DIVIDEND.—

* * *

[*Caution: Code Sec. 854(b)(1)(B), below, was added by § 302(c)(2). For sunset provision, see H.R. 2, § 303, in the amendment notes.—CCH.*]

(B) MAXIMUM RATE UNDER SECTION 1(h).—

(i) IN GENERAL.—If the aggregate dividends received by a regulated investment company during any taxable year are less than 95 percent of its gross income, then, in computing the maximum rate under section 1(h)(11), rules similar to the rules of subparagraph (A) shall apply.

(ii) GROSS INCOME.—For purposes of clause (i), in the case of 1 or more sales or other dispositions of stock or securities, the term "gross income" includes only the excess of—

(I) the net short-term capital gain from such sales or dispositions, over

(II) the net long-term capital loss from such sales or dispositions.

(iii) DIVIDENDS FROM REAL ESTATE INVESTMENT TRUSTS.—For purposes of clause (i)—

(I) paragraph (3)(B)(ii) shall not apply, and

(II) in the case of a distribution from a trust described in such paragraph, the amount of such distribution which is a dividend shall be subject to the limitations under section 857(c).

(iv) DIVIDENDS FROM QUALIFIED FOREIGN CORPORATIONS.—For purposes of clause (i), dividends received from qualified foreign corporations (as defined in section 1(h)(11)) shall also be taken into account in computing aggregate dividends received.

[*Caution: Code Sec. 854(b)(1)(C), below, was redesignated by § 302(c)(2) and amended by § 302(c)(3). For sunset provision, see H.R. 2, § 303, in the amendment notes.—CCH.*]

(C) LIMITATION.—The aggregate amount which may be designated as dividends under subparagraph (A) or (B) shall not exceed the aggregate dividends received by the company for the taxable year.

[*Caution: Code Sec. 854(b)(2), below, was amended by § 302(c)(4). For sunset provision, see H.R. 2, § 303, in the amendment notes.—CCH.*]

(2) NOTICE TO SHAREHOLDERS.—The amount of any distribution by a regulated investment company which may be taken into account as a dividend for purposes of *the maximum rate under section 1(h)(11) and* the deduction under section 243 shall not exceed the amount so designated by the company in a written notice to its shareholders mailed not later than 60 days after the close of its taxable year.

* * *

[*Caution: Code Sec. 854(b)(5), below, was added by § 302(c)(5). For sunset provision, see H.R. 2, § 303, in the amendment notes.—CCH.*]

(5) COORDINATION WITH SECTION 1(h)(11).—For purposes of paragraph (1)(B), an amount shall be treated as a dividend only if the amount is qualified dividend income (within the meaning of section 1(h)(11)(B)).

[CCH Explanation at ¶ 335. Committee Reports at ¶ 10,110.]

Amendment Notes

Act Sec. 302(c)(2) amended Code Sec. 854(b)(1) by redesignating subparagraph (B) as subparagraph (C) and by inserting after subparagraph (A) a new subparagraph (B) to read as above.

Act Sec. 302(c)(3) amended Code Sec. 854(b)(1)(C), as redesignated by Act Sec. 302(c)(2), by striking "subparagraph (A)" and inserting "subparagraph (A) or (B)".

Act Sec. 302(c)(4) amended Code Sec. 854(b)(2) by inserting "the maximum rate under section 1(h)(11) and" after "for purposes of".

Act Sec. 302(c)(5) amended Code Sec. 854(b) by adding at the end a new paragraph (5) to read as above.

The above amendments generally apply to tax years beginning after December 31, 2002. For a special rule, see Act Sec. 302(f)(2), below.

Act Sec. 302(f)(2) provides:

(2) REGULATED INVESTMENT COMPANIES AND REAL ESTATE INVESTMENT TRUSTS.—In the case of a regulated investment company or a real estate investment trust, the amendments made by this section shall apply to taxable years ending after December 31, 2002; except that dividends received by such a company or trust on or before such date shall not be treated as qualified dividend income (as defined in section 1(h)(11)(B) of the Internal Revenue Code of 1986, as added by this Act).

Act Sec. 303 provides:

SEC. 303. SUNSET OF TITLE.

¶ 5090 Code Sec. 854(b)

Law Added, Amended or Repealed

All provisions of, and amendments made by, this title shall not apply to taxable years beginning after December 31, 2008, and the Internal Revenue Code of 1986 shall be applied and administered to such years as if such provisions and amendments had never been enacted.

[¶ 5095] CODE SEC. 857. TAXATION OF REAL ESTATE INVESTMENT TRUSTS AND THEIR BENEFICIARIES.

* * *

[Caution: Code Sec. 857(c), below, was amended by § 302(d). For sunset provision, see H.R. 2, § 303, in the amendment notes.—CCH.]

(c) RESTRICTIONS APPLICABLE TO DIVIDENDS RECEIVED FROM REAL ESTATE INVESTMENT TRUSTS.—

(1) SECTION 243.—For purposes of section 243 (relating to deductions for dividends received by corporations), a dividend received from a real estate investment trust which meets the requirements of this part shall not be considered a dividend.

(2) SECTION 1(h)(11).—For purposes of section 1(h)(11) (relating to maximum rate of tax on dividends)—

(A) rules similar to the rules of subparagraphs (B) and (C) of section 854(b)(1) shall apply to dividends received from a real estate investment trust which meets the requirements of this part, and

(B) for purposes of such rules, such a trust shall be treated as receiving qualified dividend income during any taxable year in an amount equal to the sum of—

(i) the excess of real estate investment trust taxable income computed under section 857(b)(2) for the preceding taxable year over the tax payable by the trust under section 857(b)(1) for such preceding taxable year, and

(ii) the excess of the income subject to tax by reason of the application of the regulations under section 337(d) for the preceding taxable year over the tax payable by the trust on such income for such preceding taxable year.

* * *

[CCH Explanation at ¶ 335. Committee Reports at ¶ 10,110.]

Amendment Notes

Act Sec. 302(d) amended Code Sec. 857(c) to read as above. Prior to amendment, Code Sec. 857(c) read as follows:

(c) RESTRICTIONS APPLICABLE TO DIVIDENDS RECEIVED FROM REAL ESTATE INVESTMENT TRUSTS.—For purposes of section 243 (relating to deductions for dividends received by corporations), a dividend received from a real estate investment trust which meets the requirements of this part shall not be considered as a dividend.

The above amendment generally applies to tax years beginning after December 31, 2002. For a special rule, see Act Sec. 302(f)(2), below.

Act Sec. 302(f)(2) provides:

(2) REGULATED INVESTMENT COMPANIES AND REAL ESTATE INVESTMENT TRUSTS.—In the case of a regulated investment company or a real estate investment trust, the amendments made by this section shall apply to taxable years ending after December 31, 2002; except that dividends received by such a company or trust on or before such date shall not be treated as qualified dividend income (as defined in section 1(h)(11)(B) of the Internal Revenue Code of 1986, as added by this Act).

Act Sec. 303 provides:

SEC. 303. SUNSET OF TITLE.

All provisions of, and amendments made by, this title shall not apply to taxable years beginning after December 31, 2008, and the Internal Revenue Code of 1986 shall be applied and administered to such years as if such provisions and amendments had never been enacted.

[¶ 5100] CODE SEC. 1255. GAIN FROM DISPOSITION OF SECTION 126 PROPERTY.

* * *

(b) SPECIAL RULES.—Under regulations prescribed by the Secretary—

(1) rules similar to the rules applicable under section 1245 shall be applied for purposes of this section, and

150   Jobs and Growth Tax Relief Reconciliation Act of 2003

[*Caution: Code Sec. 1255(b)(2), below, was amended by § 302(e)(4)(B)(ii). For sunset provision, see H.R. 2, § 303, in the amendment notes.—CCH.*]

(2) for purposes of sections 170(e) and 751(c), amounts treated as ordinary income under this section shall be treated in the same manner as amounts treated as ordinary income under section 1245.

[CCH Explanation at ¶ 335 and ¶ 360. Committee Reports at ¶ 10,110.]

Amendment Notes

Act Sec. 302(e)(4)(B)(ii) amended Code Sec. 1255(b)(2) by striking ", 341(e)(12)," following "sections 170(e)".

The above amendment generally applies to tax years beginning after December 31, 2002. For a special rule, see Act Sec. 302(f)(2), below.

Act Sec. 302(f)(2) provides:

(2) REGULATED INVESTMENT COMPANIES AND REAL ESTATE INVESTMENT TRUSTS.—In the case of a regulated investment company or a real estate investment trust, the amendments made by this section shall apply to taxable years ending after December 31, 2002; except that dividends received by such a company or trust on or before such date shall not be treated as qualified dividend income (as defined in section 1(h)(11)(B) of the Internal Revenue Code of 1986, as added by this Act).

Act Sec. 303 provides:

SEC. 303. SUNSET OF TITLE.

All provisions of, and amendments made by, this title shall not apply to taxable years beginning after December 31, 2008, and the Internal Revenue Code of 1986 shall be applied and administered to such years as if such provisions and amendments had never been enacted.

[¶ 5105] CODE SEC. 1257. DISPOSITION OF CONVERTED WETLANDS OR HIGHLY ERODIBLE CROPLANDS.

* * *

[*Caution: Code Sec. 1257(d), below, was amended by § 302(e)(4)(B)(ii). For sunset provision, see H.R. 2, § 303, in the amendment notes.—CCH.*]

(d) SPECIAL RULES.—Under regulations prescribed by the Secretary, rules similar to the rules applicable under section 1245 shall apply for purposes of subsection (a). For purposes of sections 170(e) and 751(c), amounts treated as ordinary income under subsection (a) shall be treated in the same manner as amounts treated as ordinary income under section 1245.

[CCH Explanation at ¶ 335 and ¶ 360. Committee Reports at ¶ 10,110.]

Amendment Notes

Act Sec. 302(e)(4)(B)(ii) amended Code Sec. 1257(d) by striking ", 341(e)(12)," following "sections 170(e)".

The above amendment generally applies to tax years beginning after December 31, 2002. For a special rule, see Act Sec. 302(f)(2), below.

Act Sec. 302(f)(2) provides:

(2) REGULATED INVESTMENT COMPANIES AND REAL ESTATE INVESTMENT TRUSTS.—In the case of a regulated investment company or a real estate investment trust, the amendments made by this section shall apply to taxable years ending after December 31, 2002; except that dividends received by such a company or trust on or before such date shall not be treated as qualified dividend income (as defined in section 1(h)(11)(B) of the Internal Revenue Code of 1986, as added by this Act).

Act Sec. 303 provides:

SEC. 303. SUNSET OF TITLE.

All provisions of, and amendments made by, this title shall not apply to taxable years beginning after December 31, 2008, and the Internal Revenue Code of 1986 shall be applied and administered to such years as if such provisions and amendments had never been enacted.

[¶ 5110] CODE SEC. 1400L. TAX BENEFITS FOR NEW YORK LIBERTY ZONE.

* * *

(b) SPECIAL ALLOWANCE FOR CERTAIN PROPERTY ACQUIRED AFTER SEPTEMBER 10, 2001.—

* * *

(2) QUALIFIED NEW YORK LIBERTY ZONE PROPERTY.—For purposes of this subsection—

* * *

(C) EXCEPTIONS.—

(i) BONUS DEPRECIATION PROPERTY UNDER SECTION 168(k).—Such term shall not include property to which section 168(k) applies.

* * *

[CCH Explanation at ¶ 350. Committee Reports at ¶ 10,080.]

Amendment Notes

Act Sec. 201(c)(2) amended the heading for Code Sec. 1400L(b)(2)(C)(i) by striking "30-PERCENT ADDITIONAL ALLOWANCE PROPERTY" and inserting "BONUS DEPRECIATION PROPERTY UNDER SECTION 168(k)".

The above amendment applies to tax years ending after May 5, 2003.

¶ 5105   Code Sec. 1257(d)

Law Added, Amended or Repealed

[¶ 5115] CODE SEC. 1445. WITHHOLDING OF TAX ON DISPOSITIONS OF UNITED STATES REAL PROPERTY INTERESTS.

* * *

(e) SPECIAL RULES RELATING TO DISTRIBUTIONS, ETC., BY CORPORATIONS, PARTNERSHIPS, TRUSTS, OR ESTATES.—

[Caution: Code Sec. 1445(e)(1), below, was amended by § 301(a)(2)(C). For sunset provision, see H.R. 2, § 303, in the amendment notes.—CCH.]

(1) CERTAIN DOMESTIC PARTNERSHIPS, TRUSTS, AND ESTATES.—In the case of any disposition of a United States real property interest as defined in section 897(c) (other than a disposition described in paragraph (4) or (5)) by a domestic partnership, domestic trust, or domestic estate, such partnership, the trustee or such trust, or the executor of such estate (as the case may be) shall be required to deduct and withhold under subsection (a) a tax equal to 35 percent (or, to the extent provided in regulations, *15 percent*) of the gain realized to the extent such gain—

(A) is allocable to a foreign person who is a partner or beneficiary of such partnership, trust, or estate, or

(B) is allocable to a portion of the trust treated as owned by a foreign person under subpart E of Part I of subchapter J.

* * *

[CCH Explanation at ¶ 305. Committee Reports at ¶ 10,100.]

Amendment Notes

Act Sec. 301(a)(2)(C) amended Code Sec. 1445(e)(1) by striking "20 percent" and inserting "15 percent".

The above amendment applies to amounts paid after the date of the enactment of this Act.

Act Sec. 303 provides:
SEC. 303. SUNSET OF TITLE.

All provisions of, and amendments made by, this title shall not apply to taxable years beginning after December 31, 2008, and the Internal Revenue Code of 1986 shall be applied and administered to such years as if such provisions and amendments had never been enacted.

[Caution: Code Sec. 6429, below, was added by § 101(b)(1). For sunset provision, see H.R. 2, § 107, in the amendment notes.—CCH.]

[¶ 5120] CODE SEC. 6429. ADVANCE PAYMENT OF PORTION OF INCREASED CHILD CREDIT FOR 2003.

(a) IN GENERAL.—Each taxpayer who was allowed a credit under section 24 on the return for the taxpayer's first taxable year beginning in 2002 shall be treated as having made a payment against the tax imposed by chapter 1 for such taxable year in an amount equal to the child tax credit refund amount (if any) for such taxable year.

(b) CHILD TAX CREDIT REFUND AMOUNT.—For purposes of this section, the child tax credit refund amount is the amount by which the aggregate credits allowed under part IV of subchapter A of chapter 1 for such first taxable year would have been increased if—

(1) the per child amount under section 24(a)(2) for such year were $1,000,

(2) only qualifying children (as defined in section 24(c)) of the taxpayer for such year who had not attained age 17 as of December 31, 2003, were taken into account, and

(3) section 24(d)(1)(B)(ii) did not apply.

(c) TIMING OF PAYMENTS.—In the case of any overpayment attributable to this section, the Secretary shall, subject to the provisions of this title, refund or credit such overpayment as rapidly as possible and, to the extent practicable, before October 1, 2003. No refund or credit shall be made or allowed under this section after December 31, 2003.

(d) COORDINATION WITH CHILD TAX CREDIT.—

(1) IN GENERAL.—The amount of credit which would (but for this subsection and section 26) be allowed under section 24 for the taxpayer's first taxable year beginning in 2003 shall be reduced (but not below zero) by the payments made to the taxpayer under this section. Any failure to so reduce the credit shall be treated as arising out of a mathematical or clerical error and assessed according to section 6213(b)(1).

152 Jobs and Growth Tax Relief Reconciliation Act of 2003

(2) JOINT RETURNS.—In the case of a payment under this section with respect to a joint return, half of such payment shall be treated as having been made to each individual filing such return.

(e) NO INTEREST.—No interest shall be allowed on any overpayment attributable to this section.

[CCH Explanation at ¶ 225. Committee Reports at ¶ 10,010.]

Amendment Notes

Act Sec. 101(b)(1) amended subchapter B of chapter 65 by inserting after Code Sec. 6428 a new Code Sec. 6429 to read as above.

The above amendment is effective on the date of the enactment of this Act.

Each amendment made by this title shall be subject to title IX of the Economic Growth and Tax Relief Reconciliation Act of 2001 to the same extent and in the same manner as the provision of such Act to which such amendment relates [applicable to years beginning after December 31, 2010.—CCH].

Act Sec. 107 provides:

SEC. 107. APPLICATION OF EGTRRA SUNSET TO THIS TITLE.

[¶ 5125] CODE SEC. 7518. TAX INCENTIVES RELATING TO MERCHANT MARINE CAPITAL CONSTRUCTION FUNDS.

* * *

(g) TAX TREATMENT OF NONQUALIFIED WITHDRAWALS.—

* * *

(6) NONQUALIFIED WITHDRAWALS TAXED AT HIGHEST MARGINAL RATE.—

[*Caution: Code Sec. 7518(g)(6)(A), below, was amended by § 301(a)(2)(D). For sunset provision, see H.R. 2, § 303, in the amendment notes.—CCH.*]

(A) IN GENERAL.—In the case of any taxable year for which there is a nonqualified withdrawal (including any amount so treated under paragraph (5)), the tax imposed by chapter 1 shall be determined—

(i) by excluding such withdrawal from gross income, and

(ii) by increasing the tax imposed by chapter 1 by the product of the amount of such withdrawal and the highest rate of tax specified in section 1 (section 11 in the case of a corporation).

With respect to the portion of any nonqualified withdrawal made out of the capital gain account during a taxable year to which section 1(h) or 1201(a) applies, the rate of tax taken into account under the preceding sentence shall not exceed *15 percent* (34 percent in the case of a corporation).

* * *

[CCH Explanation at ¶ 305. Committee Reports at ¶ 10,100.]

Amendment Notes

Act Sec. 301(a)(2)(D) amended the second sentence of Code Sec. 7518(g)(6)(A) by striking "20 percent" and inserting "15 percent".

The above amendment applies to tax years ending on or after May 6, 2003.

All provisions of, and amendments made by, this title shall not apply to taxable years beginning after December 31, 2008, and the Internal Revenue Code of 1986 shall be applied and administered to such years as if such provisions and amendments had never been enacted.

Act Sec. 303 provides:

SEC. 303. SUNSET OF TITLE.

¶ 5125 Code Sec. 7518(g)

ACT SECTIONS NOT AMENDING CODE SECTIONS

JOBS AND GROWTH TAX RELIEF RECONCILIATION ACT OF 2003

[¶ 7005] ACT SEC. 1. SHORT TITLE; REFERENCES; TABLE OF CONTENTS.

(a) SHORT TITLE.—This Act may be cited as the "Jobs and Growth Tax Relief Reconciliation Act of 2003".

(b) AMENDMENT OF 1986 CODE.—Except as otherwise expressly provided, whenever in this Act an amendment or repeal is expressed in terms of an amendment to, or repeal of, a section or other provision, the reference shall be considered to be made to a section or other provision of the Internal Revenue Code of 1986.

* * *

TITLE I—ACCELERATION OF CERTAIN PREVIOUSLY ENACTED TAX REDUCTIONS

* * *

[¶ 7010] ACT SEC. 102. ACCELERATION OF 15-PERCENT INDIVIDUAL INCOME TAX RATE BRACKET EXPANSION FOR MARRIED TAXPAYERS FILING JOINT RETURNS.

* * *

(b) CONFORMING AMENDMENTS.—

* * *

(2) Section 302(c) of the Economic Growth and Tax Relief Reconciliation Act of 2001 is amended by striking "2004" and inserting "2002".

●● *EGTRRA OF 2001 ACT SEC. 302(c) AS AMENDED* ─────────

ACT SEC. 302. PHASEOUT OF MARRIAGE PENALTY IN 15-PERCENT BRACKET.

* * *

(c) EFFECTIVE DATE.—The amendments made by this section shall apply to taxable years beginning after December 31, *2002*.

(c) EFFECTIVE DATE.—The amendments made by this section shall apply to taxable years beginning after December 31, 2002.

[CCH Explanation at ¶ 215. Committee Reports at ¶ 10,020.]

[¶ 7015] ACT SEC. 103. ACCELERATION OF INCREASE IN STANDARD DEDUCTION FOR MARRIED TAXPAYERS FILING JOINT RETURNS.

* * *

(b) CONFORMING AMENDMENT.—Section 301(d) of the Economic Growth and Tax Relief Reconciliation Act of 2001 is amended by striking "2004" and inserting "2002".

●● *EGTRRA OF 2001 ACT SEC. 301(d) AS AMENDED* ─────────

ACT SEC. 301. ELIMINATION OF MARRIAGE PENALTY IN STANDARD DEDUCTION.

* * *

(d) EFFECTIVE DATE.—The amendments made by this section shall apply to taxable years beginning after December 31, *2002*.

(c) EFFECTIVE DATE.—The amendments made by this section shall apply to taxable years beginning after December 31, 2002.

[CCH Explanation at ¶ 220. Committee Reports at ¶ 10,030.]

[¶ 7020] ACT SEC. 104. ACCELERATION OF 10-PERCENT INDIVIDUAL INCOME TAX RATE BRACKET EXPANSION.

* * *

(c) EFFECTIVE DATE.—

* * *

(2) TABLES FOR 2003.—The Secretary of the Treasury shall modify each table which has been prescribed under section 1(f) of the Internal Revenue Code of 1986 for taxable years beginning in 2003 and which relates to the amendment made by subsection (a) to reflect such amendment.

* * *

[CCH Explanation at ¶ 210. Committee Reports at ¶ 10,040.]

[¶ 7025] ACT SEC. 107. APPLICATION OF EGTRRA SUNSET TO THIS TITLE.

Each amendment made by this title shall be subject to title IX of the Economic Growth and Tax Relief Reconciliation Act of 2001 to the same extent and in the same manner as the provision of such Act to which such amendment relates.

* * *

[CCH Explanation at ¶ 29,001. Committee Reports at ¶ 10,070.]

TITLE III—REDUCTION IN TAXES ON DIVIDENDS AND CAPITAL GAINS

[¶ 7030] ACT SEC. 301. REDUCTION IN CAPITAL GAINS RATES FOR INDIVIDUALS; REPEAL OF 5-YEAR HOLDING PERIOD REQUIREMENT.

(a) IN GENERAL.—

* * *

(2) The following sections are each amended by striking "20 percent" and inserting "15 percent":

* * *

(E) The second sentence of section 607(h)(6)(A) of the Merchant Marine Act, 1936.

* * *

(c) TRANSITIONAL RULES FOR TAXABLE YEARS WHICH INCLUDE MAY 6, 2003.—For purposes of applying section 1(h) of the Internal Revenue Code of 1986 in the case of a taxable year which includes May 6, 2003—

(1) The amount of tax determined under subparagraph (B) of section 1(h)(1) of such Code shall be the sum of—

(A) 5 percent of the lesser of—

(i) the net capital gain determined by taking into account only gain or loss properly taken into account for the portion of the taxable year on or after May 6, 2003 (determined without regard to collectibles gain or loss, gain described in section 1(h)(6)(A)(i) of such Code, and section 1202 gain), or

(ii) the amount on which a tax is determined under such subparagraph (without regard to this subsection),

(B) 8 percent of the lesser of—

(i) the qualified 5-year gain (as defined in section 1(h)(9) of the Internal Revenue Code of 1986, as in effect on the day before the date of the enactment of this Act) properly taken into account for the portion of the taxable year before May 6, 2003, or

(ii) the excess (if any) of—

(I) the amount on which a tax is determined under such subparagraph (without regard to this subsection), over

(II) the amount on which a tax is determined under subparagraph (A), plus

(C) 10 percent of the excess (if any) of—

(i) the amount on which a tax is determined under such subparagraph (without regard to this subsection), over

(ii) the sum of the amounts on which a tax is determined under subparagraphs (A) and (B).

(2) The amount of tax determined under subparagraph (C) of section (1)(h)(1) of such Code shall be the sum of—

(A) 15 percent of the lesser of—

(i) the excess (if any) of the amount of net capital gain determined under subparagraph (A)(i) of paragraph (1) of this subsection over the amount on which a tax is determined under subparagraph (A) of paragraph (1) of this subsection, or

(ii) the amount on which a tax is determined under such subparagraph (C) (without regard to this subsection), plus

(B) 20 percent of the excess (if any) of—

(i) the amount on which a tax is determined under such subparagraph (C) (without regard to this subsection), over

(ii) the amount on which a tax is determined under subparagraph (A) of this paragraph.

(3) For purposes of applying section 55(b)(3) of such Code, rules similar to the rules of paragraphs (1) and (2) of this subsection shall apply.

(4) In applying this subsection with respect to any pass-thru entity, the determination of when gains and losses are properly taken into account shall be made at the entity level.

(5) For purposes of applying section 1(h)(11) of such Code, as added by section 302 of this Act, to this subsection, dividends which are qualified dividend income shall be treated as gain properly taken into account for the portion of the taxable year on or after May 6, 2003.

(6) Terms used in this subsection which are also used in section 1(h) of such Code shall have the respective meanings that such terms have in such section.

* * *

[CCH Explanation at ¶ 320. Committee Reports at ¶ 10,100.]

[¶ 7035] ACT SEC. 303. SUNSET OF TITLE.

All provisions of, and amendments made by, this title shall not apply to taxable years beginning after December 31, 2008, and the Internal Revenue Code of 1986 shall be applied and administered to such years as if such provisions and amendments had never been enacted.

[CCH Explanation at ¶ 29,001. Committee Reports at ¶ 10,100 and ¶ 10,110.]

TITLE IV—TEMPORARY STATE FISCAL RELIEF

[¶ 7040] ACT SEC. 401. TEMPORARY STATE FISCAL RELIEF.

(a) $10,000,000,000 FOR A TEMPORARY INCREASE OF THE MEDICAID FMAP.—

(1) PERMITTING MAINTENANCE OF FISCAL YEAR 2002 FMAP FOR LAST 2 CALENDAR QUARTERS OF FISCAL YEAR 2003.—Subject to paragraph (5), if the FMAP determined without regard to this subsection for a State for fiscal year 2003 is less than the FMAP as so determined for fiscal year 2002, the FMAP for the State for fiscal year 2002 shall be substituted for the State's FMAP for the third and fourth calendar quarters of fiscal year 2003, before the application of this subsection.

(2) PERMITTING MAINTENANCE OF FISCAL YEAR 2003 FMAP FOR FIRST 3 QUARTERS OF FISCAL YEAR 2004.—Subject to paragraph (5), if the FMAP determined without regard to this subsection for a State for fiscal year 2004 is less than the FMAP as so determined for fiscal year 2003, the FMAP for the State for fiscal year 2003 shall be substituted for the State's FMAP for the first, second, and third calendar quarters of fiscal year 2004, before the application of this subsection.

(3) GENERAL 2.95 PERCENTAGE POINTS INCREASE FOR LAST 2 CALENDAR QUARTERS OF FISCAL YEAR 2003 AND FIRST 3 CALENDAR QUARTERS OF FISCAL YEAR 2004.—Subject to paragraphs (5), (6), and (7), for each State for the third and fourth calendar quarters of fiscal year 2003 and for the first, second,

and third calendar quarters of fiscal year 2004, the FMAP (taking into account the application of paragraphs (1) and (2)) shall be increased by 2.95 percentage points.

(4) INCREASE IN CAP ON MEDICAID PAYMENTS TO TERRITORIES.—Subject to paragraphs (6) and (7), with respect to the third and fourth calendar quarters of fiscal year 2003 and the first, second, and third calendar quarters of fiscal year 2004, the amounts otherwise determined for Puerto Rico, the Virgin Islands, Guam, the Northern Mariana Islands, and American Samoa under subsections (f) and (g) of section 1108 of the Social Security Act (42 U.S.C. 1308) shall each be increased by an amount equal to 5.90 percent of such amounts.

(5) SCOPE OF APPLICATION.—The increases in the FMAP for a State under this subsection shall apply only for purposes of title XIX of the Social Security Act and shall not apply with respect to—

(A) disproportionate share hospital payments described in section 1923 of such Act (42 U.S.C. 1396r-4);

(B) payments under title IV or XXI of such Act (42 U.S.C. 601 et seq. and 1397aa et seq.); or

(C) any payments under XIX of such Act that are based on the enhanced FMAP described in section 2105(b) of such Act (42 U.S.C. 1397ee(b)).

(6) STATE ELIGIBILITY.—

(A) IN GENERAL.—Subject to subparagraph (B), a State is eligible for an increase in its FMAP under paragraph (3) or an increase in a cap amount under paragraph (4) only if the eligibility under its State plan under title XIX of the Social Security Act (including any waiver under such title or under section 1115 of such Act (42 U.S.C. 1315)) is no more restrictive than the eligibility under such plan (or waiver) as in effect on September 2, 2003.

(B) STATE REINSTATEMENT OF ELIGIBILITY PERMITTED.—A State that has restricted eligibility under its State plan under title XIX of the Social Security Act (including any waiver under such title or under section 1115 of such Act (42 U.S.C. 1315)) after September 2, 2003, is eligible for an increase in its FMAP under paragraph (3) or an increase in a cap amount under paragraph (4) in the first calendar quarter (and subsequent calendar quarters) in which the State has reinstated eligibility that is no more restrictive than the eligibility under such plan (or waiver) as in effect on September 2, 2003.

(C) RULE OF CONSTRUCTION.—Nothing in subparagraph (A) or (B) shall be construed as affecting a State's flexibility with respect to benefits offered under the State medicaid program under title XIX of the Social Security Act (42 U.S.C. 1396 et seq.) (including any waiver under such title or under section 1115 of such Act (42 U.S.C. 1315)).

(7) REQUIREMENT FOR CERTAIN STATES.—In the case of a State that requires political subdivisions within the State to contribute toward the non-Federal share of expenditures under the State medicaid plan required under section 1902(a)(2) of the Social Security Act (42 U.S.C. 1396a(a)(2)), the State shall not require that such political subdivisions pay a greater percentage of the non-Federal share of such expenditures for the third and fourth calendar quarters of fiscal year 2003 and the first, second and third calendar quarters of fiscal year 2004, than the percentage that was required by the State under such plan on April 1, 2003, prior to application of this subsection.

(8) DEFINITIONS.—In this subsection:

(A) FMAP.—The term "FMAP" means the Federal medical assistance percentage, as defined in section 1905(b) of the Social Security Act (42 U.S.C. 1396d(b)).

(B) STATE.—The term "State" has the meaning given such term for purposes of title XIX of the Social Security Act (42 U.S.C. 1396 et seq.).

(9) REPEAL.—Effective as of October 1, 2004, this subsection is repealed.

(b) $10,000,000,000 TO ASSIST STATES IN PROVIDING GOVERNMENT SERVICES.—The Social Security Act (42 U.S.C. 301 et seq.) is amended by inserting after title V the following:

"TITLE VI—TEMPORARY STATE FISCAL RELIEF

"SEC. 601. TEMPORARY STATE FISCAL RELIEF.

"(a) APPROPRIATION.—There is authorized to be appropriated and is appropriated for making payments to States under this section, $5,000,000,000 for each of fiscal years 2003 and 2004.

"(b) PAYMENTS.—

"(1) FISCAL YEAR 2003.—From the amount appropriated under subsection (a) for fiscal year 2003, the Secretary of the Treasury shall, not later than the later of the date that is 45 days after the date of enactment of this Act or the date that a State provides the certification required by subsection (e) for fiscal year 2003, pay each State the amount determined for the State for fiscal year 2003 under subsection (c).

"(2) FISCAL YEAR 2004.—From the amount appropriated under subsection (a) for fiscal year 2004, the Secretary of the Treasury shall, not later than the later of October 1, 2003, or the date that a State provides the certification required by subsection (e) for fiscal year 2004, pay each State the amount determined for the State for fiscal year 2004 under subsection (c).

"(c) PAYMENTS BASED ON POPULATION.—

"(1) IN GENERAL.—Subject to paragraph (2), the amount appropriated under subsection (a) for each of fiscal years 2003 and 2004 shall be used to pay each State an amount equal to the relative population proportion amount described in paragraph (3) for such fiscal year.

"(2) MINIMUM PAYMENT.—

"(A) IN GENERAL.—No State shall receive a payment under this section for a fiscal year that is less than—

"(i) in the case of 1 of the 50 States or the District of Columbia, 1/2 of 1 percent of the amount appropriated for such fiscal year under subsection (a); and

"(ii) in the case of the Commonwealth of Puerto Rico, the United States Virgin Islands, Guam, the Commonwealth of the Northern Mariana Islands, or American Samoa, 1/10 of 1 percent of the amount appropriated for such fiscal year under subsection (a).

"(B) PRO RATA ADJUSTMENTS.—The Secretary of the Treasury shall adjust on a pro rata basis the amount of the payments to States determined under this section without regard to this subparagraph to the extent necessary to comply with the requirements of subparagraph (A).

"(3) RELATIVE POPULATION PROPORTION AMOUNT.—The relative population proportion amount described in this paragraph is the product of—

"(A) the amount described in subsection (a) for a fiscal year; and

"(B) the relative State population proportion (as defined in paragraph (4)).

"(4) RELATIVE STATE POPULATION PROPORTION DEFINED.—For purposes of paragraph (3)(B), the term 'relative State population proportion' means, with respect to a State, the amount equal to the quotient of—

"(A) the population of the State (as reported in the most recent decennial census); and

"(B) the total population of all States (as reported in the most recent decennial census).

"(d) USE OF PAYMENT.—

"(1) IN GENERAL.—Subject to paragraph (2), a State shall use the funds provided under a payment made under this section for a fiscal year to—

"(A) provide essential government services; or

"(B) cover the costs to the State of complying with any Federal intergovernmental mandate (as defined in section 421(5) of the Congressional Budget Act of 1974) to the extent that the mandate applies to the State, and the Federal Government has not provided funds to cover the costs.

"(2) LIMITATION.—A State may only use funds provided under a payment made under this section for types of expenditures permitted under the most recently approved budget for the State.

"(e) CERTIFICATION.—In order to receive a payment under this section for a fiscal year, the State shall provide the Secretary of the Treasury with a certification that the State's proposed uses of the funds are consistent with subsection (d).

"(f) DEFINITION OF STATE.—In this section, the term 'State' means the 50 States, the District of Columbia, the Commonwealth of Puerto Rico, the United States Virgin Islands, Guam, the Commonwealth of the Northern Mariana Islands, and American Samoa.

"(g) REPEAL.—Effective as of October 1, 2004, this title is repealed.".

[CCH Explanation at ¶ 240. Committee Reports at ¶ 10,120.]

TITLE V—CORPORATE ESTIMATED TAX PAYMENTS FOR 2003

[¶ 7045] ACT SEC. 501. TIME FOR PAYMENT OF CORPORATE ESTIMATED TAXES.

Notwithstanding section 6655 of the Internal Revenue Code of 1986, 25 percent of the amount of any required installment of corporate estimated tax which is otherwise due in September 2003 shall not be due until October 1, 2003.

[CCH Explanation at ¶ 375. Committee Reports at ¶ 10,130.]

Committee Reports

Jobs and Growth Tax Relief Reconciliation Act of 2003

Introduction

[¶ 10,001]

The "Jobs and Growth Tax Act of 2003" was introduced in the House of Representatives (House) on February 27, 2003, as H.R. 2. The House Ways and Means Committee favorably reported an amendment in the nature of a substitute to H.R. 2, which retitled the act as the "Jobs and Growth Reconciliation Tax Act of 2003," on May 8, 2003 (H.R. REP. NO. 108-94). On May 9, 2003, the House adopted amendments by voice vote and passed the bill. A reconciliation tax cut package, the "Jobs and Growth Tax Relief Reconciliation Act of 2003" (S. 1054), was favorably reported by the Senate Finance Committee (SFC) on May 13, 2003, without a published official report. S. 1054 replaced an earlier Senate version of a reconciliation tax bill (S. 2) because a parliamentarian ruling on May 12, 2003, forced the SFC to correct a technical glitch and report the measure out of committee as an original bill.

On May 15, 2003, the Senate approved an amended version of the "Jobs and Growth Tax Relief Reconciliation Act of 2003" (H.R. 2). A manager's amendment was inserted prior to the final vote and was approved by voice vote. The Senate insisted on its version of the legislation and requested a conference with the House to reconcile differences.

A conference report on H.R. 2 was filed in the House on May 22, 2003 (H.R. CONF. REP. NO. 108-126). The House and Senate passed the conference agreement on May 23, 2003.

This section includes the pertinent text of committee reports that provide guidance for the tax law changes enacted in the Jobs and Growth Tax Relief Reconciliation Act of 2003. The following material is the official wording of the relevant House and Conference committee reports accompanying the 2003 Act. In one instance, an excerpt from the Congressional Record is included to aid in the reader's understanding of the relevant provision. Headings have been added for convenience. Any omission of text is indicated by asterisks (* * *). References are to the following official reports:

- The Jobs and Growth Tax Relief Reconciliation Act of 2003 (H.R. 2) House Ways and Means Committee Report, reported on May 8, 2003, is referred to as **House Committee Report** (H.R. REP. NO. 108-94).

- Senate debate on the Jobs and Growth Tax Relief Reconciliation Act of 2003, as included in the Congressional Record on May 15, 2003, is referred to as **Senate Floor Debate** (149 CONG. REC. 73, S6414), May 15, 2003.

- The Conference Committee Report on the Jobs and Growth Tax Relief Reconciliation Act of 2003, as released on May 23, 2003, is referred to as **Conference Committee Report** (H.R. CONF. REP. NO. 108-126).

¶ 10,001

160 Jobs and Growth Tax Relief Reconciliation Act of 2003

[¶ 10,010]   Act Sec. 101.   Accelerate the increase in the child tax credit

Conference Committee Report (H.R. CONF. REP. NO. 108-126)

[Code Sec. 24 and New Code Sec. 6429]

Present Law

In general

For 2003, an individual may claim a $600 tax credit for each qualifying child under the age of 17. In general, a qualifying child is an individual for whom the taxpayer can claim a dependency exemption and who is the taxpayer's son or daughter (or descendent of either), stepson or stepdaughter (or descendent of either), or eligible foster child.

The child tax credit is scheduled to increase to $1,000, phased-in over several years.

Table 1, below, shows the scheduled increases of the child tax credit as provided under the Economic Growth and Tax Relief Reconciliation Act of 2001 ("EGTRRA").

Table 1.—Scheduled Increase of the Child Tax Credit

Taxable Year	Credit Amount Per Child
2003–2004	$600
2005–2008	$700
2009	$800
2010[1]	$1,000

[1] The credit reverts to $500 in taxable years beginning after December 31, 2010, under the sunset provision of EGTRRA.

The child tax credit is phased-out for individuals with income over certain thresholds. Specifically, the otherwise allowable child tax credit is reduced by $50 for each $1,000 (or fraction thereof) of modified adjusted gross income over $75,000 for single individuals or heads of households, $110,000 for married individuals filing joint returns, and $55,000 for married individuals filing separate returns.[1] The length of the phase-out range depends on the number of qualifying children. For example, the phase-out range for a single individual with one qualifying child is between $75,000 and $87,000 of modified adjusted gross income. The phase-out range for a single individual with two qualifying children is between $75,000 and $99,000.

The amount of the tax credit and the phase-out ranges are not adjusted annually for inflation.

Refundability

For 2003, the child credit is refundable to the extent of 10 percent of the taxpayer's earned income in excess of $10,500.[2] The percentage is increased to 15 percent for taxable years 2005 and thereafter. Families with three or more children are allowed a refundable credit for the amount by which the taxpayer's social security taxes exceed the taxpayer's earned income credit, if that amount is greater than the refundable credit based on the taxpayer's earned income in excess of $10,500 (for 2003). The refundable portion of the child credit does not constitute income and is not treated as resources for purposes of determining eligibility or the amount or nature of benefits or assistance under any Federal program or any State or local program financed with Federal funds. For taxable years beginning after December 31, 2010, the sunset provision of EGTRRA applies to the rules allowing refundable child credits.

Alternative minimum tax liability

The child credit is allowed against the individual's regular income tax and alternative minimum tax. For taxable years beginning after December 31, 2010, the sunset provision of EGTRRA applies to the rules allowing the child credit against the alternative minimum tax.

House Bill

Under the House bill, the amount of the child credit is increased to $1,000 for 2003 through 2005.[3] After 2005, the child credit will revert to the levels provided under present law. For 2003, the increased amount of the child credit will be paid in advance beginning in July, 2003, on the basis of information on each taxpayer's 2002 return filed in 2003. Such payments will be made in a manner similar to the advance payment checks issued by the Treasury in 2001 to reflect the

---

[1] Modified adjusted gross income is the taxpayer's total gross income plus certain amounts excluded from gross income (i.e., excluded income of: U.S. citizens or residents living abroad (sec. 911), residents of Guam, American Samoa, and the Northern Mariana Islands (sec. 931), and residents of Puerto Rico (sec. 933)).

[2] The $10,500 amount is indexed for inflation.
[3] The increase in refundability to 15 percent of the taxpayer's earned income, scheduled for calendar years 2005 and thereafter, is not accelerated under the provision.

¶ 10,010   Act Sec. 101

Committee Reports

creation of the 10-percent regular income tax rate bracket.

Effective Date

The House bill provision is effective for taxable years beginning after December 31, 2002, and before January 1, 2006.

Senate Amendment

The amount of the child credit is increased to $1,000 for 2003 and thereafter. For 2003, the increased amount of the child credit will be paid in advance beginning in July 2003 on the basis of information on each taxpayer's 2002 return filed in 2003. Advance payments will be made in a similar manner to the advance payment checks issued by the Treasury in 2001 to reflect the creation of the 10-percent regular income tax rate bracket. The increase in the refundable portion of the credit from 10 percent to 15 percent of the taxpayer's earned income in excess of the threshold amount is accelerated to 2003 from 2005.

Effective Date

The Senate amendment provision is effective for taxable years beginning after December 31, 2002.

Conference Agreement

Under the conference agreement, the amount of the child credit is increased to $1,000 for 2003 and 2004.[4] After 2004, the child credit will revert to the levels provided under present law. For 2003, the increased amount of the child credit will be paid in advance beginning in July, 2003, on the basis of information on each taxpayer's 2002 return filed in 2003. The IRS is not expected to issue advance payment checks to an individual who did not claim the child credit for 2002. Such payments will be made in a manner similar to the advance payment checks issued by the Treasury in 2001 to reflect the creation of the 10-percent regular income tax rate bracket.

Effective Date

The conference agreement provision is effective for taxable years beginning after December 31, 2002, and before January 1, 2005.

[Law at ¶ 5010 and ¶ 5120. CCH Explanation at ¶ 225.]

[¶ 10,020] Act Sec. 102. Accelerate the expansion of the 15-percent rate bracket for married couples filing joint returns

Conference Committee Report (H.R. CONF. REP. NO. 108-126)

[Code Sec. 1(f)]

Present Law

In general

Under the Federal individual income tax system, an individual who is a citizen or resident of the United States generally is subject to tax on worldwide taxable income. Taxable income is total gross income less certain exclusions, exemptions, and deductions. An individual may claim either a standard deduction or itemized deductions.

An individual's income tax liability is determined by computing his or her regular income tax liability and, if applicable, alternative minimum tax liability.

Regular income tax liability

Regular income tax liability is determined by applying the regular income tax rate schedules (or tax tables) to the individual's taxable income and then is reduced by any applicable tax credits. The regular income tax rate schedules are divided into several ranges of income, known as income brackets, and the marginal tax rate increases as the individual's income increases. The income bracket amounts are adjusted annually for inflation. Separate rate schedules apply based on filing status: single individuals (other than heads of households and surviving spouses), heads of households, married individuals filing joint returns (including surviving spouses), married individuals filing separate returns, and estates and trusts. Lower rates may apply to capital gains.

In general, the bracket breakpoints for single individuals are approximately 60 percent of the rate bracket breakpoints for married couples filing joint returns.[8] The rate bracket breakpoints for married individuals filing separate returns are exactly one-half of the rate brackets for married individuals filing joint returns. A separate, compressed rate schedule applies to estates and trusts.

15-percent regular income tax rate bracket

EGTRRA increased the size of the 15-percent regular income tax rate bracket for a married couple filing a joint return to twice the size of the corresponding rate bracket for a single individual filing a single return. The increase is phased-in over four years, beginning in 2005. Therefore, this provision is fully effective (i.e., the size of the 15-percent regular income tax rate bracket for a married couple filing a joint return is twice the size of the 15-percent regular income tax rate bracket for an unmarried individual filing a single

---

[4] The increase in refundability to 15 percent of the taxpayer's earned income, scheduled for calendar years 2005 and thereafter, is not accelerated under the provision.

[8] Under present law, the rate bracket breakpoint for the 38.6 percent marginal tax rate is the same for single individuals and married couples filing joint returns.

162 Jobs and Growth Tax Relief Reconciliation Act of 2003

return) for taxable years beginning after December 31, 2007. Table 3, below, shows the increase in the size of the 15-percent bracket during the phase-in period.

Table 3.—Scheduled Increase in Size of the 15-Percent Rate Bracket for Married Couples Filing Joint Returns

Taxable year	End Point of 15-Percent Rate Bracket for Married Couples Filing Joint Returns as Percentage of End Point of 15-Percent Rate Bracket for Unmarried Individuals
2005	180
2006	187
2007	193
2008 through 2010[1]	200

[1] The increases in the 15-percent rate bracket for married couples filing a joint return are repealed for taxable years beginning after December 31, 2010, under the sunset of EGTRRA.

House Bill

The House bill accelerates the increase of the size of the 15-percent regular income tax rate bracket for joint returns to twice the width of the 15-percent regular income tax rate bracket for single returns for taxable years beginning in 2003, 2004, and 2005. For taxable years beginning after 2005, the applicable percentages will revert to those allowed under present law, as described above.

Effective Date

The House bill provision is effective for taxable years beginning after December 31, 2002, and before January 1, 2006.

Senate Amendment

The Senate amendment increases in the size of the 15-percent regular income tax rate bracket for joint returns to 195 percent of the size of the 15-percent regular income tax rate bracket for single returns effective for 2003. The Senate amendment also increases in the size of the 15-percent regular income tax rate bracket for joint returns to twice the size of the 15-percent regular income tax rate bracket for single returns effective for 2004. For taxable years beginning after 2004, the applicable percentages will revert to those allowed under present law, as described above.

Effective Date

The provision is effective for taxable years beginning after December 31, 2002 and before January 1, 2005.

Conference Agreement

The conference agreement increases of the size of the 15-percent regular income tax rate bracket for joint returns to twice the width of the 15-percent regular income tax rate bracket for single returns for taxable years beginning in 2003 and 2004. For taxable years beginning after 2004, the applicable percentages will revert to those allowed under present law, as described above.

Effective Date

The conference agreement provision is effective for taxable years beginning after December 31, 2002, and before January 1, 2005.

[Law at ¶ 5005 and ¶ 7010. CCH Explanation at ¶ 215.]

[¶ 10,030] Act Sec. 103. Standard deduction marriage penalty relief

Conference Committee Report (H.R. Conf. Rep. No. 108-126)

[Code Sec. 63(c)]

Present Law

Marriage penalty

A married couple generally is treated as one tax unit that must pay tax on the couple's total taxable income. Although married couples may elect to file separate returns, the rate schedules and other provisions are structured so that filing separate returns usually results in a higher tax than filing a joint return. Other rate schedules apply to single persons and to single heads of households.

A "marriage penalty" exists when the combined tax liability of a married couple filing a joint return is greater than the sum of the tax liabilities of each individual computed as if they were not married. A "marriage bonus" exists when the combined tax liability of a married couple filing a joint return is less than the sum of the tax liabilities of each individual computed as if they were not married.

Basic standard deduction

Taxpayers who do not itemize deductions may choose the basic standard deduction (and addi-

¶ 10,030 Act Sec. 103

tional standard deductions, if applicable),[5] which is subtracted from adjusted gross income ("AGI") in arriving at taxable income. The size of the basic standard deduction varies according to filing status and is adjusted annually for inflation.[6] For 2003, the basic standard deduction for married couples filing a joint return is 167 percent of the basic standard deduction for single filers. (Alternatively, the basic standard deduction amount for single filers is 60 percent of the basic standard deduction amount for married couples filing joint returns.) Thus, two unmarried individuals have standard deductions whose sum exceeds the standard deduction for a married couple filing a joint return.

EGTRRA increased the basic standard deduction for a married couple filing a joint return to twice the basic standard deduction for an unmarried individual filing a single return.[7] The increase in the standard deduction for married taxpayers filing a joint return is scheduled to be phased-in over five years beginning in 2005 and will be fully phased-in for 2009 and thereafter. Table 2, below, shows the standard deduction for married couples filing a joint return as a percentage of the standard deduction for single individuals during the phase-in period.

Table 2.—Scheduled Phase-In of Increase of the Basic Standard Deduction for Married Couples Filing Joint Returns

Taxable Year	Standard Deduction for Married Couples Filing Joint Returns as Percentage of Standard Deduction for Unmarried Individual Returns
2005	174
2006	184
2007	187
2008	190
2009 and 2010[1]	200

[1]The basic standard deduction increases are repealed for taxable years beginning after December 31, 2010, under the sunset provision of EGTRRA.

House Bill

The House bill accelerates the increase in the basic standard deduction amount for joint returns to twice the basic standard deduction amount for single returns effective for 2003, 2004, and 2005. For taxable years beginning after 2005, the applicable percentages will revert to those allowed under present law, as described above.

Effective Date

The House bill provision is effective for taxable years beginning after December 31, 2002, and before January 1, 2006.

Senate Amendment

The Senate amendment increases in the basic standard deduction amount for joint returns to 195 percent of the basic standard deduction amount for single returns effective for 2003. The Senate amendment also increases in the basic standard deduction amount for joint returns to twice the basic standard deduction amount for single returns effective for 2004. For taxable years beginning after 2004, the applicable percentages will revert to those allowed under present law, as described above.

Effective Date

The Senate amendment provision is effective for taxable years beginning after December 31, 2002 and before January 1, 2005.

Conference Agreement

The conference agreement increases the basic standard deduction amount for joint returns to twice the basic standard deduction amount for single returns effective for 2003 and 2004. For taxable years beginning after 2004, the applicable percentages will revert to those allowed under present law, as described above.

---

[5] Additional standard deductions are allowed with respect to any individual who is elderly (age 65 or over) or blind.

[6] For 2003 the basic standard deduction amounts are: (1) $4,750 for unmarried individuals; (2) $7,950 for married individuals filing a joint return; (3) $7,000 for heads of households; and (4) $3,975 for married individuals filing separately.

[7] The basic standard deduction for a married taxpayer filing separately will continue to equal one-half of the basic standard deduction for a married couple filing jointly; thus, the basic standard deduction for unmarried individuals filing a single return and for married couples filing separately will be the same after the phase-in period.

Act Sec. 103   ¶ 10,030

Jobs and Growth Tax Relief Reconciliation Act of 2003

Effective Date

The conference agreement provision is effective for taxable years beginning after December 31, 2002, and before January 1, 2005.

[Law at ¶ 5025 and ¶ 7015. CCH Explanation at ¶ 220.]

[¶ 10,040]   Act Sec. 101 [104].   **Accelerate reductions in individual income tax rates (ten-percent regular income tax rate)**

Conference Committee Report (H.R. CONF. REP. NO. 108-126)

[Code Sec. 1]

Present Law

In general

Under the Federal individual income tax system, an individual who is a citizen or a resident of the United States generally is subject to tax on worldwide taxable income. Taxable income is total gross income less certain exclusions, exemptions, and deductions. An individual may claim either a standard deduction or itemized deductions.

An individual's income tax liability is determined by computing his or her regular income tax liability and, if applicable, alternative minimum tax liability.

* * *

Ten-percent regular income tax rate

Under present law, the 10-percent rate applies to the first $6,000 of taxable income for single individuals, $10,000 of taxable income for heads of households, and $12,000 of taxable income for married couples filing joint returns. Effective beginning in 2008, the $6,000 amount will increase to $7,000 and the $12,000 amount will increase to $14,000.

The taxable income levels for the 10-percent rate bracket will be adjusted annually for inflation for taxable years beginning after December 31, 2008. The bracket for single individuals and married individuals filing separately is one-half for joint returns (after adjustment of that bracket for inflation).

The 10-percent rate bracket will expire for taxable years beginning after December 31, 2010, under the sunset provision of the Economic Growth and Tax Relief Reconciliation Act of 2001 ("EGTRRA").

* * *

House Bill

Ten-percent regular income tax rate

The House bill accelerates the increase in the taxable income levels for the 10-percent rate bracket now scheduled for 2008 to be effective in 2003, 2004, and 2005. Specifically, for 2003, 2004, and 2005, the proposal increases the taxable income level for the 10-percent regular income tax rate brackets for unmarried individuals from $6,000 to $7,000 and for married individuals filing jointly from $12,000 to $14,000. The taxable income levels for the 10-percent regular income tax rate bracket will be adjusted annually for inflation for taxable years beginning after December 31, 2003.

For taxable years beginning after December 31, 2005, the taxable income levels for the 10-percent rate bracket will revert to the levels allowed under present law. Therefore, for 2006 and 2007, the levels will revert to $6,000 for unmarried individuals and $12,000 for married individuals filing jointly. In 2008, the taxable income levels for the 10-percent regular income tax rate brackets will be $7,000 for unmarried individuals and $14,000 for married individuals filing jointly. The taxable income levels for the 10-percent rate bracket will be adjusted annually for inflation for taxable years beginning after December 31, 2008.

* * *

Effective Date

The House bill provision is effective for taxable years beginning after December 31, 2002 and before January 1, 2006.

Senate Amendment

Ten-percent regular income tax rate

The Senate amendment accelerates the scheduled increase in the taxable income levels for the 10-percent rate bracket. Specifically, beginning in 2003, the Senate amendment increases the taxable income level for the 10-percent regular income tax rate brackets for single individuals from $6,000 to $7,000 and for married individuals filing jointly from $12,000 to $14,000. The taxable income levels for the 10-percent regular income tax rate bracket will be adjusted annually for inflation for taxable years beginning after December 31, 2003.

* * *

Effective Date

The Senate amendment provision is effective for taxable years beginning after December 31, 2002 and before January 1, 2006.

Conference Agreement

Ten-percent regular income tax rate

The conference agreement accelerates the increase in the taxable income levels for the 10-percent rate bracket now scheduled for 2008 to be effective in 2003 and 2004. Specifically, for 2003 and 2004, the conference agreement increases the taxable income level for the 10-percent regular income tax rate brackets for unmarried individuals from $6,000 to $7,000 and for married individ-

¶ 10,040   Act Sec. 101

uals filing jointly from $12,000 to $14,000. The taxable income levels for the 10-percent regular income tax rate bracket will be adjusted annually for inflation for taxable years beginning after December 31, 2003.

For taxable years beginning after December 31, 2004, the taxable income levels for the 10-percent rate bracket will revert to the levels allowed under present law. Therefore, for 2005, 2006, and 2007, the levels will revert to $6,000 for unmarried individuals and $12,000 for married individuals filing jointly. In 2008, the taxable income levels for the 10-percent regular income tax rate brackets will be $7,000 for unmarried individuals and $14,000 for married individuals filing jointly. The taxable income levels for the 10-percent rate bracket will be adjusted annually for inflation for taxable years beginning after December 31, 2008.

* * *

Effective Date

The conference agreement generally is effective for taxable years beginning after December 31, 2002. The conferees recognize that withholding at statutorily mandated rates (such as pursuant to backup withholding under section 3406) has already occurred. The conferees intend that taxpayers who have been overwithheld as a consequence of this obtain a refund of this overwithholding through the normal process of filing an income tax return, and not through the payor. In addition, the conferees anticipate that the Treasury will provide a brief, reasonable period of transition for payors to implement these changes in these statutorily mandated withholding rates.

[Law at ¶ 5005 and ¶ 7020. CCH Explanation at ¶ 210.]

[¶ 10,050]   Act Sec. 102 [105].   **Accelerate reductions in individual income tax rates (regular income tax liability)**

Conference Committee Report (H.R. CONF. REP. NO. 108-126)

[Code Sec. 1]

Present Law

In general

Under the Federal individual income tax system, an individual who is a citizen or a resident of the United States generally is subject to tax on worldwide taxable income. Taxable income is total gross income less certain exclusions, exemptions, and deductions. An individual may claim either a standard deduction or itemized deductions.

An individual's income tax liability is determined by computing his or her regular income tax liability and, if applicable, alternative minimum tax liability.

Regular income tax liability

Regular income tax liability is determined by applying the regular income tax rate schedules (or tax tables) to the individual's taxable income. This tax liability is then reduced by any applicable tax credits. The regular income tax rate schedules are divided into several ranges of income, known as income brackets, and the marginal tax rate increases as the individual's income increases. The income bracket amounts are adjusted annually for inflation. Separate rate schedules apply based on filing status: single individuals (other than heads of households and surviving spouses), heads of households, married individuals filing joint returns (including surviving spouses), married individuals filing separate returns, and estates and trusts. Lower rates may apply to capital gains.

For 2003, the regular income tax rate schedules for individuals are shown in Table 4, below. The rate bracket breakpoints for married individuals filing separate returns are exactly one-half of the rate brackets for married individuals filing joint returns. A separate, compressed rate schedule applies to estates and trusts.

Table 4.—Individual Regular Income Tax Rates for 2003

If taxable income is over:	But not over:	Then regular income tax equals:
	Single Individuals	
$0	$6,000	10% of taxable income
$6,000	$28,400	$600, plus 15% of the amount over $6,000
$28,400	$68,800	$3,960.00, plus 27% of the amount over $28,400
$68,800	$143,500	$14,868.00, plus 30% of the amount over $68,800
$143,500	$311,950	$37,278.00, plus 35% of the amount over $143,500
Over 311,950		$96,235.50, plus 38.6% of the amount over $311,950

Act Sec. 102   ¶ 10,050

Jobs and Growth Tax Relief Reconciliation Act of 2003

Head of Households

$0	$10,000	10% of taxable income
$10,000	$38,050	$1,000, plus 15% of the amount over $10,000
$38,050	$98,250	$5,207.50, plus 27% of the amount over $38,050
$98,250	$159,100	$21,461.50, plus 30% of the amount over $98,250
$159,100	$311,950	$39,716.50, plus 35% of the amount over $159,100
Over 311,950		$93,214, plus 38.6% of the amount over $311,950

Married Individuals Filing Joint Returns

$0	$12,000	10% of taxable income
$12,000	$47,450	$1,200, plus 15% of the amount over $12,000
$47,450	$114,650	$6,517.50, plus 27% of the amount over $47,450
$114,650	$174,700	$24,661.50, plus 30% of the amount over $114,650
$174,700	$311,950	$42,676.50, plus 35% of the amount over $174,700
Over 311,950		$90,714, plus 38.6% of the amount over $311,950

* * *

Reduction of other regular income tax rates

Prior to EGTRRA, the regular income tax rates were 15 percent, 28 percent, 31 percent, 36 percent, and 39.6 percent.[9] EGTRRA added the 10-percent regular income tax rate, described above, and retained the 15-percent regular income tax rate. Also, the 15-percent regular income tax bracket was modified to begin at the end of the 10-percent regular income tax bracket. EGTRRA also made other changes to the 15-percent regular income tax bracket.[10]

Also, under EGTRRA, the 28 percent, 31 percent, 36 percent, and 39.6 percent rates are phased down over six years to 25 percent, 28 percent, 33 percent, and 35 percent, effective after June 30, 2001. The taxable income levels for the rates above the 15-percent rate in all taxable years are the same as the taxable income levels that apply under the prior-law rates.

Table 5, below, shows the schedule of regular income tax rate reductions.

Table 5.—Scheduled Regular Income Tax Rate Reductions

Taxable Year	28% rate reduced to:	31% rate reduced to:	36% rate reduced to:	39.6% rate reduced to:
2001[1]-2003	27%	30%	35%	38.6%
2004-2005	26%	29%	34%	37.6%
2006 thru 2010[2]	25%	28%	33%	35.0%

[1] Effective July 1, 2001.

[2] The reduction in the regular income tax rates are repealed for taxable years beginning after December 31, 2010, under the sunset provision of EGTRRA.

* * *

House Bill
* * *

Reduction of other regular income tax rates

The House bill accelerates the reductions in the regular income tax rates in excess of the 15-percent regular income tax rate that are scheduled for 2004 and 2006. Therefore, for 2003 and thereafter, the regular income tax rates in excess of 15 percent under the bill are 25 percent, 28 percent, 33 percent, and 35 percent.

* * *

Effective Date

The House bill provision is effective for taxable years beginning after December 31, 2002 and before January 1, 2006.

Senate Amendment
* * *

---

[9] The regular income tax rates will revert to these percentages for taxable years beginning after December 31, 2010, under the sunset of EGTRRA.

[10] See the discussion of the provision regarding marriage penalty relief in the 15-percent regular income tax bracket, above.

¶ 10,050   Act Sec. 102

Reduction of other regular income tax rates

The Senate amendment accelerates the reductions in the regular income tax rates in excess of the 15-percent regular income tax rate that are scheduled for 2004 and 2006. Therefore, for 2003 and thereafter, the regular income tax rates in excess of 15 percent under the bill are 25 percent, 28 percent, 33 percent, and 35 percent.

* * *

Effective Date

The Senate amendment provision is effective for taxable years beginning after December 31, 2002 and before January 1, 2006.

Conference Agreement

* * *

Reduction of other regular income tax rates

The conference agreement follows the House bill and the Senate amendment.

* * *

Effective Date

The conference agreement generally is effective for taxable years beginning after December 31, 2002. The conferees recognize that withholding at statutorily mandated rates (such as pursuant to backup withholding under section 3406) has already occurred. The conferees intend that taxpayers who have been overwithheld as a consequence of this obtain a refund of this overwithholding through the normal process of filing an income tax return, and not through the payor. In addition, the conferees anticipate that the Treasury will provide a brief, reasonable period of transition for payors to implement these changes in these statutorily mandated withholding rates.

[Law at ¶ 5005. CCH Explanation at ¶ 205.]

[¶ 10,060] Act Sec. 103 [106]. Accelerate reductions in individual income tax rates (alternative minimum tax)

Conference Committee Report (H.R. Conf. Rep. No. 108-126)

[Code Sec. 55]

Present Law

* * *

In general

An individual's income tax liability is determined by computing his or her regular income tax liability and, if applicable, alternative minimum tax liability.

* * *

Alternative minimum tax

The alternative minimum tax is the amount by which the tentative minimum tax exceeds the regular income tax. An individual's tentative minimum tax is an amount equal to (1) 26 percent of the first $175,000 ($87,500 in the case of a married individual filing a separate return) of alternative minimum taxable income ("AMTI") in excess of a phased-out exemption amount and (2) 28 percent of the remaining AMTI. The maximum tax rates on net capital gain used in computing the tentative minimum tax are the same as under the regular tax. AMTI is the individual's taxable income adjusted to take account of specified preferences and adjustments. The exemption amounts are: (1) $49,000 ($45,000 in taxable years beginning after 2004) in the case of married individuals filing a joint return and surviving spouses; (2) $35,750 ($33,750 in taxable years beginning after 2004) in the case of other unmarried individuals; (3) $24,500 ($22,500 in taxable years beginning after 2004) in the case of married individuals filing a separate return; and (4) $22,500 in the case of an estate or trust. The exemption amounts are phased out by an amount equal to 25 percent of the amount by which the individual's AMTI exceeds (1) $150,000 in the case of married individuals filing a joint return and surviving spouses, (2) $112,500 in the case of other unmarried individuals, and (3) $75,000 in the case of married individuals filing separate returns or an estate or a trust. These amounts are not indexed for inflation.

House Bill

* * *

Alternative minimum tax exemption amounts

The House bill increases the AMT exemption amount for married taxpayers filing a joint return and surviving spouses to $64,000, and for unmarried taxpayers to $43,250, for taxable years beginning in 2003, 2004, and 2005.

Effective Date

The House bill provision is effective for taxable years beginning after December 31, 2002 and before January 1, 2006.

Senate Amendment

* * *

Alternative minimum tax exemption amounts

The Senate amendment increases the AMT exemption amount for married taxpayers filing a joint return and surviving spouses to $60,500, and for unmarried taxpayers to $41,500, for taxable years beginning in 2003, 2004, and 2005.

Effective Date

The Senate amendment provision is effective for taxable years beginning after December 31, 2002 and before January 1, 2006.

Jobs and Growth Tax Relief Reconciliation Act of 2003

Conference Agreement

* * *

Alternative minimum tax exemption amounts

The conference agreement increases the AMT exemption amount for married taxpayers filing a joint return and surviving spouses to $58,000, and for unmarried taxpayers to $40,250 for taxable years beginning in 2003 and 2004.

Effective Date

The conference agreement generally is effective for taxable years beginning after December 31, 2002.

* * *

[Law at ¶ 5015. CCH Explanation at ¶ 230.]

[¶ 10,070] Act Sec. 1001 [107]. Termination of certain provisions

Conference Committee Report (H.R. Conf. Rep. No. 108-126)

[Caution: The provision of the Joint Explanatory Statement of the Committee of Conference pertaining to section 1001 of the Senate amendment, below, is included to assist the reader's understanding. Section 1001 of the Senate amendment was not included in the conference agreement.—CCH.]

[Act Sec. 107]

Present Law

Budget reconciliation is a procedure under the Congressional Budget Act of 1974 (the "Budget Act") by which Congress implements spending and tax policies contained in a budget resolution. The Budget Act contains numerous rules enforcing the scope of items permitted to be considered under the budget reconciliation process. One such rule, the so-called "Byrd rule," was incorporated into the Budget Act in 1990. The Byrd rule, named after its principal sponsor, Senator Robert C. Byrd, is contained in section 313 of the Budget Act. The Byrd rule generally permits members to raise a point of order against extraneous provisions (those which are unrelated to the goals of the reconciliation process) from either a reconciliation bill or a conference report on such bill.

Under the Byrd rule, a provision is considered to be extraneous if it falls under one or more of the following six definitions: (1) it does not produce a change in outlays or revenues; (2) it produces an outlay increase or revenue decrease when the instructed committee is not in compliance with its instructions; (3) it is outside of the jurisdiction of the committee that submitted the title or provision for inclusion in the reconciliation measure; (4) it produces a change in outlays or revenues which is merely incidental to the nonbudgetary components of the provision; (5) it would increase the deficit for a fiscal year beyond those covered by the reconciliation measure; or (6) it recommends changes in Social Security.

House Bill

No provision.

Senate Amendment

To ensure compliance with the Budget Act, the Senate amendment provides that certain provisions of, and amendments made by, the bill do not apply for taxable years beginning after December 31, 2012.

Effective Date

The Senate amendment provision is effective on the date of enactment.

Conference Agreement

The conference agreement does not include the Senate amendment.

The conference agreement does not modify the application of the Economic Growth Tax Reconciliation Relief Act of 2001 ("EGTRRA") sunset provision. The EGTRRA provision is contained in Title IX of Pub. L. No. 107-16.

[Law at ¶ 7025. CCH Explanation at ¶ 29,001.]

[¶ 10,080] Act Sec. 201. Special depreciation allowance for certain property

House Committee Report (H.R. Rep. No. 108-94)

[Code Sec. 168(k)]

Present Law

In general

A taxpayer is allowed to recover, through annual depreciation deductions, the cost of certain property used in a trade or business or for the production of income. The amount of the depreciation deduction allowed with respect to tangible property for a taxable year is determined under the modified accelerated cost recovery system ("MACRS"). Under MACRS, different types of property generally are assigned applicable recovery periods and depreciation methods. The recovery periods applicable to most tangible personal property (generally tangible property other than residential rental property and nonresidential real property) range from 3 to 25 years. The depreciation methods generally applicable to tangible per-

¶ 10,070   Act Sec. 1001

sonal property are the 200-percent and 150-percent declining balance methods, switching to the straight-line method for the taxable year in which the depreciation deduction would be maximized.

Section 280F limits the annual depreciation deductions with respect to passenger automobiles to specified dollar amounts, indexed for inflation.

Section 167(f)(1) provides that capitalized computer software costs, other than computer software to which section 197 applies, are recovered ratably over 36 months.

In lieu of depreciation, a taxpayer with a sufficiently small amount of annual investment generally may elect to deduct up to $25,000 of the cost of qualifying property placed in service for the taxable year (sec. 179). In general, qualifying property is defined as depreciable tangible personal property that is purchased for use in the active conduct of a trade or business.

Additional first year depreciation deduction

The Job Creation and Worker Assistance Act of 2002[10] ("JCWAA") allows an additional first-year depreciation deduction equal to 30 percent of the adjusted basis of qualified property.[11] The amount of the additional first-year depreciation deduction is not affected by a short taxable year. The additional first-year depreciation deduction is allowed for both regular tax and alternative minimum tax purposes for the taxable year in which the property is placed in service.[12] The basis for the property and the depreciation allowances in the year of purchase and later years are appropriately adjusted to reflect the additional first-year depreciation deduction. In addition, there are no adjustments to the allowable amount of depreciation for purposes of computing a taxpayer's alternative minimum taxable income with respect to property to which the provision applies. A taxpayer is allowed to elect out of the additional first-year depreciation for any class of property for any taxable year.

In order for property to qualify for the additional first-year depreciation deduction it must meet all of the following requirements. First, the property must be property (1) to which MACRS applies with an applicable recovery period of 20 years or less, (2) water utility property (as defined in section 168(e)(5)), (3) computer software other than computer software covered by section 197, or (4) qualified leasehold improvement property (as defined in section 168(k)(3)).[13] Second, the original use[14] of the property must commence with the taxpayer on or after September 11, 2001.[15] Third, the taxpayer must purchase the property within the applicable time period. Finally, the property must be placed in service before January 1, 2005. An extension of the placed in service date of one year (i.e., January 1, 2006) is provided for certain property with a recovery period of ten years or longer and certain transportation property.[16] Transportation property is defined as tangible personal property used in the trade or business of transporting persons or property.

The applicable time period for acquired property is (1) after September 10, 2001 and before September 11, 2004, but only if no binding written contract for the acquisition is in effect before September 11, 2001, or (2) pursuant to a binding written contract which was entered into after September 10, 2001, and before September 11, 2004.[17] With respect to property that is manufactured, constructed, or produced by the taxpayer for use by the taxpayer, the taxpayer must begin the manufacture, construction, or production or the property after September 10, 2001, and before September 11, 2004. Property that is manufactured, constructed, or produced for the taxpayer by another person under a contract that is entered into prior to the manufacture, construction, or production of the property is considered to be manufactured, constructed, or produced by the taxpayer. For property eligible for the extended placed in service date, a special rule limits the amount of costs eligible for the additional first

---

[10] Pub. Law No. 107-147, sec. 101 (2002).
[11] The additional first-year depreciation deduction is subject to the general rules regarding whether an item is deductible under section 162 or subject to capitalization under section 263 or section 263A.
[12] However, the additional first-year depreciation deduction is not allowed for purposes of computing earnings and profits.
[13] A special rule precludes the additional first-year depreciation deduction for any property that is required to be depreciated under the alternative depreciation system of MACRS.
[14] The term "original use" means the first use to which the property is put, whether or not such use corresponds to the use of such property by the taxpayer. If in the normal course of its business a taxpayer sells fractional interests in property to unrelated third parties, then the original use of such property begins with the first user of each fractional interest (i.e., each fractional owner is considered the original user of its proportionate share of the property.
[15] A special rule applies in the case of certain leased property. In the case of any property that is originally placed in service by a person and that is sold to the taxpayer and leased back to such person by the taxpayer within three months after the date that the property was placed in service, the property would be treated as originally placed in service by the taxpayer not earlier than the date that the property misused under the lease back.

If property is originally placed in service by a lessor (including by operation of section 168(k)(2)(D)(i)), such property is sold within three months after the date that the property was placed service, and the user of such property does not change, then the property is treated as originally placed in service by the taxpayer not earlier than the date of such sale. A technical correction may be needed so the statute reflects this intent.
[16] In order for property to qualify for the extended placed in service data, the property is required to have a production period exceeding two years or an estimated production period exceeding one year and a cost exceeding $1 million.
[17] Property does not fail to qualify for the additional first-year depreciation merely because a binding written contract to acquire a component of the property is in effect prior to September 11, 2001.

Act Sec. 201   ¶ 10,080

year depreciation. With respect to such property, only the portion of the basis that is properly attributable to the costs incurred before September 11, 2004 ("progress expenditures") is eligible for the additional first-year depreciation.[18]

Property does not qualify for the additional first-year depreciation deduction when the user of such property (or a related party) would not have been eligible for the additional first-year depreciation deduction if the user (or a related party) were treated as the owner.[19] For example, if a taxpayer sells to a related party property that was under construction prior to September 11, 2001, the property does not qualify for the additional first-year depreciation deduction. Similarly, if a taxpayer sells to a related party property that was subject to a binding written contract prior to September 11, 2001, the property does not qualify for the additional first-year depreciation deduction. As a further example, if a taxpayer (the lessee) sells property in a sale-leaseback arrangement, and the property otherwise would not have qualified for the additional first-year depreciation deduction if it were owned by the taxpayer-lessee, then the lessor is not entitled to the additional first-year depreciation deduction.

The limitation on the amount of depreciation deductions allowed with respect to certain passenger automobiles (sec. 280F) is increased in the first year by $4,600 for automobiles that qualify (and do not elect out of the increased first year deduction). The $4,600 increase is not indexed for inflation.

Reasons For Change

The Committee believes that increasing and extending the additional first-year depreciation will accelerate purchases of equipment, promote capital investment, modernization, and growth, and will help to spur an economic recovery. As businesses accelerate their purchases of equipment current employment will increase to produce that equipment. Current business expansion also will increase employment opportunities in the years ahead.

Explanation Of Provision

The provision provides an additional first-year depreciation deduction equal to 50 percent of the adjusted basis of qualified property.[20] Qualified property is defined in the same manner as for purposes of the 30-percent additional first-year depreciation deduction provided by the JCWAA except that the applicable time period for acquisition (or self construction) of the property is modified. In addition, property must be placed in service before January 1, 2006 to qualify.[21] Property eligible for the 50-percent additional first year depreciation deduction is not eligible for the 30-percent additional first year depreciation deduction.

Under the provision, in order to qualify the property must be acquired after May 5, 2003 and before January 1, 2006, and no binding written contract for the acquisition is in effect before May 6, 2003.[22] With respect to property that is manufactured, constructed, or produced by the taxpayer for use by the taxpayer, the taxpayer must begin the manufacture, construction, or production of the property after May 5, 2003. For property eligible for the extended placed in service date (i.e., certain property with a recovery period of ten years or longer and certain transportation property), a special rule limits the amount of costs eligible for the additional first year depreciation. With respect to such property, only progress expenditures properly attributable to the costs incurred before January 1, 2006 shall be eligible for the additional first year depreciation.[23]

The Committee wishes to clarify that the adjusted basis of qualified property acquired by a taxpayer in a like kind exchange or an involuntary conversion is eligible for the additional first year depreciation deduction.

The provision also increases the limitation on the amount of depreciation deductions allowed with respect to certain passenger automobiles (sec. 280F of the Code) in the first year by $9,200 (in lieu of the $4,600 provided under the JCWAA) for automobiles that qualify (and do not elect out of the increased first year deduction). The $9,200 increase is not indexed for inflation.

For property eligible for the present law 30-percent additional first year depreciation, the provision extends the date of the placed in service requirement to property placed in service prior to January 1, 2006 (from January 1, 2005). Thus, property otherwise qualifying for the 30-percent additional first year depreciation deduction will now qualify if placed in service prior to January 1, 2006. The provision also extends the placed in

---

[18] For purposes of determining the amount of eligible progress expenditures, it is intended that rules similar to sec. 46(d)(3) as in effect prior to the Tax Reform Act of 1986 shall apply.

[19] A technical correction may be needed so that the statute reflects this intent.

[20] A taxpayer is permitted to elect out of the additional first-year depreciation deduction for any class of property for any taxable year.

[21] An extension of the placed in service date of one year (i.e., January 1, 2007) is provided for certain property with a recovery period of ten years or longer and certain transportation property as defined for purposes of the JCWAA.

[22] Property does not fail to qualify for the additional first-year depreciation merely because a binding written contract to acquire a component of the property is in effect prior to May 6, 2003. However, no additional first-year depreciation is permitted on any such component. No inference is intended as to the proper treatment of components placed in service under the 30% additional first-year depreciation provided by the JCWAA.

[23] For purposes of determining the amount of eligible progress expenditures, it is intended that rules similar to sec. 46(d)(3) as in effect prior to the Tax Reform Act of 1986 shall apply.

¶ 10,080 Act Sec. 201

Committee Reports

service date requirement for certain property with a recovery period of ten years or longer and certain transportation property to property placed in service prior to January 1, 2007 (instead of January 1, 2006). In addition, progress expenditures eligible for the 30-percent additional first year depreciation is extended to include costs incurred prior to January 1, 2006 (instead of September 11, 2004).

Effective Date

The provision applies to property placed in service after May 5, 2003.

Conference Committee Report (H.R. CONF. REP. NO. 108-126)

Senate Amendment

No provision.

Conference Agreement

The conference agreement follows the House bill provision with the following modifications. The conference agreement terminates the provision one year earlier than under the House bill provision. Thus, all references to January 1, 2007, and January 1, 2006, are modified to January 1, 2006, and January 1, 2005, respectively. In addition, the conference agreement provides that the increase on the amount of depreciation deductions allowed with respect to certain passenger automobiles (sec. 280F of the Code) in the first year is $7,650 for automobiles that qualify. The $7,650 increase is not indexed for inflation.

Effective Date

The conference agreement applies to taxable years ending after May 5, 2003.

[Law at ¶ 5035 and ¶ 5110. CCH Explanation at ¶ 350.]

[¶ 10,090]   Act Sec. 202.   Increase Section 179 expensing

House Committee Report (H.R. REP. NO. 108-94)

[Code Sec. 179]

Present Law

Present law provides that, in lieu of depreciation, a taxpayer with a sufficiently small amount of annual investment may elect to deduct up to $25,000 (for taxable years beginning in 2003 and thereafter) of the cost of qualifying property placed in service for the taxable year (sec. 179).[24] In general, qualifying property is defined as depreciable tangible personal property that is purchased for use in the active conduct of a trade or business. The $25,000 amount is reduced (but not below zero) by the amount by which the cost of qualifying property placed in service during the taxable year exceeds $200,000. An election to expense these items generally is made on the taxpayer's original return for the taxable year to which the election relates, and may be revoked only with the consent of the Commissioner.[25] In general, taxpayers may not elect to expense off-the-shelf computer software.[26]

The amount eligible to be expensed for a taxable year may not exceed the taxable income for a taxable year that is derived from the active conduct of a trade or business (determined without regard to this provision). Any amount that is not allowed as a deduction because of the taxable income limitation may be carried forward to succeeding taxable years (subject to similar limitations). No general business credit under section 38 is allowed with respect to any amount for which a deduction is allowed under section 179.

Reasons For Change

The Committee believes that section 179 expensing provides two important benefits for small businesses. First, it lowers the cost of capital for tangible property used in a trade or business. With a lower cost of capital, the Committee believes small business will invest in more equipment and employ more workers. Second, it eliminates depreciation recordkeeping requirements with respect to expensed property. In order to increase the value of these benefits and to increase the number of taxpayers eligible, the Committee bill increases the amount allowed to be expensed under section 179 and increases the amount of the phase-out threshold, as well as indexing these amounts.

The Committee also believes that purchased computer software should be included in the section 179 expensing provision so that it is not disadvantaged relative to developed software. In addition, the Committee believes that the process of making and revoking section 179 elections should be made simpler and more efficient for taxpayers by eliminating the requirement for the consent of the Commissioner.

Explanation Of Provision

The provision provides that the maximum dollar amount that may be deducted under section

---

[24] Additional section 179 incentives are provided with respect to a qualified property used by a business in the New York Liberty Zone (sec. 1400(f)) or an empowerment zone (sec. 1397A).

[25] Section 179(c)(2).
[26] Section 179(d)(1) requires that property be tangible to be eligible for expensing; in general, computer software is intangible property.

Jobs and Growth Tax Relief Reconciliation Act of 2003

179 is increased to $100,000 for property placed in service in taxable years beginning in 2003, 2004, 2005, 2006, and 2007. In addition, the $200,000 amount is increased to $400,000 for property placed in service in taxable years beginning in 2003, 2004, 2005, 2006, and 2007. The dollar limitations are indexed annually for inflation for taxable years beginning after 2003 and before 2008. The provision also includes off-the-shelf computer software placed in service in a taxable year beginning in 2003, 2004, 2005, 2006, or 2007, as qualifying property. With respect to a taxable year beginning after 2002 and before 2008, the provision permits taxpayers to make or revoke expensing elections on amended returns without the consent of the Commissioner.

Effective Date

The provision is effective for taxable years beginning after December 31, 2002.

Conference Committee Report (H.R. CONF. REP. NO. 108-126)

Senate Amendment

The Senate amendment is the same as the House bill.

Conference Agreement

The conference agreement follows the House bill and the Senate amendment, with modifications. The conference agreement provides that the increase in the dollar limitations, as well as the provision relating to off-the-shelf computer software, apply for property placed in service in taxable years beginning in 2003, 2004, and 2005. The conference agreement provides that the dollar limitations are indexed annually for inflation for taxable years beginning after 2003 and before 2006. With respect to a taxable year beginning after 2002 and before 2006, the conference agreement permits taxpayers to make or revoke expensing elections on amended returns without the consent of the Commissioner.

[Law at ¶ 5040. CCH Explanation at ¶ 355.]

[¶ 10,100]   Act Sec. 301 and Act Sec. 303.   Reduce individual capital gains rates

House Committee Report (H.R. REP. NO. 108-94)

[Code Sec. 1(h), Code Sec. 55(b), Code Sec. 57(a), Code Sec. 1445(e) and Code Sec. 7518(g)]

Present Law

In general, gain or loss reflected in the value of an asset is not recognized for income tax purposes until a taxpayer disposes of the asset. On the sale or exchange of a capital asset, any gain generally is included in income. Any net capital gain of an individual is taxed at maximum rates lower than the rates applicable to ordinary income. Net capital gain is the excess of the net long-term capital gain for the taxable year over the net short-term capital loss for the year. Gain or loss is treated as long-term if the asset is held for more than one year.

Capital losses generally are deductible in full against capital gains. In addition, individual taxpayers may deduct capital losses against up to $3,000 of ordinary income in each year. Any remaining unused capital losses may be carried forward indefinitely to another taxable year.

A capital asset generally means any property except (1) inventory, stock in trade, or property held primarily for sale to customers in the ordinary course of the taxpayer's trade or business, (2) depreciable or real property used in the taxpayer's trade or business, (3) specified literary or artistic property, (4) business accounts or notes receivable, (5) certain U.S. publications, (6) certain commodity derivative financial instruments, (7) hedging transactions, and (8) business supplies. In addition, the net gain from the disposition of certain property used in the taxpayer's trade or business is treated as long-term capital gain. Gain from the disposition of depreciable personal property is not treated as capital gain to the extent of all previous depreciation allowances. Gain from the disposition of depreciable real property is generally not treated as capital gain to the extent of the depreciation allowances in excess of the allowances that would have been available under the straight-line method of depreciation.

The maximum rate of tax on the adjusted net capital gain of an individual is 20 percent. In addition, any adjusted net capital gain which otherwise would be taxed at a 15-percent rate is taxed at a 10-percent rate. These rates apply for purposes of both the regular tax and the alternative minimum tax.

The "adjusted net capital gain" of an individual is the net capital gain reduced (but not below zero) by the sum of the 28-percent rate gain and the unrecaptured section 1250 gain. The net capital gain is reduced by the amount of gain that the individual treats as investment income for purposes of determining the investment interest limitation under section 163(d).

The term "28-percent rate gain" means the amount of net gain attributable to long-term capital gains and losses from the sale or exchange of collectibles (as defined in section 408(m) without regard to paragraph (3) thereof), an amount of gain equal to the amount of gain excluded from

¶ 10,100   Act Sec. 301

gross income under section 1202 (relating to certain small business stock),[32] the net short-term capital loss for the taxable year, and any long-term capital loss carryover to the taxable year.

"Unrecaptured section 1250 gain" means any long-term capital gain from the sale or exchange of section 1250 property (i.e., depreciable real estate) held more than one year to the extent of the gain that would have been treated as ordinary income if section 1250 applied to all depreciation, reduced by the net loss (if any) attributable to the items taken into account in computing 28=percent rate gain. The amount of unrecaptured section 1250 gain (before the reduction for the net loss) attributable to the disposition of property to which section 1231 applies shall not exceed the net section 1231 gain for the year.

The unrecaptured section 1250 gain is taxed at a maximum rate of 25 percent, and the 28-percent rate gain is taxed at a maximum rate of 28 percent. Any amount of unrecaptured section 1250 gain or 28-percent rate gain otherwise taxed at a 15-percent rate is taxed at the 15-percent rate.

Any gain from the sale or exchange of property held more than five years that would otherwise be taxed at the 10-percent rate is taxed at an 8-percent rate. Any gain from the sale or exchange of property held more than five years and the holding period for which begins after December 31, 2000, which would otherwise be taxed at a 20-percent rate is taxed at an 18-percent rate.

Reasons For Change

The Committee believes it is important that tax policy be conducive to economic growth. The Committee believes that reducing the capital gains tax lowers the cost of capital and will lead to economic growth and the creation of jobs. Economic growth cannot occur without savings, investment, and the willingness of individuals to take risks. The greater the pool of savings, the greater will be the monies available for business investment. It is through such investment that the United States' economy can increase output, productivity, and employment. It is through increases in productivity that workers earn higher real wages. Increases in investment create more employment opportunities. Hence, a greater saving rate is necessary for all Americans to benefit from a higher standard of living.

The Committee believes that, by reducing the effective tax rates on capital gains, American households will respond by increasing savings. The Committee believes it is important to encourage risk-taking and believes a reduction in the taxation of capital gains will have that effect. The Committee also believes that a reduction in the taxation of capital gains will improve the efficiency of the markets, because the taxation of capital gains upon realization encourages investors who have accrued past gains to keep their monies "locked in" to such investments even when better investment opportunities present themselves. A reduction in the taxation of capital gains should reduce this "look in" effect.

Explanation Of Provision

The provision reduces the 10 and 20 percent rates on the adjusted net capital gain to five and 15 percent, respectively. These lower rates apply to both the regular tax and the alternative minimum tax. The lower rates apply to assets held more than one year.

Effective Date

The provision applies to taxable years ending on or after May 6, 2003, and beginning before January 1, 2013.

For taxable years that include May 6, 2003, the lower rates apply to amounts properly taken into account for the portion of the year on or after that date. This generally has the effect of applying the lower rates to capital assets sold or exchanged (and installment payments received) on or after May 6, 2003. In the case of gain and loss taken into account by a pass-through entity, the date taken into account by the entity is the appropriate date for applying this rule.

Conference Committee Report (H.R. CONF. REP. NO. 108-126)

Senate Amendment

No provision.

Conference Agreement

The conference agreement follows the House bill, except that the 5-percent tax rate is reduced to zero percent for taxable years beginning after December 31, 2007.

Effective Date

The effective date is the same as the House bill, except that the provision does not apply to taxable years beginning after December 31, 2008.

[Law at ¶ 5005, ¶ 5015, ¶ 5020, ¶ 5115, ¶ 5125, ¶ 7030 and ¶ 7035. CCH Explanation at ¶ 305, ¶ 310, ¶ 315, ¶ 320 and ¶ 29,001.]

---

[32] This results in a maximum effective regular tax rate on qualified gain from small business stock of 14 percent.

Act Sec. 301   ¶ 10,100

[¶ 10,110] Act Sec. 302 and Act Sec. 303. Treatment of dividend income of individuals

House Committee Report (H.R. REP. NO. 108-94)

[Code Sec. 1(h), Code Sec. 163(d), Code Sec. 854 and Code Sec. 857(c)]

Present Law

Under present law, dividends received by an individual are included in gross income and taxed as ordinary income at rates up to 38.6 percent.[33]

The rate of tax on the net capital gain of an individual generally is 20 percent (10 percent[34] with respect to income which would otherwise be taxed at the 10- or 15-percent rate).[35] Net capital gain means net gain from the sale or exchange of capital assets held for more than one year in excess of net loss from the sale or exchange of capital assets held not more than one year.

Reasons For Change

The Committee believes it is important that tax policy be conducive to economic growth. The Committee believes that reducing the individual tax on dividends lowers the cost of capital and will lead to economic growth and the creation of jobs. Economic growth is impeded by tax-induced distortions in the capital markets. Mitigating these distortions will improve the efficiency of the capital markets. In addition, reducing the aggregate tax burden on investments made by corporations will lower the cost of capital needed to finance new investments and lead to increases in aggregate national investment and increases in private sector employment. It is through such investment that the United States' economy can increase output, employment, and productivity. It is through increases in productivity that workers earn higher real wages and all Americans benefit from a higher standard of living.

The Committee observes that present law imposes different total tax burdens on income from different investments. The Committee believes that, by placing different tax burdens on different investments, the present system results in economic distortions. The Committee observes that present law distorts individual and corporate financial decisions. The Committee observes that because interest payments on the debt are deductible, present law encourages corporations to finance using debt rather than equity. The Committee believes that the increase in corporate leverage, while beneficial to each corporation from a tax perspective, may place the economy at risk of more bankruptcies during an economic downturn. In addition, the Committee finds that present law, by taxing dividend income at a higher rate than income from capital gains, encourages corporations to retain earnings rather than to distribute them as taxable dividends. If dividends are discouraged, shareholders may prefer that corporate management retain and reinvest earnings rather than pay out dividends, even if the shareholder might have an alternative use for the funds that could offer a higher rate of return than that earned on the retained earnings. This is another source of inefficiency as the opportunity to earn higher pre-tax returns is bypassed in favor of lower pre-tax returns.

Explanation of Provision

Under the provision, dividends received by an individual shareholder from domestic corporations are taxed at the same rates that apply to net capital gain. This treatment applies for purposes of both the regular tax and the alternative minimum tax. Thus, under the provision, dividends will be taxed at rates of five and 15 percent.[36]

If a shareholder does not hold a share of stock for more than 45 days during the 90-day period beginning 45 days before the ex-dividend date (as measured under section 246(c)),[37] dividends received on the stock are not eligible for the reduced rates. Also, the reduced rates are not available for dividends to the extent that the taxpayer is obligated to make related payments with respect to positions in substantially similar or related property.

If an individual receives an extraordinary dividend (within the meaning of section 1059(c)) eligible for the reduced rates with respect to any share of stock, any loss on the sale of the stock is treated as a long-term capital loss to the extent of the dividend.

A dividend is treated as investment income for purposes of determining the amount of deductible investment interest only if the taxpayer elects to treat the dividend as not eligible for the reduced rates.

The amount of dividends qualifying for reduced rates that may be paid by a regulated investment company or real estate investment trust, for any taxable year that the aggregate qualifying dividends received by the company or trust are less than 95 percent of its gross income (as specially

---

[33] Section 105 of the bill reduces the maximum rate to 35 percent.
[34] An eight percent rate applies to property held more than five years.
[35] Section 301 of the bill reduces the capital gain rates to five and 15 percent, respectively.

[36] Payments in lieu of dividends are not eligible for the lower rates. See section 6045(d) relating to statements required to be furnished by brokers regarding these payments.
[37] In the case of preferred stock, the periods are doubled.

computed), may not exceed the amount of the aggregate qualifying dividends received by the company or trust.

The reduced rates do not apply to dividends received from an organization that was exempt from tax under section 501 or was a tax-exempt farmers' cooperative in either the taxable year of the distribution or the preceding taxable year; dividends received from a mutual savings bank that received a deduction under section 591; or deductible dividends paid on employer securities.

The tax rate for the accumulated earnings tax (sec. 531) and the personal holding company tax (sec. 541) is reduced to 15 percent.

Amounts treated as ordinary income on the disposition of certain preferred stock (sec. 306) are treated as dividends for purposes of applying the reduced rates.

The collapsible corporation rules (sec. 341) are repealed.

Effective Date

The provision is effective for taxable years beginning after December 31, 2002, and beginning before January 1, 2013.

Conference Committee Report (H.R. CONF. REP. NO. 108-126)

Conference Agreement

The conference agreement follows the House bill taxing dividends at the same rates as net capital gain with the following modifications:

The 45-day holding period requirement is increased to 60 days during the 120-day period beginning 60 days before the ex-dividend date.

Qualified dividend income includes otherwise qualified dividends received from qualified foreign corporations. The term "qualified foreign corporation" includes a foreign corporation that is eligible for the benefits of a comprehensive income tax treaty with the United States which the Treasury Department determines to be satisfactory for purposes of this provision, and which includes an exchange of information program. The conferees do not believe that the current income tax treaty between the United States and Barbados is satisfactory for this purpose because that treaty may operate to provide benefits that are intended for the purpose of mitigating or eliminating double taxation to corporations that are not at risk of double taxation. The conferees intend that, until the Treasury Department issues guidance regarding the determination of treaties as satisfactory for this purpose, a foreign corporation will be considered to be a qualified foreign corporation if it is eligible for the benefits of a comprehensive income tax treaty with the United States that includes an exchange of information program other than the current U.S.-Barbados income tax treaty. The conferees further intend that a company will be eligible for benefits of a comprehensive income tax treaty within the meaning of this provision if it would qualify for the benefits of the treaty with respect to substantially all of its income in the taxable year in which the dividend is paid.

In addition, a foreign corporation is treated as a qualified foreign corporation with respect to any dividend paid by the corporation with respect to stock that is readily tradable on an established securities market in the United States.[41]

Dividends received from a foreign corporation that was a foreign investment company (a defined in section 1246(b)), a passive foreign investment company (as defined in section 1297), or a foreign personal holding company (as defined in section 552) in either the taxable year of the distribution or the preceding taxable year are not qualified dividends.

Special rules apply in determining a taxpayer's foreign tax credit limitation under section 904 in the case of qualified dividend income. For these purposes, rules similar to the rules of section 904(b)(2)(B) concerning adjustments to the foreign tax credit limitation to reflect any capital gain rate differential will apply to any qualified dividend income. Additionally, it is anticipated that regulations promulgated under this provision will coordinate the operation of the rules applicable to qualified dividend income and capital gain.

In the case of a REIT, an amount equal to the excess of the income subject to the taxes imposed by section 857(b)(1) and the regulations prescribed under section 337(d) for the preceding taxable year over the amount of these taxes for the preceding taxable year is treated as qualified dividend income.

In the case of brokers and dealers who engage in securities lending transactions, short sales, or other similar transactions on behalf of their customers in the normal course of their trade or business, the conferees intend that the IRS will exercise its authority under section 6724(a) to waive penalties where dealers and brokers attempt in good faith to comply with the information reporting requirements under sections 6042 and 6045, but are unable to reasonably comply because of the period necessary to conform their

---

[41] For this purpose, a share shall be treated as so traded if an American Depository Receipt (ADR) backed by such share is so traded.

information reporting systems to the retroactive rate reductions on qualified dividends provided by the conference agreement. In addition, the conferees expect that individual taxpayers who receive payments in lieu of dividends from these transactions may treat the payments as dividend income to the extent that the payments are reported to them as dividend income on their Forms 1099-DIV received for calendar year 2003, unless they know or have reason to know that the payments are in fact payments in lieu of dividends rather than actual dividends. The conferees expect that the Treasury Department will issue guidance as rapidly as possible on information reporting with respect to payments in lieu of dividends made to individuals.

The conference agreement provides that the amendment to section 306 treating certain ordinary income as a dividend for purposes of the rate computation under section 1(h) may also apply to such other provisions as the Secretary may provide, including provisions at the corporate level.

Effective Date

The provision is effective for taxable years beginning after December 31, 2002, and beginning before January 1, 2009.

[Law at ¶ 5005, ¶ 5030, ¶ 5045, ¶ 5050, ¶ 5055, ¶ 5060, ¶ 5065, ¶ 5070, ¶ 5075, ¶ 5080, ¶ 5085, ¶ 5090, ¶ 5095, ¶ 5100, ¶ 5105 and ¶ 7035. CCH Explanation at ¶ 325, ¶ 335, ¶ 360, ¶ 365, ¶ 370 and ¶ 29,001.]

[¶ 10,120] Act Sec. 381 [401]. Temporary state and local fiscal relief

Senate Floor Debate (149 CONG. REC. 73, S6414), May 15, 2003

[Caution: The following excerpt from the Congressional Record is included to assist the reader's understanding. The amendment discussed below on the floor of the Senate was renumbered in the final version of the bill.— CCH.]

[Act Sec. 401]
* * *

Mr. GRASSLEY. Mr. President, Senator Collins is ready to speak on her amendment.

The PRESIDING OFFICER. Without objection, the Senate will proceed to the Collins amendment.

The Senator from Maine is recognized.

Ms. COLLINS. Mr. President, this bipartisan amendment would provide $20 billion in much needed fiscal aid to the States. Forty-nine States are struggling with budget deficits. This won't relieve them of the obligation to make painful budget choices, but it will recognize the difficult financial strains under which they are operating.

Half of the money would go for an increase in the FMAP rate under Medicaid. The other half would be used for a flexible grant program that would be allocated between the States and localities.

I yield the remainder of my time in favor of the amendment to the Senator from Nevada, if he wishes to speak.

The PRESIDING OFFICER. The Senator from Nevada is recognized.

Mr. REID. Mr. President, I compliment the Senator from Maine for her vision in offering this amendment. The State of Nevada is one of the 49 States that is desperate for money. I think this amendment is one of the best we have had. Again, I compliment the Senator from Maine.

The PRESIDING OFFICER. Who yields time in opposition?

Mr. REID. Mr. President, we yield back whatever time is left.

The PRESIDING OFFICER. Without objection, the opposition time is yielded back.

The question is on agreeing to the amendment.

The yeas and nays have previously been ordered.

The clerk will call the roll.

The bill clerk called the roll.

Mr. McCONNELL. I announce that the Senator from Idaho (Mr. Craig) and the Senator from Alabama (Mr. Sessions) are necessarily absent.

The PRESIDING OFFICER. Are there any other Senators in the Chamber desiring to vote?

The result was announced—yeas 95, nays 3, as follows:
* * *

Conference Committee Report (H.R. CONF. REP. NO. 108-126)

Present Law

No provision.

House Bill

No provision.

Senate Amendment

The Senate amendment extends relief to States by establishing a temporary fund to provide $10 billion, divided among State and local governments, to be used for health care, education or job training; transportation or infrastructure; law enforcement or public safety; and other essential governmental services, and $10 billion for Medicaid (FMAP).

Effective Date

The Senate amendment provision is effective on the date of enactment.

Conference Agreement

The conference agreement provides relief to States by establishing a temporary fund to provide $10 billion divided among the States to be used for essential government services, and $10 billion for Medicaid (FMAP). Nothing in this subsection shall be construed to preclude consideration of reforms to improve the Medicaid program.

Effective Date

The Senate amendment provision is effective on the date of enactment.

[Law at ¶ 7040. CCH Explanation at ¶ 240.]

[¶ 10,130] Act Sec. 501. Modification to corporate estimated tax requirements

House Committee Report (H.R. REP. NO. 108-94)

[Act Sec. 501]

Present Law

In general, corporations are required to make quarterly estimated tax payments of their income tax liability (section 6655). For a corporation whose taxable year is a calendar year, these estimated tax payments must be made by April 15, June 15, September 15, and December 15.

Reasons For Change

The Committee believes that it is appropriate to modify these corporate estimated tax requirements.

Explanation Of Provisions

With respect to corporate estimated tax payments due on September 15, 2003, 52 percent is required to be paid by October 1, 2003.

Effective Date

The provision is effective on the date of enactment.

Conference Committee Report (H.R. CONF. REP. NO. 108-126)

Senate Amendment

No provision.

Conference Agreement

With respect to corporate estimated tax payments due on September 15, 2003, 25 percent is required to be paid by October 1, 2003.

Effective Date

The provision is effective on the date of enactment.

[Law at ¶ 7045. CCH Explanation at ¶ 375.]

Effective Dates

Jobs and Growth Tax Relief Reconciliation Act of 2003

¶ 20,001

This CCH-prepared table presents the general effective dates for major law provisions added, amended or repealed by the Jobs and Growth Tax Relief Reconciliation Act of 2003, enacted May 28, 2003. Entries are listed in Code Section order.

Code Sec.	Act Sec.	Act Provision Subject	Effective Date
1(f)(8)(A)	102(b)(1)	Acceleration of 15-percent individual income tax rate bracket expansion for married taxpayers filing joint returns—conforming amendment	Tax years beginning after December 31, 2002
1(f)(8)(B)	102(a)	Acceleration of 15-percent individual income tax rate bracket expansion for married taxpayers filing joint returns	Tax years beginning after December 31, 2002
1(h)(1)(B)	301(a)(1)	Reduction in capital gains rates for individuals; repeal of 5-year holding period requirement	Tax years ending on or after May 6, 2003
1(h)(1)(C)	301(a)(2)(A)	Reduction in capital gains rates for individuals; repeal of 5-year holding period requirement	Tax years ending on or after May 6, 2003
1(h)(2)-(8)	301(b)(1)(B)	Reduction in capital gains rates for individuals; repeal of 5-year holding period requirement—conforming amendment	Tax years ending on or after May 6, 2003
1(h)(2)	301(b)(1)(A)	Reduction in capital gains rates for individuals; repeal of 5-year holding period requirement—conforming amendment	Tax years ending on or after May 6, 2003
1(h)(3)	302(e)(1)	Dividends of individuals taxed at capital gain rates—conforming amendment	Tax years beginning after December 31, 2002
1(h)(8)-(12)	301(b)(1)(C)	Reduction in capital gains rates for individuals; repeal of 5-year holding period requirement—conforming amendment	Tax years ending on or after May 6, 2003
1(h)(9)	301(b)(1)(A)	Reduction in capital gains rates for individuals; repeal of 5-year holding period requirement—conforming amendment	Tax years ending on or after May 6, 2003
1(h)(11)	302(a)	Dividends of individuals taxed at capital gain rates	Tax years beginning after December 31, 2002

¶ 20,001

Code Sec.	Act Sec.	Act Provision Subject	Effective Date
1(i)(1)(B)	104(a)	Acceleration of 10-percent individual income tax rate bracket expansion	Tax years beginning after December 31, 2002
1(i)(1)(C)	104(b)	Acceleration of 10-percent individual income tax rate bracket expansion—inflation adjustment	Tax years beginning after December 31, 2002
1(i)(2)	105(a)	Acceleration of reduction in individual income tax rates	Tax years beginning after December 31, 2002
24(a)(2)	101(a)	Acceleration of increase in child tax credit	Tax years beginning after December 31, 2002
55(b)(3)(B)	301(a)(1)	Reduction in capital gains rates for individuals; repeal of 5-year holding period requirement	Tax years ending on or after May 6, 2003
55(b)(3)(C)	301(a)(2)(B)	Reduction in capital gains rates for individuals; repeal of 5-year holding period requirement	Tax years ending on or after May 6, 2003
55(b)(3)	301(b)(2)	Reduction in capital gains rates for individuals; repeal of 5-year holding period requirement—conforming amendment	Tax years ending on or after May 6, 2003
55(d)(1)(A)	106(a)(1)	Minimum tax relief to individuals	Tax years beginning after December 31, 2002
55(d)(1)(B)	106(a)(2)	Minimum tax relief to individuals	Tax years beginning after December 31, 2002
57(a)(7)	301(b)(3)(A)	Reduction in capital gains rates for individuals; repeal of 5-year holding period requirement—conforming amendment	Dispositions on or after May 6, 2003
57(a)(7)	301(b)(3)(B)	Reduction in capital gains rates for individuals; repeal of 5-year holding period requirement—conforming amendment	Dispositions on or after May 6, 2003
63(c)(7)	103(a)	Acceleration of increase in standard deduction for married taxpayers filing joint returns	Tax years beginning after December 31, 2002
163(d)(4)(B)	302(b)	Dividends of individuals taxed at capital gain rates—exclusion of dividends from investment income	Tax years beginning after December 31, 2002
168(k)(2)(A)	201(b)(2)	Increase and extension of bonus depreciation—extension of certain dates for 30-percent bonus depreciation property—acquisition date	Tax years ending after May 5, 2003
168(k)(2)(B)	201(b)(1)(A)	Increase and extension of bonus depreciation—extension of certain dates for 30-percent bonus depre-	Tax years ending after May 5, 2003

¶ 20,001

Effective Dates

Code Sec.	Act Sec.	Act Provision Subject	Effective Date
		ciation property—portion of basis taken into account	
168(k)(2)(B)	201(b)(1)(B)	Increase and extension of bonus depreciation—extension of certain dates for 30-percent bonus depreciation property—portion of basis taken into account	Tax years ending after May 5, 2003
168(k)(2)(C)	201(b)(3)	Increase and extension of bonus depreciation—extension of certain dates for 30-percent bonus depreciation property—election	Tax years ending after May 5, 2003
168(k)(2)(D)	201(b)(1)(A)	Increase and extension of bonus depreciation—extension of certain dates for 30-percent bonus depreciation property—portion of basis taken into account	Tax years ending after May 5, 2003
168(k)(4)	201(a)	Increase and extension of bonus depreciation	Tax years ending after May 5, 2003
168(k)	201(c)(1)	Increase and extension of bonus depreciation—conforming amendment	Tax years ending after May 5, 2003
179(b)(1)	202(a)	Increased expensing for small business	Tax years beginning after December 31, 2002
179(b)(2)	202(b)	Increased expensing for small business—increase in qualifying investment at which phaseout begins	Tax years beginning after December 31, 2002
179(b)(5)	202(d)	Increased expensing for small business—adjustment of dollar limit and phaseout threshold for inflation	Tax years beginning after December 31, 2002
179(c)(2)	202(e)	Increased expensing for small business—revocation of election	Tax years beginning after December 31, 2002
179(d)(1)	202(c)	Increased expensing for small business—off-the-shelf computer software	Tax years beginning after December 31, 2002
301(f)(4)	302(e)(2)	Dividends of individuals taxed at capital gain rates—conforming amendment	Tax years beginning after December 31, 2002
306(a)(1)(D)	302(e)(3)	Dividends of individuals taxed at capital gain rates—conforming amendment	Tax years beginning after December 31, 2002
338(h)(14)	302(e)(4)(B)	Dividends of individuals taxed at capital gain rates—conforming amendment	Tax years beginning after December 31, 2002
341	302(e)(4)(A)	Dividends of individuals taxed at capital gain rates—conforming amendment	Tax years beginning after December 31, 2002

Code Sec.	Act Sec.	Act Provision Subject	Effective Date
467(c)(5)(C)	302(e)(4)(B)	Dividends of individuals taxed at capital gain rates—conforming amendment	Tax years beginning after December 31, 2002
531	302(e)(5)	Dividends of individuals taxed at capital gain rates—conforming amendment	Tax years beginning after December 31, 2002
541	302(e)(6)	Dividends of individuals taxed at capital gain rates—conforming amendment	Tax years beginning after December 31, 2002
584(c)	302(e)(7)	Dividends of individuals taxed at capital gain rates—conforming amendment	Tax years beginning after December 31, 2002
702(a)(5)	302(e)(8)	Dividends of individuals taxed at capital gain rates—conforming amendment	Tax years beginning after December 31, 2002
854(a)	302(c)(1)	Dividends of individuals taxed at capital gain rates—treatment of dividends from regulated investment companies	Tax years ending after December 31, 2002, generally
854(b)(1)(B)-(C)	302(c)(2)	Dividends of individuals taxed at capital gain rates—treatment of dividends from regulated investment companies	Tax years ending after December 31, 2002, generally
854(b)(1)(C)	302(c)(3)	Dividends of individuals taxed at capital gain rates—treatment of dividends from regulated investment companies	Tax years ending after December 31, 2002, generally
854(b)(2)	302(c)(4)	Dividends of individuals taxed at capital gain rates—treatment of dividends from regulated investment companies	Tax years ending after December 31, 2002, generally
854(b)(5)	302(c)(5)	Dividends of individuals taxed at capital gain rates—treatment of dividends from regulated investment companies	Tax years ending after December 31, 2002, generally
857(c)	302(d)	Dividends of individuals taxed at capital gain rates—treatment of dividends received from real estate investment trusts	Tax years ending after December 31, 2002, generally
1255(b)(2)	302(e)(4)(B)	Dividends of individuals taxed at capital gain rates—conforming amendment	Tax years beginning after December 31, 2002
1257(d)	302(e)(4)(B)	Dividends of individuals taxed at capital gain rates—conforming amendment	Tax years beginning after December 31, 2002
1400L(b)(2)(C)(i)	201(c)(2)	Increase and extension of bonus depreciation—conforming amendment	Tax years ending after May 5, 2003

¶ 20,001

Effective Dates

Code Sec.	Act Sec.	Act Provision Subject	Effective Date
1445(e)(1)	301(a)(2)(C)	Reduction in capital gains rates for individuals; repeal of 5-year holding period requirement	Amounts paid after date of enactment
6429	101(b)(1)	Advance payment of portion of increased credit in 2003	Date of enactment
7518(g)(6)(A)	301(a)(2)(D)	Reduction in capital gains rates for individuals; repeal of 5-year holding period requirement	Tax years ending on or after May 6, 2003
.....	101(b)(2)	Advance payment of portion of increased credit in 2003—clerical amendment	Date of enactment
.....	102(b)(2)	Acceleration of 15-percent individual income tax rate bracket expansion for married taxpayers filing joint returns—conforming amendment	Tax years beginning after December 31, 2002
.....	103(b)	Acceleration of increase in standard deduction for married taxpayers filing joint returns—conforming amendment	Tax years beginning after December 31, 2002
.....	107	Application of EGTRRA sunset to this title	Date of enactment
.....	301(a)(2)(E)	Reduction in capital gains rates for individuals; repeal of 5-year holding period requirement	Tax years ending on or after May 6, 2003
.....	301(c)(1)-(6)	Reduction in capital gains rates for individuals; repeal of 5-year holding period requirement—transitional rules for taxable years which include May 6, 2003	Tax years ending on or after May 6, 2003
.....	302(e)(4)(B)	Dividends of individuals taxed at capital gain rates—conforming amendment	Tax years beginning after December 31, 2002
.....	303	Sunset of title	Date of enactment
.....	401(a)(1)	Temporary state fiscal relief—$10,000,000,000 for a temporary increase of the Medicaid FMAP—permitting maintenance of fiscal year 2002 FMAP for last 2 calendar quarters of fiscal year 2003	Date of enactment
.....	401(a)(2)	Temporary state fiscal relief—$10,000,000,000 for a temporary increase of the Medicaid FMAP—permitting maintenance of fiscal year 2003 FMAP for first 3 quarters of fiscal year 2004	Date of enactment
.....	401(a)(3)	Temporary state fiscal relief—$10,000,000,000 for a temporary increase of the Medicaid FMAP—general 2.95 percentage points in-	Date of enactment

¶ 20,001

184 Jobs and Growth Tax Relief Reconciliation Act of 2003

Code Sec.	Act Sec.	Act Provision Subject	Effective Date
.....		crease for last 2 calendar quarters of fiscal year 2003 and first 3 calendar quarters of fiscal year 2004	
.....	401(a)(4)	Temporary state fiscal relief—$10,000,000,000 for a temporary increase of the Medicaid FMAP—increase in cap on Medicaid payments to territories	Date of enactment
.....	401(a)(5)	Temporary state fiscal relief—$10,000,000,000 for a temporary increase of the Medicaid FMAP—scope of application	Date of enactment
.....	401(a)(6)(A)	Temporary state fiscal relief—$10,000,000,000 for a temporary increase of the Medicaid FMAP—state eligibility	Date of enactment
.....	401(a)(6)(B)	Temporary state fiscal relief—$10,000,000,000 for a temporary increase of the Medicaid FMAP—state eligibility—state reinstatement of eligibility permitted	Date of enactment
.....	401(a)(6)(C)	Temporary state fiscal relief—$10,000,000,000 for a temporary increase of the Medicaid FMAP—state eligibility—rule of construction	Date of enactment
.....	401(a)(7)	Temporary state fiscal relief—$10,000,000,000 for a temporary increase of the Medicaid FMAP—requirement for certain states	Date of enactment
.....	401(a)(8)(A)	Temporary state fiscal relief—$10,000,000,000 for a temporary increase of the Medicaid FMAP—definitions—FMAP	Date of enactment
.....	401(a)(8)(B)	Temporary state fiscal relief—$10,000,000,000 for a temporary increase of the Medicaid FMAP—definitions—state	Date of enactment
.....	401(a)(9)	Temporary state fiscal relief—$10,000,000,000 for a temporary increase of the Medicaid FMAP—repeal	Date of enactment
.....	401(b)	Temporary state fiscal relief—$10,000,000,000 to assist states in providing government services	Date of enactment
.....	501	Time for payment of corporate estimated taxes	Date of enactment

¶ 20,001

Code Section to Explanation Table
¶ 25,001

Code Sec.	Explanation	Code Sec.	Explanation
1(f)(8)	¶ 215	179(c)(2)	¶ 355
1(h)	¶ 305	179(d)(1)	¶ 355
1(h)(1)(B)	¶ 305	301(f)(4)	¶ 325
1(h)(1)(C)	¶ 305	306(a)(1)(D)	¶ 325
1(h)(2)	¶ 310	338(h)	¶ 360
1(h)(3)	¶ 325	341	¶ 360
1(h)(3)-(12)	¶ 310	467(c)(5)(C)	¶ 360
1(h)(9)	¶ 310	531	¶ 365
1(h)(11)	¶ 325	541	¶ 370
1(i)(1)	¶ 210	584(c)	¶ 335
1(i)(2)	¶ 205	702(a)(5)	¶ 335
24(a)(2)	¶ 225	854(a)	¶ 335
55(b)(3)	¶ 305, ¶ 310	854(b)(1)(B)	¶ 335
55(b)(3)(B)	¶ 305	854(b)(1)(C)	¶ 335
55(b)(3)(C)	¶ 305	854(b)(2)	¶ 335
55(d)(1)	¶ 230	854(b)(5)	¶ 335
57(a)(7)	¶ 315	857(c)	¶ 335
63(c)(7)	¶ 220	1255(b)(2)	¶ 360
163(d)(4)(B)	¶ 325	1257(d)	¶ 360
168(k)(2)	¶ 350	1400L(b)(2)(C)	¶ 350
168(k)(4)	¶ 350	1445(e)(1)	¶ 305
179(b)(1)	¶ 355	6429	¶ 225
179(b)(2)	¶ 355	7518(g)(6)(A)	¶ 305
179(b)(5)	¶ 355		

¶ 25,001

Code Sections Added, Amended or Repealed

The list below notes all the Code Sections or subsections of the Internal Revenue Code that were added, amended or repealed by the Jobs and Growth Tax Relief Reconciliation Act of 2003 (H.R. 2). The first column indicates the Code Section added, amended or repealed and the second column indicates the Act Section.

¶ 25,005

Code Sec.	Act Sec.	Code Sec.	Act Sec.
1(f)(8)(A)	102(b)(1)	179(b)(1)	202(a)
1(f)(8)(B)	102(a)	179(b)(2)	202(b)
1(h)(1)(B)	301(a)(1)	179(b)(5)	202(d)
1(h)(1)(C)	301(a)(2)(A)	179(c)(2)	202(e)
1(h)(2)-(12)	301(b)(1)(A)-(C)	179(d)(1)	202(c)
1(h)(3)	302(e)(1)	301(f)(4)	302(e)(2)
1(h)(11)	302(a)	306(a)(1)(D)	302(e)(3)
1(i)(1)(B)(i)	104(a)	338(h)(14)	302(e)(4)(B)(i)
1(i)(1)(C)	104(b)	341	302(e)(4)(A)
1(i)(2)	105(a)	467(c)(5)(C)	302(e)(4)(B)(ii)
24(a)(2)	101(a)	531	302(e)(5)
55(b)(3)	301(b)(2)	541	302(e)(6)
55(b)(3)(B)	301(a)(1)	584(c)	302(e)(7)
55(b)(3)(C)	301(a)(2)(B)	702(a)(5)	302(e)(8)
55(d)(1)(A)	106(a)(1)	854(a)	302(c)(1)
55(d)(1)(B)	106(a)(2)	854(b)(1)(B)-(C)	302(c)(2)
57(a)(7)	301(b)(3)(A)-(B)	854(b)(1)(C)	302(c)(3)
63(c)(7)	103(a)	854(b)(2)	302(c)(4)
163(d)(4)(B)	302(b)	854(b)(5)	302(c)(5)
168(k)	201(c)(1)	857(c)	302(d)
168(k)(2)(A)(iii)	201(b)(2)	1255(b)(2)	302(e)(4)(B)(ii)
168(k)(2)(B)(ii)	201(b)(1)(A)	1257(d)	302(e)(4)(B)(ii)
168(k)(2)(B)(ii)	201(b)(1)(B)	1400L(b)(2)(C)(i)	201(c)(2)
168(k)(2)(C)(iii)	201(b)(3)	1445(e)(1)	301(a)(2)(C)
168(k)(2)(D)(i)	201(b)(1)(A)	6429	101(b)(1)
168(k)(4)	201(a)	7518(g)(6)(A)	301(a)(2)(D)

Table of Amendments to Other Acts
¶ 25,010
Jobs and Growth Tax Relief Reconciliation Act of 2003

Amended Act Sec.	H.R. 2 Sec.	Par.	Amended Act Sec.	H.R. 2 Sec.	Par.
ECONOMIC GROWTH AND TAX RELIEF RECONCILIATION ACT OF 2001			**SOCIAL SECURITY ACT**		
			601	401(b)	7040
301(d)	103(b)	7015	**MERCHANT MARINE ACT, 1936**		
302(c)	102(b)(2)	7010	607(h)(6)(A)	301(a)(2)(E)	7030

Table of Act Sections Not Amending Internal Revenue Code Sections

¶ 25,015

Jobs and Growth Tax Relief Reconciliation Act of 2003

	Paragraph		Paragraph
Short title; references; table of contents	7005	Reduction in capital gains rates for individuals; repeal of 5-year holding period requirement	7030
Acceleration of 10-percent individual income tax rate bracket expansion	7020	Sunset of title	7035
Application of EGTRRA sunset to this title	7025	Temporary State fiscal relief	7040
		Time for payment of corporate estimated taxes	7045

Act Sections Amending Code Sections
¶ 25,020

Act Sec.	Code Sec.	Act Sec.	Code Sec.
101(a)	24(a)(2)	301(a)(2)(B)	55(b)(3)(C)
101(b)(1)	6429	301(a)(2)(C)	1445(e)(1)
102(a)	1(f)(8)(B)	301(a)(2)(D)	7518(g)(6)(A)
102(b)(1)	1(f)(8)(A)	301(b)(1)(A)-(C)	1(h)(2)-(12)
103(a)	63(c)(7)	301(b)(2)	55(b)(3)
104(a)	1(i)(1)(B)(i)	301(b)(3)(A)-(B)	57(a)(7)
104(b)	1(i)(1)(C)	302(a)	1(h)(11)
105(a)	1(i)(2)	302(b)	163(d)(4)(B)
106(a)(1)	55(d)(1)(A)	302(c)(1)	854(a)
106(a)(2)	55(d)(1)(B)	302(c)(2)	854(b)(1)(B)-(C)
201(a)	168(k)(4)	302(c)(3)	854(b)(1)(C)
201(b)(1)(A)	168(k)(2)(B)(ii)	302(c)(4)	854(b)(2)
201(b)(1)(A)	168(k)(2)(D)(i)	302(c)(5)	854(b)(5)
201(b)(1)(B)	168(k)(2)(B)(ii)	302(d)	857(c)
201(b)(2)	168(k)(2)(A)(iii)	302(e)(1)	1(h)(3)
201(b)(3)	168(k)(2)(C)(iii)	302(e)(2)	301(f)(4)
201(c)(1)	168(k)	302(e)(3)	306(a)(1)(D)
201(c)(2)	1400L(b)(2)(C)(i)	302(e)(4)(A)	341
202(a)	179(b)(1)	302(e)(4)(B)(i)	338(h)(14)
202(b)	179(b)(2)	302(e)(4)(B)(ii)	467(c)(5)(C)
202(c)	179(d)(1)	302(e)(4)(B)(ii)	1255(b)(2)
202(d)	179(b)(5)	302(e)(4)(B)(ii)	1257(d)
202(e)	179(c)(2)	302(e)(5)	531
301(a)(1)	1(h)(1)(B)	302(e)(6)	541
301(a)(1)	55(b)(3)(B)	302(e)(7)	584(c)
301(a)(2)(A)	1(h)(1)(C)	302(e)(8)	702(a)(5)

¶ 25,020

Sunset Provisions

¶ 29,001

The Jobs and Growth Tax Relief Reconciliation Act of 2003 contains two provisions that sunset some of the changes made by the new law. Provisions in Title I of the 2003 Act that have been made subject to the sunset in the Economic Growth and Tax Relief Reconciliation Act of 2001 (EGTRRA) (P.L. 107-16) will not apply to tax years beginning after December 31, 2010. Provisions in Title III of the 2003 Act are subject to a separate sunset under which such provisions will not apply to tax years beginning after December 31, 2008. The inclusion of the sunset language means that Congress will eventually need to pass legislation that restores the provisions before the scheduled expiration date. If Congress takes no action, the expiration of the provisions will take effect.

The sunset provisions are necessary to comply with Section 313 of the Congressional Budget Act of 1974 (2 U.S.C. 644). Section 313, which was permanently incorporated into the Budget Act in 1990, is commonly referred to as the "Byrd rule" and was named after its principal sponsor, Senator Robert C. Byrd. The Byrd rule generally permits Senators to raise a point of order on the Senate floor against "extraneous" provisions contained in a reconciliation bill that are unrelated to the goals of the reconciliation process. One of the six types of extraneous provisions is a provision that would increase net outlays or decrease revenues for a fiscal year beyond those covered by the reconciliation measure. Use of sunset language prevents provisions from violating the Byrd rule and becoming subject to a point of order in the Senate.

Specifically, Act Section 107 of the Jobs and Growth Tax Relief Reconciliation Act of 2003 provides:

SEC. 107. APPLICATION OF EGTRRA SUNSET TO THIS TITLE.

Each amendment made by this title [Title I] shall be subject to title IX of the Economic Growth and Tax Relief Reconciliation Act of 2001 to the same extent and in the same manner as the provision of such Act to which such amendment relates.

The Committee Report for Section 107 is at ¶ 10,070.

Specifically, Act Section 303 of the Jobs and Growth Tax Relief Reconciliation Act of 2003 provides:

SEC. 303. SUNSET OF TITLE.

All provisions of, and amendments made by, this title [Title III] shall not apply to taxable years beginning after December 31, 2008, and the Internal Revenue Code of 1986 shall be applied and administered to such years as if such provisions and amendments had never been enacted.

Provisions Dropped in Conference
¶ 30,001

The following proposed law changes were originally included in the House or Senate amendment versions of the Jobs and Growth Tax Relief Reconciliation Act of 2003, but were dropped by the conferees. References to the House bill are to the Jobs and Growth Reconciliation Tax bill of 2003 (H.R. 2) as passed by the House on May 9, 2003. References to the Senate bill are to the Jobs and Growth Tax Relief Reconciliation bill of 2003 as passed by the Senate on May 15, 2003 (originally S. 1054, H.R. 2 as passed), with floor amendments.

DEPRECIATION AND EXPENSING PROVISIONS

- Five-year carryback of net operating losses (House Sec. 203).

REVENUE PROVISIONS

A. Provisions Designed to Curtail Tax Shelters

- Clarification of the economic substance doctrine (Senate amendment Sec. 301).

- Penalty for failure to disclose reportable transactions (Senate amendment Sec. 302).

- Modifications to the accuracy-related penalties for listed transactions and reportable transactions having a significant tax avoidance purpose (Senate amendment Sec. 303).

- Penalty for understatements from transactions lacking economic substance (Senate amendment Sec. 304).

- Modifications to the substantial understatement penalty (Senate amendment Sec. 305).

- Tax shelter exception to confidentiality privileges relating to taxpayer communications (Senate amendment Sec. 306).

- Disclosure of reportable transactions by material advisors (Senate amendment Secs. 307 and 308).

- Investor lists and modification of penalty for failure to maintain investor lists (Senate amendment Secs. 307 and 309).

- Actions to enjoin conduct with respect to tax shelters and reportable transactions (Senate amendment Sec. 310).

- Understatement of taxpayer's liability by income tax return preparer (Senate amendment Sec. 311).

- Penalty for failure to report interests in foreign financial accounts (Senate amendment Sec. 312).

- Frivolous tax returns and submissions (Senate amendment Sec. 313).

- Penalties on promoters of tax shelters (Senate amendment Sec. 314).

- Extend statute of limitations for certain undisclosed transactions (Senate amendment Sec. 315).

- Deny deduction for interest paid to IRS on underpayments involving certain tax-motivated transactions (Senate amendment Sec. 316).

B. Enron-Related Tax Shelter Related Provisions

- Limitation of transfer and importation of built-in losses (Senate amendment Sec. 321).

- No reduction of basis under section 734 in stock held by partnership in corporate partner (Senate amendment Sec. 322).
- Repeal of special rules for FASITs (Senate amendment Sec. 323).
- Expanded disallowance of deduction for interest on convertible debt (Senate amendment Sec. 324).
- Expanded authority to disallow tax benefits under section 269 (Senate amendment Sec. 325).
- Modification of controlled foreign corporation-passive foreign investment company coordination rules (Senate amendment Sec. 326).
- Modify treatment of closely-held REITs (Senate amendment Sec. 327).

C. Other Corporate Governance Provisions

- Affirmation of consolidated return regulation authority (Senate amendment Sec. 331).
- Chief Executive Officer required to sign corporate income tax returns (Senate amendment Sec. 332).
- Denial of deduction for certain fines, penalties and other amounts (Senate amendment Sec. 333).
- Denial of deduction for punitive damages (Senate amendment Sec. 334).
- Criminal tax fraud (Senate amendment Sec. 335).
- Executive compensation reforms (Senate amendment Secs. 336 through 338).
- Increase in withholding from supplemental wage payments in excess of $1 million (Senate amendment Sec. 339).

D. International Provisions

- Impose mark-to-market on individuals who expatriate (Senate amendment Sec. 340).
- Provisions to discourage corporate expatriation (Senate amendment Secs. 341 through 343).
- Doubling of certain penalties, fines, and interest on underpayments related to certain offshore financial arrangements (Senate amendment Sec. 344).
- Effectively connected income to include certain foreign source income (Senate amendment Sec. 345).
- Determination of basis amounts paid from foreign pension plans (Senate amendment Sec. 346).
- Recapture of overall foreign losses on sale of controlled foreign corporation stock (Senate amendment Sec. 347).
- Prevention of mismatching of interest and original issue deductions and income inclusions in transactions with related foreign persons (Senate amendment Sec. 348).
- Sale of gasoline and diesel fuel at duty-free sales enterprises (Senate amendment Sec. 349).
- Repeal of earned income exclusion for citizens or residents living abroad (Senate amendment Sec. 350).

E. Other Revenue Provisions

- Extension of IRS user fees (Senate amendment Sec. 351).
- Add vaccines against hepatitis A to the list of taxable vaccines (Senate amendment Sec. 352).

¶ 30,001

Provisions Dropped in Conference

- Disallowance of certain partnership loss transfers (Senate amendment Sec. 353).
- Treatment of stripped bonds to apply to stripped interests in bond and preferred stock funds (Senate amendment Sec. 354).
- Reporting of taxable mergers and acquisitions (Senate amendment Sec. 355).
- Minimum holding period for foreign tax credit with respect to withholding taxes on income other than dividends (Senate amendment Sec. 356).
- Qualified tax collection contracts (Senate amendment Sec. 357).
- Extension of customs user fees (Senate amendment Sec. 358).
- Modify qualification rules for tax-exempt property and casualty insurance companies (Senate amendment Sec. 359).
- Authorize IRS to enter into installment agreements that provide for partial payment (Senate amendment Sec. 360).
- Extend intangible amortization (Senate amendment Sec. 361).
- Deposits made to suspend the running of interest on potential underpayments (Senate amendment Sec. 362).
- Clarification of rules for payment of estimated tax for certain deemed asset sales (Senate amendment Sec. 363).
- Limit deduction for charitable contributions of patents and similar property (Senate amendment Sec. 364).
- Extension of provision permitting qualified transfers of excess pension assets to retiree health accounts (Senate amendment Sec. 365).
- Proration rules for life insurance business of property and casualty insurance companies (Senate amendment Sec. 366).
- Modify treatment of transfers to creditors in divisive reorganizations (Senate amendment Sec. 367).
- Taxation of minor children (Senate amendment Sec. 368).
- Provide consistent amortization period for intangibles (Senate amendment Sec. 369).
- Clarify definition of nonqualified preferred stock (Senate amendment Sec. 370).
- Establish specific class lives for utility grading costs (Senate amendment Sec. 371).
- Prohibition on nonrecognition of gain through complete liquidation of holding company (Senate amendment Sec. 372).
- Lease term to include certain service contracts (Senate amendment Sec. 373).
- Exclusion of like-kind exchange property from nonrecognition treatment on the sale or exchange of a principal residence (Senate amendment Sec. 374).

F. Other Provisions

- Review of State agency blindness and disability determinations (Senate amendment Sec. 382).
- Prohibition on use of SCHIP funds to provide coverage for childless adults (Senate amendment Sec. 383).
- Increase Medicaid payments to states with extremely low disproportionate share hospitals (Senate amendment Sec. 384).

¶ 30,001

SMALL BUSINESS AND AGRICULTURAL PROVISIONS

A. Small Business Provisions

• Exclusion of certain indebtedness of small business investment companies from acquisition indebtedness (Senate amendment Sec. 401).

• Repeal of occupational taxes relating to distilled spirits, wine, and beer (Senate amendment Sec. 402).

• Custom gunsmiths (Senate amendment Sec. 403).

• Simplification of excise tax imposed on bows and arrows (Senate amendment Sec. 404).

B. Agricultural Provisions

• Capital gains treatment to apply to outright sales of timber by landowner (Senate amendment Sec. 411).

• Special rules for livestock sold on account of weather-related conditions (Senate amendment Sec. 412).

• Exclusion from gross income for amounts paid under National Health Service Corps load repayment program (Senate amendment Sec. 413).

• Payment of dividends on stock of cooperatives without reducing patronage dividends (Senate amendment Sec. 414).

SIMPLIFICATION AND OTHER PROVISIONS

A. Establish Uniform Definition of a Qualifying Child (Senate amendment Secs. 501 through 508).

B. Other Simplification Provisions

• Consolidation of life insurance and nonlife companies (Senate amendment Sec. 511).

• Suspension of reduction of deductions for mutual life insurance companies and of policyholder surplus accounts of life insurance companies (Senate amendment Sec. 512).

• Section 355 "active business test" applied to chains of affiliated corporations (Senate amendment Sec. 513).

C. Other Provisions

• Civil rights tax relief (Senate amendment Sec. 521).

• Increase section 382 limitation for certain corporations in bankruptcy (Senate amendment Sec. 522).

• Increase in historic rehabilitation credit for residential housing for the elderly (Senate amendment Sec. 523).

• Modification of application of income forecast method of depreciation (Senate amendment Sec. 524).

• Additional advance refunding of certain governmental bonds (Senate amendment Sec. 525).

• Exclusion of income derived from certain wagers on horse races from gross income of nonresident alien individuals (Senate amendment Sec. 526).

• Federal reimbursement of emergency health services furnished to undocumented aliens (Senate amendment Sec. 527).

• Treatment of premiums for mortgage insurance (Senate amendment Sec. 528).

¶ 30,001

Provisions Dropped in Conference

- Sense of the Senate on repealing the 1993 tax hike on Social Security Benefits (Senate amendment Sec. 529).
- Flat tax (Senate amendment Sec. 530).
- Temporary rate reduction for certain dividends received from controlled foreign corporations (Senate amendment Sec. 531).
- Repeal of ten-percent rehabilitation tax credit (Senate amendment Sec. 531).
- Income inclusion for certain delinquent child support (Senate amendment Sec. 532).
- Sense of the Senate regarding the low-income housing tax credit (Senate amendment Sec. 533).
- Expensing of investment in broadband equipment (Senate amendment Sec. 534).
- Income tax credit for cost of carrying tax-paid distilled spirits in wholesale inventories and in control State bailment warehouses (Senate amendment Sec. 535).
- Contribution in aid of construction (Senate amendment Sec. 536).
- Travel expenses for spouses (Senate amendment Sec. 537).
- Certain sightseeing flights exempt from taxes on air transportation (Senate amendment Sec. 538).
- Required coverage for reconstructive surgery following mastectomies (Senate amendment Sec. 539).
- Renewal community modifications (Senate amendment Secs. 540 and 541).
- Combat zone expansions (Senate amendment Secs. 542 and 543).
- Ratable income inclusion for citrus canker tree payments (Senate amendment Sec. 544).
- Exclusion of certain punitive damage awards (Senate amendment Sec. 545).
- Repeal of pre-1997 tax on certain imported recycled halons (Senate amendment Sec. 546).
- Modification of involuntary conversion rules for businesses affected by the September 11, 2001 terrorist attacks (Senate amendment Sec. 547).

D. Medicare Provisions (Senate amendment Secs. 561 through 576).

E. Provisions Relating to S Corporations (Senate amendment Secs. 581 through 594).

- Shareholders of an S corporation.
- Termination of election and additions to tax due to passive investment income.
- Treatment of S corporation shareholders.
- Provisions relating to banks.
- Qualified subchapter S subsidiaries.
- Elimination of all earnings and profits attributable to pre-1983 years.

BLUE RIBBON COMMISSION ON COMPREHENSIVE TAX REFORM
(Senate amendment Secs. 601 through 607).

REIT PROVISIONS

A. REIT Modification Provisions (Senate amendment Secs. 701 through 707).

B. REIT Savings Provisions (Senate amendment Sec. 711).

¶ 30,001

EXTENSION OF CERTAIN EXPIRING PROVISIONS

- Tax on failure to comply with mental health parity requirements (Senate amendment Sec. 801).
- Extend alternative minimum tax relief for individuals (Senate amendment Sec. 802).
- Extension of electricity production credit for electricity produced from certain renewable resources (Senate amendment Sec. 803).
- Extend the work opportunity tax credit (Senate amendment Sec. 804).
- Extend the welfare-to-work tax credit (Senate amendment Sec. 805).
- Taxable income limit on percentage depletion for oil and natural gas produced from marginal properties (Senate amendment Sec. 806).
- Qualified zone academy bonds (Senate amendment Sec. 807).
- Cover over of tax on distilled spirits (Senate amendment Sec. 808).
- Extend deduction for corporate donations of computer technology (Senate amendment Sec. 809).
- Extension of credit for electric vehicles (Senate amendment Sec. 810).
- Extension of deduction for clean-fuel vehicles (Senate amendment Sec. 811).
- Adjusted gross income determined by taking into account certain expenses of elementary and secondary school teachers (Senate amendment Sec. 812).
- Extend Archer Medical Savings Accounts ("MSAs") (Senate amendment Sec. 813).
- Extension of expensing of brownsfield remediation expenses (Senate amendment Sec. 814).

IMPROVING TAX EQUITY FOR MILITARY PERSONNEL

- Exclusion of gain on sale of a principal residence by a member of the uniformed services or the foreign service (Senate amendment Sec. 901).
- Exclusion from gross income of certain death gratuity payments (Senate amendment Sec. 902).
- Exclusion for amounts received under Department of Defense Homeowners Assistance Program (Senate amendment Sec. 903).
- Expansion of combat zone filing rules to contingency operations (Senate amendment Sec. 904).
- Modification of membership requirement for exemption from tax for certain veteran's organizations (Senate amendment Sec. 905).
- Clarification of treatment of certain dependent care assistance programs provided to members of the uniformed services of the United States (Senate amendment Sec. 906).
- Treatment of service academy appointments as scholarships for purposes of qualified tuition programs and Coverdell Education Savings Accounts (Senate amendment Sec. 907).
- Suspension of tax-exempt status of designated terrorist organizations (Senate amendment Sec. 908).
- Above-the-line deduction for overnight travel expenses of National Guard and reserve members (Senate amendment Sec. 909).
- Extension of certain tax relief provisions to astronauts (Senate amendment Sec. 910).

SUNSET PROVISION (Senate amendment Sec. 1001).

¶ 30,001

INDEX

References are to explanation paragraph (¶) numbers.

Accumulated earnings tax
. corporations...205; 365

Additional first-year depreciation allowance—see Bonus depreciation

Alternative minimum tax
. capital gains...305
. dividends...325
. exemption amount...230
. exemption phaseouts...230
. individuals
. . increase in AMT exemption amount...230
. married separately AMT add-back...230

Amended returns
. capital gains...310

Bonus depreciation
. election out...350
. like-kind exchanges...350
. luxury auto depreciation cap...350
. New York Liberty Zone...350
. progress expenditures...350
. property with longer production periods...350
. rate increased to 50 percent...350
. sale-leasebacks...350
. self-constructed property...350

Capital gains
. alternative minimum tax...305
. amended returns...310
. collectibles...305
. deemed sales
. . elections...310
. dividend income...305; 325
. elimination of five-year holding period...310
. nonqualified withdrawals of construction funds
. . Merchant Marine Act...305
. reduction in rates for individuals...305
. small business stock...315
. transitional rules...310; 320
. withholding
. . foreign person gain from U.S. real property...305

Child tax credit
. advance payment of credit...225
. tax credit increase...225

Closely held corporations
. accumulated earnings...365
. dividends
. . capital gains rate...325

"Code Sec. 306 stock"
. stock dispositions
. . tax rate...325

Collapsible corporations
. rules
. . repealed...360

Collectibles
. capital gains...305

Computer software
. small business expenses...355

Conference report
. provisions dropped...30,001

Corporations
Taxpayer Impact...140; 145; 150; 160
. accumulated earnings
. . tax rate reduced...205; 365
. collapsible corporation rules repealed...360

Corporations—continued
. dividends
. . capital gains...325
. estimated tax payments...375
. personal holding company
. . tax rate reduced...205; 370

Credits against tax
. child tax credit
. . advance payment of credit...225
. . tax credit increase...225
. foreign tax credit
. . dividend income...325

Deductions
. small businesses
. . increased expensing...355

Deemed sales
. capital gains...310

Depreciation
. increase and extension of bonus depreciation...350

Dividend income
. capital gains...305
. "Code Sec. 306 stock"...325
. constructive dividends...325
. estate planning...305; 325
. ex-dividend date
. . 60-day holding period...325
. extraordinary dividends...325
. foreign corporation stock
. . tax rate reduction...325
. . treaty requirements...325
. foreign tax credit
. . tax rate differential...325
. individual tax rate
. . capital gains rate...325
. investment interest deduction...325
. leveraged stock investments...325
. mutual funds
. . reduced tax rate...325
. real estate investment trust
. . reduced tax rate...325
. tax rate reduction...325
. transitional rules...320

Dividends
. individuals taxed at capital gains rate...325
. non-profit entities...325
. real estate investment trust (REIT)
. . pass-through dividends...335
. regulated investment company (RIC)
. . pass-through dividends...335

Elections
. bonus depreciation...350
. capital gains
. . deemed sales...310
. small business expenses
. . revocation...355

Estate planning
. capital gains rate...305
. dividends...325

Estimated tax payments
. corporations...375

Federal Medical Assistance Program
. Medicaid
. . temporary state fiscal relief...240

Foreign corporation stock
. dividend income
. . tax rate reduction...325

FOR

Index

References are to explanation paragraph (¶) numbers.

Foreign tax credit
. dividend income
. . tax rate differential...325
Holding period
. capital gains
. . five-year holding period eliminated...310
Individuals
Taxpayer Impact...110; 112
. 2003 projected rate schedules...205
. alternative minimum tax
. . increase in AMT exemption amount...230
. capital gain tax rate reduction...305; 325
. credits
. . child tax credit...225
. marriage penalty relief
. . acceleration of 15-percent tax bracket expansion for joint filers...215
. . acceleration of increase in standard deduction...220
. rate reductions
. . 10-percent bracket increase...210
. . acceleration of reduction in income tax rates...205
. withholding...205
Installment sales
. transitional rules...320
Joint filers
. acceleration of increase in standard deduction...220
. tax rates
. . 15-percent bracket...215
Like-kind exchanges
. bonus depreciation...350
Marriage penalty relief
Taxpayer Impact...122; 124
. joint filers
. . 10-percent tax bracket...210
. . 15-percent tax bracket...215
. . standard deduction...220
. standard deduction...220
Medicaid
. temporary state fiscal relief...240
Mutual funds
. dividend income
. . reduced tax rate...325
. gain or loss
. . transitional rules...320
New York Liberty Zone
. bonus depreciation...350
Pass-through entities
. depreciation...350; 355
. dividends...320; 325
Personal holding company tax
. rate reduction...370
. tax rates...205
Qualified dividend income
. real estate investment trust (REIT)...335
. regulated investment company (RIC)...335
Qualifying investment
. small business expenses...355
Rate reductions
. 10-percent bracket increase...210
. capital gains
. . individuals...305
. corporations
. . personal holding company...370
. marriage tax penalty...220
. married persons...220
. standard deduction...220
Real estate investment trust (REIT)
. qualified dividend income...335

Regulated investment company (RIC)
. qualified dividend income...335
Sale-leasebacks
. bonus depreciation...350
Small business expenses
. capital purchases...355
. election to expense property
. . revocation...355
. off-the-shelf computer software...355
. qualifying investment...355
. qualifying property
. . inflationary adjustment...355
. vehicles...355
Small business stock
. exclusion from alternative minimum tax...315
. holding period...315
Standard deduction
. joint filers...220
. married filing separately...220
State aid
. temporary Medicaid expenditure increase
. . Federal Medical Assistance Program...240
Stocks
. 60-day holding period
. . ex-dividend date...325
. extraordinary dividends
. . individual tax rate...325
Sunset provisions
. explanation...29,001
Tax credits
. child tax credit...225
. foreign tax credit...325
Tax preference items
. small business stock...315
Tax rates
. 2003 projected rate schedules...205
. acceleration of reduction in income tax rates...205
. accumulated earnings
. . rate reduced...205; 365
. dividend income
. . "Code Sec. 306 stock"...325
. . rate reductions...325
. foreign corporation stock dividends
. . rate reduction...325
. income tax rate reduction
. . 10-percent bracket increase...210
. joint filers
. . 15-percent bracket...215
. personal holding company tax...205; 370
. withholding...205
Taxpayer impact
. businesses
. . capital-intensive...165
. . generally...140
. . labor-intensive...167
. . multi-national...175
. . small businesses...160
. . technology...170
. collapsible corporations...184
. corporations
. . closely held...147
. . collapsible...184
. . generally...145
. employee stock ownership plans (ESOPs)...192
. financial entities...180
. governmental entities...195
. high-income taxpayers...112
. individual taxpayers...110; 122
. investors
. education...134

FOR

Index

References are to explanation paragraph (¶) numbers.

Taxpayer impact—continued
. investors—continued
. . estate planning...136
. . generally...130
. . retirement...132
. . wealthy...138
. Jobs and Growth Act sample scenarios...198
. low-income taxpayers...116
. married taxpayers...120; 124
. middle-income taxpayers...114
. not-for-profit entities...190
. overview...105
. pass-through entities
. . generally...150
. . partnerships and LLCs...152
. . real estate investment trust (REIT)...156
. . S corporations...154

Taxpayer impact—continued
. personal holding companies...182
. real estate investment trust (REIT)...186
. senior citizens...126

Transitional rules
. application of...320
. capital gains...310; 320
. dividend income...320
. gain or loss from mutual funds...320
. installment sale gain...320

Treaty requirements
. dividend income...325

Vehicles
. small business expenses...355

Withholding
. tax rate reductions...205

WIT